JAKE BERNSTEIN'S NEW GUIDE TO INVESTING IN METALS

JAKE BERNSTEIN'S
NEW GUIDE TO
INVESTING IN METALS

Jacob Bernstein

John Wiley & Sons, Inc.

New York • Chichester • Brisbane • Toronto • Singapore

Copyright © 1991 by Jacob Bernstein

Published by John Wiley & Sons, Inc.
All rights reserved. Published simultaneously in Canada.

Library of Congress Cataloging-in-Publication Data

Bernstein, Jacob, 1946–
  Jake Bernstein's new guide to investing in metals / Jacob Bernstein.
    p. cm.
  Includes bibliographical references.
  ISBN 0-471-51251-6 (alk. paper)
  1. Metals as an investment. I. Title. II. Title: New guide to investing in metals.
HG6047.M48B47 1991
332.63—dc200   90-20035

Printed in the United States of America

91 92 10 9 8 7 6 5 4 3 2 1

CONTENTS

1   Emotions, the Investor, and the Metals Markets
Controlling Risk in the Metals Markets   2
Metals Mania   5
How This Book Can Help   7

2   The Base Metals
Copper   11
Tin   22
The Base Metals as Investment Vehicles   31

3   Gold
Sources of Gold   38
Gold Mining   49
The Marketing of Gold   52
Uses of Gold   53
Supply and Demand Factors   55
The Role of Gold in International Economics   60

4   The Other Precious Metals
Silver   63
Platinum and Palladium   76

5   **The Strategic Metals**

Antimony 84	Lithium 101	Tellurium 114
Beryllium 86	Magnesium 102	Titanium 115
Cadmium 88	Manganese 104	Tungsten 117
Chromium 90	Mercury 106	Vanadium 118
Cobalt 92	Molybdenum 108	Yttrium 120
Columbium 94	Platinum-Group	Zirconium 120
Gallium 96	Metals 109	Investment Oppor-
Germanium 97	Selenium 110	tunities in Stra-
Hafnium 99	Silicon 112	tegic Metals 121
Indium 100	Tantalum 113	

6   **Investing in Metals Through the Stock and Futures Market**
Investing in Metals Shares   124
Futures Trading in Metals   127

7   **Investing in Coins**
Bullion Coins   144
Numismatics and Numismatic Coin Funds   148
Guidelines for Investing in Coins   149

8   **A Precious-Metals Strategy for Our Times**
Evaluate Your Financial Condition   155
Determine the Optimum Allocation of Funds   156
Historical Cycles in Metals Prices   156
Technical Factors in Metals Prices   163
Developing a Precious-Metals Strategy   170
Timing with Cyclical and Technical Factors   172
Risk and Reward in Metals Investing   203

9   **Seasonal Price Tendencies in Metals**

Copper 209	Platinum 223
Silver 217	Palladium 234
Gold 223	

10   **The Future of Metals Prices**
International Conflict   236
Inflation   237
Industrial Usage   238
Stock Market Trends   239

Currency Instability   243
Japanese Economic Trends   243

11   **Suggestions for the Metals Investor**

Major Metals Producers in the United States and Canada   249

Reference and Reading List   251

Index   255

JAKE BERNSTEIN'S
NEW GUIDE TO
INVESTING IN METALS

1 EMOTIONS, THE INVESTOR, AND THE METALS MARKETS

FEW INVESTMENT OPPORTUNITIES arouse as much interest and emotion as do the various types of metals. Whether precious metals, industrial metals, or strategic metals, investors and speculators have had a long-standing love-hate relationship with these markets. In particular, the precious metals have, for literally thousands of years, driven speculators to risk their fortunes, armies to risk their lives, and leaders to risk their power.

Precious metals have always been considered a safe haven during times of turmoil, whether political, economic, or monetary. In fact, the right to own, trade, and invest in precious metals has acquired the status of an inalienable, or even God-given, right. While we have come a long way from the arcane and mystical teachings of alchemists, our continued fascination with metals, particularly the precious kind, has grown steadily. While stocks may come and go, while bonds eventually mature, and while businesses may flourish and dissolve precious metals endure.

Why have metals created such strong emotions among investors and speculators? What makes them so attractive? What is the long-term investment potential of the metals markets? What are the premier metals investments of today? And which metals are likely to attract a future following? These are some of the questions this book will answer.

Why should the average investor be interested in metals? Why be interested in a topic that has had such a volatile, and at times violent, history? Why take the time to learn about strategic metals, a seemingly esoteric subject? I suggest that you keep some of these questions in mind as you read the pages that follow. If you do, then you will be convinced, as I am, that the future is likely to be a bright one indeed for all three of the metals groups. You will see that your own future could be even brighter if you can use your knowledge of metals in a comprehensive program of investment and/or speculation.

Controlling Risk in the Metals Markets

You need to understand the risks associated with precious-metals investments. Although many of you are well aware of the potential risk that accompanies virtually all investments, it is even more important to be aware and to recognize the particularly large risks associated with investments in metals. What exactly are the risks? Why are they especially large in the metals markets? What can be done to minimize risk? How can we recognize and analyze risk? As you read on you will become more familiar with the answers to these questions, however, at this juncture a few brief and general statements will be sufficient:

1. The metals markets, particularly silver, platinum, gold, and copper, have an international following. They are considered important barometers of economic activity, and they are followed closely throughout the world by both investors and speculators. As a consequence, these metals and others are especially sensitive to virtually all types of economic and political events. At times these events will have a major impact upon prices, causing them to gyrate wildly, and at other times the effects of international developments will be only minimal. Regardless of the particular events that affect prices, the fact remains that investments in the metals have always been, and will likely continue to be, speculative and, therefore, subject to wide price fluctuations over both the long run and the short run.

While many investment advisors tout the value of investing in precious metals as a hedge against uncertainty, it must be said that investing in precious metals is itself uncertain at times. The vehicle that is purported to be the hedge against destabilizing and/or unexpected events is often unstable itself, and you must be prepared for this possibility.

2. Because metals have attracted such a wide and persistent following among investors and speculators, they have also attracted a plethora of con artists, swindlers, and other undesirables. These individuals and firms have hatched literally hundreds of schemes designed to relieve investors of their money. While some of these programs are clearly illegal and fraudulent, others are on the fringe of legality, and still others are legal but based upon high-pressure sales tactics. As an investor or potential investor, you must always be cautious. "Investigate before you invest," we are told. It's a simple rule to follow, but when dealing in metals it's a very important one!

3. The risk of loss in futures and options trading is substantial. In fact, the odds of coming out ahead are small enough for this topic to warrant in-depth discussion later in this book. Futures contracts are highly leveraged. The speculator is frequently required to use a margin of less than 5 percent of the total value of the underlying contract being traded. Leverage is a two-sided coin. It can work for you or it can work against you, but most often it tends to work against you.

Trading in futures options is even more speculative. Those who buy or sell options, as opposed to those who employ options strategies, rarely make money on their speculation. Most futures options are worthless when they expire. Hence, it is especially important that you be careful not to place your money with a firm that specializes in metals-options trading only. The odds of success are minimal, and in most cases these firms charge large commissions, which are frequently several times larger than discount commissions. It often takes a very large move in the underlying metals futures contract to make enough profit to pay your commissions alone.

4. From time to time, investments in strategic metals have come into vogue. While there are several ethical firms that specialize in strategic-metals investments, there are numerous fly-by-night firms that prey on public ignorance, greed, and gullibility. There are many things these firms fail to tell you about the lack of liquidity in strategic-metals investments. Before you plunge into this area of metals investing, make sure you know what you're getting in to, how easy it will be to get out, where your investments will be stored, and how reliable your dealer is. More about this later on.

5. Bull markets in precious metals stimulate the growth of all sorts of metals investments. Among these are such things as gold-backed bonds, insurance, and others. As with any other investment, you must take the time and effort to investigate them thoroughly and carefully. I urge you to consult your accountant, attorney, or investment advisor. Don't be afraid to ask specific questions. And don't hesitate to contact the proper government regulatory agencies to check on registrations, claims, and credentials of firms and/or individuals with whom you are doing business.

Emotion has always been one of the primary driving forces in the metals markets, and it is emotion that prompts investors to become greedy or fearful. When greedy, the investor will take imprudent risks, making investments that are neither logical nor sound. Greed will drive an investor or speculator to remain with an investment too long. And greed will diminish judgment.

Fear, on the other hand, will cause investors to liquidate sound investments and to shy away from profitable opportunities. Whether you are involved in mining stocks, futures, options, or other metals-related investments, you are more susceptible to the effects of fear that you would be in most other investments. Be aware of this and you will fare well. Forget my warnings, or ignore them consciously and your odds of success will be greatly diminished!

Metals Mania

My first investment in stocks was made in 1968 while I was in my last year of college. With borrowed money I bought several hundred shares of Wright Hargreaves Mines, a small Canadian producer. If memory serves me, the stock was in the $3 range. I recall with great fondness my excitement and anticipation. This, I felt was the stock that would start me on my way to millions. And I remember my trips to the local brokerage offices of what was then Hayden-Stone in Champaign, Illinois. With tremendous anticipation I watched WRT move back and forth between 3 and 4 as it traded in sixteenths of a point.

Not too many years later the precious metals began major bull moves that culminated in 1980 all-time highs. The years between the late 1960s and the early 1980s marked one of the most volatile periods in the history of all metals prices. Legalization of gold ownership by U.S. citizens during this period provided an additional impetus to hopeful investors. Vast fortunes were made and lost during this two-decade span that was also, and not surprisingly, characterized by unprecedented economic volatility and instability in virtually every corner of the world. Investors rushed into virtually any proposition that involved metals. This was the age of the "gold bugs." Virtually every investor, regardless of financial status, was interested in capitalizing on the fantastic opportunities still to be reaped. The average investor was faced with literally hundreds of different vehicles. And the choices were further complicated by questions of timing, disagreement among the experts, unethical operators, and by extremely volatile international and domestic political and economic environments.

During this period literally hundreds of metals "experts" were born and grew to maturity seemingly overnight. While some, such as the late Verne Myers of Canada, the outspoken Harry Schultz, and Jim Dines, were bona fide experts who were in on the "movement" from well before its inception, many others sought to claim their fame riding on the coattails of the true experts. As the bull markets in precious metals pushed prices ever higher in what seemed to be a never-ending story, price projections and expectations increased as well. Some experts claimed that gold prices would rise well in excess of $1,000/ounce and that platinum would easily reach $1,500. "Silver to $100/ounce, we were told, as the Hunt brothers steadily increased their corner on the market.

During those days of metals mania the investor was never quite sure where to turn. Would mining stocks be the best way to participate? After all, they paid dividends, and some of them had vast yet-unmined gold deposits. And if gold-mining stocks were the best vehicles, then which mines would be best? Would the Canadians do well, or was their cost of producing gold too high? Would the South Africans be ideal since their cost of production was so much lower, or would they be too speculative due to the continuing racial unrest? And what about metals mutual funds? Which might perform best in the months and year ahead? Or would bullion coins be the way to go? Perhaps numismatic coins would be even better, since they combined the benefits of rarity with the attraction of precious metals?

As you can see, there were many questions to answer. And the answers were not easily found. Virtually every precious metals expert had his or her recommended portfolio. While some favored mutual funds, coins, and gold-backed bonds, others were convinced that a healthy selection of penny mining stocks would bring the greatest results. And the experts disagreed with one another, which was even more confusing to the public. One thing that a majority of experts did agree upon was the fact that precious metals were headed higher and higher and higher. And the closer prices came to their long-term tops, the more adamant the experts became.

But this was not the first time that metals mania had swept the markets. There have been numerous periods throughout economic history during which precious metals have been considered premier investment panaceas. Each of these periods was characterized by similar emotions and mass hysteria. The history of metals has been cyclical. While the cycles have not been predictable to the very day or month, all of the more widely known metals, such as copper, silver, and gold have had lengthy cyclical histories.

Various researchers, including E. R. Dewey, the Foundation for the Study of Cycles, and others, have demonstrated cyclical phenomena in metals prices. And my own research has confirmed the existence of these cycles, not only in the metals themselves, but in metal-shares prices as well. In-depth studies suggest that the cyclical patterns in metals may be nothing more than a reflection of underlying economic cycles, but even if this is the case, the validity of cycles in metals prices is not undermined.

Knowledge of the various cyclical patterns in metals is important. It can alert you to the approximate high and low turning points in these markets. Since timing is critical in virtually all investments, knowledge of metals cycles can yield considerable benefits. But there are still several other ingredients essential to success. Knowing that something will happen is important, but knowing what to do about it may be even more important. The knowledge that metals are likely to turn higher or lower is potentially quite valuable, however, it must be translated into a plan of action that will maximize dollar return on the information. In a rising market, not all investment vehicles move at the same pace. And in a falling market, not all investment vehicles drop as quickly or as far. Some may even rise.

How This Book Can Help

I have written this book to assist average investors in finding answers to the many questions that face them when they seek to invest in the metals markets. Although I cannot hope to provide all answers to all questions, I am confident that I will be able to assist you in the following areas:

1. **Understanding the fundamentals of each market.** My main task is to provide you with concise information about the basics of each major metals market. While such information is generally known to many investors, there are important facts about the metals that are not generally known.

2. **Learning if, how, and when to invest in each market.** While some metals are ideal investment vehicles, others are not,

since they are not in short supply or heavy demand. Still other metals prices are tightly controlled by a small group of producers or suppliers. These metals may or may not be suitable for investors. And still other metals may never be liquid enough to be suitable to any investor at any time.

3. **Learning about the various investment vehicles available to you, including stocks, futures, options, coins, mutual funds, and others.** While you may know a little about each of these areas, you may wish to know more, and in particular you may want to know when each of these choices is best for you.

4. **Helping you plan a strategy for future moves in the metals markets.** While this book will answer many questions, it cannot possibly answer all of your questions. However, there are numerous sources to which you can turn for assistance. Some of these are in book form (see the Reference and Reading List at the back of this book). Still other questions can be answered by your investment advisor, financial planner, broker, or tax consultant. But remember that opinions about the direction or expected direction of the metals markets are only opinions. Any opinion stands a good chance of being right. If you have done your homework, if you have done your research, and if you have studied hard to anticipate the direction of the next major market shift then do not allow your opinion to be swayed by others. While it may be reasonable to solicit their input regarding how much money you should commit, how much risk you can take, or what the tax consequences of your investments might be, you might want to ignore their input about the anticipated direction of the markets since their knowledge and studies may not be at all as intense or as complete as are yours.

Finally, remember that investing in metals is, as I have stated previously, a highly emotional thing. The psychology of investing is a field unto itself. I have two books on this subject to which I will refer at various points. While you may have done a thorough job of researching your plan and in preparing it, you may fail if you lack the discipline to implement your program thoroughly, consistently, and without the fear or greed that often prove to be the undoing of otherwise successful programs. Keep your emotions in check and be aware of your motivation for taking specific actions at given times.

While I have attempted to provide as much pertinent information as possible about each of the metals, I realize that conditions are changing rapidly in our modern world. Technology is growing at an exponential pace and with it new applications for metals are found virtually every day. Recently, for example, researchers have introduced a powerful new drug for cancer treatment which uses platinum as its base. While the use of certain metals is declining, applications for other metals are on the rise. By the time you read this book some of my comments may be out of date; however, the core elements of this book will likely never be out of date. As long as human beings continue to advance their technology, metals will continue to play an essential role in their efforts.

2 THE BASE METALS

THE BASE METALS constitute the largest and economically most important group of metals. Their importance is primarily a function of their numerous industrial applications. While the price histories of the base metals have not been as volatile as those of the precious metals, there have been some significant price fluctuations through the years, particularly in copper prices; and price variations give rise to investment opportunities.

In this chapter, we'll examine the base metals in detail, beginning with copper.

Copper

Sometime around 8000 B.C., prehistoric peoples discovered a "new" kind of red rock. Having already learned to create crude implements from various kinds of stones by beating them or by heating them in their fires, these prehistoric people were probably surprised to find a stone that was malleable when struck. Beating the stone into various shapes, they found that it made superior weapons and useful implements for digging and cooking.

Copper was probably the first metal known to man. Its widespread use among a people historically has marked their passage from the Stone Age into the first of the ages of metals—the Copper Age. The mixture of tin with copper to make bronze created a superior metal, and the Copper Age flowed quickly into the Bronze Age, nevertheless, the Copper Age was a significant period in the development of civilizations.

The earliest copper mining occurred in regions where there were rich copper deposits—where copper existed in its nearly pure state in the form of nuggets—and the earliest use of the metal, as we have seen, involved hammering it into shape. Later metal workers learned to melt the metal and cast it, and still later, copper was smelted from its ores. Each succeeding stage required more advanced technology and a more sophisticated knowledge of the properties of the metal. The earliest widespread use of copper was probably on the island of Cyprus, where Stone Age people beat the red stones into implements. A continuing source of copper through the ages, Cyprus gave the red metal its name. Rediscovered in the early twentieth century by an American geologist, the famous old mines of Cyprus produced copper for the Phoenicians, the Greeks, and, later, the Romans.

In the Timna Valley in Israel are found the ancient copper mines thought to be the legendary King Solomon's mines. Located in a desolate area between the southern tip of the Dead Sea and the Gulf of Aqabah, the Timna Valley is the source of several types of copper mineralization, including the exotic green malachite and blue azurite. Evidence indicates that copper was smelted at this location from as early as 4000 B.C. up to Roman times.

The Rio Tinto mines in southern Spain are the sight of another very ancient source of copper. Mining activity there dates to the seventh millennium B.C., where first the Phoenicians and later the Romans extracted millions of tons of copper ore. Rediscovered by the Spanish in 1556, the Rio Tinto mines returned to profitable production in the middle of the eighteenth century. A group of private British entrepreneurs purchased the mines from the Spanish government in 1873 and developed them into a modern mining operation that continues to this day.

In the eighteenth century, Britain became the center of the world's copper industry, with most of the copper coming from the Cornish and Devon areas. As early as 1500 B.C., Phoenicians had obtained copper from those sights. By the end of the eighteenth century, Britain was producing three-fourths of the world's supply of copper. Today, Britain imports most of her copper needs.

Worldwide consumption of copper increased greatly with the advent of brass cannon and other brass implements of war around the end of the Middle Ages. Then, during the second half of the nineteenth century, the Industrial Revolution and the age of electricity brought on burgeoning growth in the copper industry. Every few years, world demand for copper for use in electrical wiring and equipment would double. In 1860, total world production of copper was approximately 100,000 metric tons. In 1912, production had grown to 1 million metric tons, and in 1929 to 2 million. In 1960, production stood at 4 million metric tons, and in 1980, over 7.5 metric tons. By the end of the 1980s, total world production of copper was approaching 9 million metric tons.

During the 1870s, Chile became the most important exporter of copper and remains so today, accounting for more than 16 percent of worldwide copper production in 1987. The second largest producer of copper is the United States. By 1988, U.S. production nearly equaled that of Chile. In third place is the Soviet Union, with nearly 12 percent of world production, while Canada runs a distant fourth.

Copper Mining

With the passage of time, the richest copper deposits have long been exhausted. As with most other metals, present-day copper production depends on sophisticated mining and smelting techniques that extract copper from low-grade ores profitably. An American engineer named Daniel C. Jackling was the first to demonstrate the viability of recovering copper from low-grade ores at the Bingham Canyon open-pit mine in Utah. Applying techniques of mass production to copper mining, his methods made it possible to mine copper ore as low as 2 percent grade. More recent developments have allowed copper ore of 5 percent grade to be mined profitably in open-pit mines.

Demand for copper has increased significantly in recent years, leading to major expansions of several mining projects, including the Ok Tedi mine in Papua New Guinea and the Escondida project in Chile. In addition, the U.S. mining industry continues to improve its smelting capacity by installing flash-furnace technology. During the past two decades, this newer smelting technology has generally replaced the older reverberatory furnaces, which were used in Britain as early as 1698. The new furnaces allow a larger quantity of copper to be smelted at a cost lower than that permitted by earlier techniques.

In recent years the technology of mining and processing copper has seen tremendous advances. Yet the basic principles have changed very little throughout the ages. Like most other metals, copper deposits in the earth's crust occurred as solutions from the extremely hot interior were thrust up through cracks created by volcanic disturbances that shattered the rocks. In places, the hot copper solutions were forced into small veins and fissures in the rocks, often in close proximity to quartz veins. At other times, the solutions would penetrate the minute pores in certain rock formations, or actually replace other minerals in those formations, and remain as microscopic grains within the massive rock structure. Copper, then, is most often found in one of these two forms: in a system of veins or lodes, or as minute specks in a huge mass of rock.

Because most of the so-called native copper—pure copper found in its metallic state and not in chemical combination with other elements—has long been exhausted, most remaining copper occurs in the form of minerals, primarily sulfides and oxides, that are scattered in irregular patterns among the rock in the earth's crust. Sometimes copper ore is found close to the earth's surface; other times copper deposits occur far below the earth's surface. Thus, two different types of mining operations are used to recover copper ore: open mining and shaft mining. In open-pit mining, huge earth-moving equipment is used to uncover the copper ore, which is then scooped up from the quarry and taken directly to the processing plant. With ore that occurs deeper underground, a series of shafts and tunnels are drilled and blasted in the ground, giving access to the ore. The ore obtained from this hard-rock mining must be crushed and concentrated before the smelting and refining process can begin.

Because the underground lode mines produce a higher grade of ore, most of the world's copper from ancient times until the early part of the twentieth century was produced from these underground mines. Most such deposits were discovered by locating outcrops of copper that occurred at the surface. As demand for copper grew in the twentieth century, however, so did the need to locate alternative sources. Lode reserves were obviously limited and would be unable to meet the growing demand indefinitely.

Geologists had long known of the copper ores that were widely disseminated in microscopic specks among huge rock formations. Recovery of the ore from such low-grade deposits, however, was not viable economically. Then, at the Bingham Canyon open-pit mine in 1905, Daniel C. Jackling demonstrated a method to recover such low-grade ores economically. The porphyries—disseminated copper deposits—have since become the most important source of the world's copper. Porphyry deposits are huge in size, covering vast areas of the earth's surface. Within the deposit, the copper minerals themselves appear to be spread uniformly throughout the mass, which produces a very low amount of copper per ton of ore. These porphyry deposits constitute over 60 percent of known copper reserves and account for 45 percent of the world's mined copper. The best-known porphyry deposits are found along a narrow, but almost continuous, belt beginning in central Chile and running through the northern part of South America into Central America and then into Mexico and several western states, then on into British Columbia and north into Alaska and the Yukon. The second belt is found along the Pacific "Ring of Fire," extending from the Philippines through New Guinea and into the Solomon Islands. A third belt occurs in the Near East, extending through Iran, Turkey, and southern Europe.

Uses of Copper

Copper is a desirable commodity for a number of reasons. First is its high electrical and thermal conductivity. Second, it is quite malleable and can be worked and formed quite easily. Third, as we have seen, copper can easily be alloyed to produce other materials like brass and bronze that take on properties important to

numerous applications. Fourth, copper is easily joined by soldering and brazing. Fifth, copper is highly resistant to corrosive elements. Sixth, copper is aesthetically pleasing.

Through the ages, right up to the present, copper has been
formed into tubes used for piping water. For centuries, copper has
been a popular material in architecture. The Romans used it to
sheathe the Pantheon and for many other vast engineering and
building projects. Today, many fine homes display copper sheathing on the roofs, as well as copper gutters. In these applications,
copper—though expensive—is chosen both for its beauty and its
long life.

From ancient times to the present, bronze has been an extremely popular medium for statues and other art forms. The Co-
lossus at Rhodes, one of the Seven Wonders of the Ancient
World, utilized more bronze than any other single statue ever
wrought. If you walk or drive through many of the parks or pla-
zas of the world's cities, you will see that bronze is still the alloy
of choice for statuary.

The Industrial Revolution created tremendous changes in the
way copper was used. From a metal used primarily in statuary,
art, and common utensils of the day, copper and brass became
central to the industrial development of the world. Engines required cylinders, valves, flanges, and all manner of other parts
made of brass. As more and more houses and buildings were built
with indoor plumbing, the demand for copper piping increased
dramatically. The growth of the modern electrical industry, however—more than any other development—created a huge
demand for copper. Early in the development of electrical gener-
ating devices, many inventors discovered that copper was the
most practical and economical medium for the generation and
transmission of electrical current.

Today, the largest consumer of copper in the United States by
far is the construction industry, for use in plumbing, heating, air
conditioning, and electrical cable. In 1988, total consumption of
copper for these uses was just under 3 million pounds, while over
1.5 million pounds was used in the electrical and electronic industry. Industrial machinery accounted for nearly 1 million
pounds, while 860,000 pounds was used by the transportation

industry, primarily in automobiles. Various consumer products that use copper accounted for another 700,000 pounds in 1988.

Supply and Demand Factors

Concentration of copper in the earth's crust is approximately 70 parts per million (ppm). Copper's relative scarcity belies its annual production, which is exceeded only by aluminum and iron. Unlike many other metals—notably tin and zinc—copper is relatively abundant in the Northern Hemisphere, particularly in North America. This means that supplies of copper are less dependent on developing countries, with their periodic political and economic instability.

In the world of mining, there are distinct ways in which geologists measure the relative long-term and short-term availability of a particular mineral. First, there is an estimate of the total resources of a mineral. These include identified and unidentified or undiscovered resources. In 1989, the total land-based resources of copper were estimated at 1.6 billion tons, while deep-sea resources—mineral-rich nodules on the ocean floor—accounted for another 0.7 billion tons.

A copper-ore deposit or a copper reserve is defined as the total share of identified resources from which copper can be produced economically, using current technology, at the time the measurement is made. An even more precise determination is called an identified copper reserve. This would include only that part of a deposit that has been precisely located and has been precisely measured in terms of quality and quantity.

Because the mining of any metal is primarily an economic activity, there is little incentive to search for new resources or identify additional reserves unless and until worldwide demand for the material makes such activity economically feasible. Thus, as worldwide consumption of copper has increased during the past few decades, so have the estimates of copper resources. In 1977, for example, the total of the world's copper resources was estimated at approximately 2.2 billion metric tons, while in 1988, the total estimated resources, including those in the oceans, amounted to approximately 2.3 billion tons. In that same period of time, total mine production of copper increased from approximately 7.8 million tons in 1977 to just under 8.7 million tons in 1988.

Although worldwide resources of copper seem adequate to meet increased demand for the foreseeable future, several factors will significantly affect future supplies: (1) recycling from scrap; (2) the ability to recover copper ore from the oceans; and (3) environmental regulations that have a direct impact on the exploration, mining, and smelting of copper. In the state of Michigan, for example, a local battle with national implications has been raging recently. The copper industry wants to develop the area for mining. People who live in the area are strongly opposed to the potential for localized pollution of rivers, streams, and air. Although the industry sources are promising that preservation of the environment will be a primary consideration, many citizens in the area simply don't believe them and want to keep them out at all costs.

Approximately 30 percent of worldwide copper resources can be found in the oceans in one of two forms: either in sea water itself or along the floor of the ocean. Although sea water is an unlikely source for copper in the near future, many of the copper deposits occurring on the floor of the ocean seem ready for exploitation.

Offshore copper deposits take two primary forms. First, the consolidated rocks of the continental shelf contain the same types of deposits that occur on land. Second, sedimentary nodules, comprised primarily of manganese, are also rich in copper and other metals. These nodules have been successfully mined on an experimental basis, using surface ships with equipment that can reach to the floor of the ocean and scoop them up. In places, these nodules form an almost continuous layer on the floor of the sea. Most of the time they occur with little or no cover of sediment. In some of the samples that have been recovered, the nodules contain almost 50 percent manganese but also large proportions of iron, silica, and lime. The proportion of copper and nickel amounts to approximately 2 percent each, as does cobalt. Most of the sampling of the seabed nodules has been done by private companies, who have kept most of their information confidential. The U.S. Department of the Interior estimates that between 190 and 460 ocean-mining sites exist, each of which could probably be exploited economically.

In addition to newly mined copper, scrap copper—copper that has already been used in one form but is then recycled and melted down for reuse—is an important source of available copper. Unlike some other metals for which scrap is limited to certain specific uses, copper produced from scrap is virtually a perfect substitute for primary copper. Known as secondary production, scrap is primarily processed in the developed countries. In the United States, the total amount of copper produced from scrap averages just about a third of the total copper produced each year.

The development of a new copper mine requires extensive exploration and development. In some of the Arizona copper mines, exploration took anywhere from one to fifteen years, followed by construction that required from one to eight years. Although expansion of existing mining operations can be done in a shorter period of time, it still requires anywhere from one and a half to three years. Development of new mining capacity also requires huge amounts of capital. Because of these factors, the copper-mining industry cannot respond quickly to changes in the demand for copper. Therefore, in periods of high demand, such as those we have seen in recent years, available supplies can be very tight, resulting in high prices. As with any commodity, however, high prices not only encourage expansion of production, but also substitution of more readily available and less costly materials. In plumbing applications, either plastic or cast iron can easily be substituted for copper. In water pipes, plastic is becoming more and more the material of choice, because it not only costs significantly less but can be installed by the do-it-yourselfer or a less-skilled workman. In big cities like Chicago, the only major hurdle standing in the way of replacing copper pipes with plastic in most new construction is the power wielded by the trade unions, who do not want to see union labor replaced by do-it-yourself labor. With union power waning, however, Chicago has taken significant steps toward relaxing building codes and allowing the use of plastic water pipes in some situations.

In a broad range of applications that require corrosion resistance, hardness, heat resistance, ductility, and tensile strength, stainless steel is a popular substitute for copper. In the telecommunications industry, fiber optics are rapidly replacing copper, since fiber-optic cables are much lighter and can carry significantly more information than a similar volume of copper.

Aluminum, which is much more abundant than copper but more expensive and difficult to produce, nevertheless can easily be substituted for copper in strip and sheet production as well as in electrical cables. In high-voltage transmission lines, in fact, copper has been almost completely replaced by the lighter aluminum coaxial cables. The primary advantage that aluminum enjoys is its much lighter weight. A given volume of aluminum weighs only one-third the amount of a similar volume of copper. Therefore, even though the electrical conductivity of aluminum is less than two-thirds that of copper, the actual amount of electricity that can be transmitted per unit of weight is greater for aluminum. Not only that, but in their finished form, both metals exhibit similar heat conductivity and workability characteristics. Thus, in applications where heat exchange is an important consideration—such as automotive radiators, air conditioners, and refrigerators—aluminum and copper are virtually interchangeable.

Even though extensive substitution of materials for copper has increased in the past few decades, the demand for copper has continued to grow as the global economy has expanded. In the developing countries, higher standards of living have led to ever-greater demand for consumer products that use copper in their construction. As the electronics industry continues to expand, so does the demand for copper and brass for use in the circuitry. During those periods when demand exceeds readily available supply, prices are driven up and substitution is encouraged—but likewise the copper-mining industry is encouraged to expand its production facilities and further modernize and improve its smelting capacity, as we have seen during the 1980s and into the 1990s.

In most applications, copper is not a final product, but rather a component of some other product. In the construction industry, copper wiring and copper plumbing, and occasionally copper sheathing, roofing, and gutters, are but a small part of the total project. In electronics, the copper used in the electronic circuits is very small compared to the quantity of other materials used. The same situation exists in consumer products and industrial machinery. Therefore, the demand for copper is primarily derived demand; for example, when the construction industry is booming, there is a greater demand for copper. When the economy is expanding, there is a greater demand for consumer products and electronic gadgetry. Just as important, when the economy is shrinking, demand for these products is reduced. The price of copper itself, however, has little effect on the demand for these end products. Therefore, the price of copper can increase or decrease significantly without affecting the demand for copper usage in a significant way. This is known as inelasticity of demand. In the short run, very little substitution occurs as a result of higher prices.

The Role of Copper in International Economics

Throughout history, copper has played an important role in international politics, trade, and economics. In ancient times—whether at Timna, in Elam, or in Cyprus, the three earliest sites of copper activity—the discovery of copper was followed very quickly by the development of important trade routes. As with any important resource, civilizations that did not have copper wanted it once they discovered the ways in which it could improve their quality of life. Cyprus was perhaps the first exporter of raw copper—in the *Odyssey,* Homer mentioned a ship's setting sail for Cyprus with iron to barter for copper. But by the third and second centuries B.C. almost every country that conducted normal commercial relations was trading in copper. Much of the far-flung Roman empire was built on copper mining and production. Near the end of the Middle Ages, Britain became first a major producer of copper and then a major trade center—a position it maintains today. During the depression, Britain encouraged the development of copper production in much of its overseas empire—particularly in northern Rhodesia (Zimbabwe), Canada, Australia, and southern Africa, and in the Belgian Congo (Zaire).

The growing copper trade from these countries, particularly those in Africa, contributed significantly to the development of railways and roads and, ultimately, to economic and political development of a number of African countries. In several other developing countries around the world, copper production has become an essential part of the economy. In 1987, 46 percent of the world's copper production came from developing countries.

While the United States remains largely self-sufficient in the production of copper, most of Europe's supplies come from Zambia and Zaire in Africa, and from Chile, Canada, and South Africa. In Japan, phenomenal industrial growth has led to greatly expanded demand for copper. During the decade of the 1980s, local production of copper in Japan steadily declined to a low of only 16,700 metric tons of copper in 1988, compared with 1.3 million metric tons of refined copper consumption. Rather than develop its own copper-mining industry, Japan has chosen to establish long-term contracts with copper-mining centers worldwide, thus assuring itself of a relatively stable supply of copper, regardless of local economic and political events. In recent years in the United States, however, Japanese industrialists have begun establishing part-ownership in several copper mines and designating a portion of the production of those mines for export directly to Japan.

Tin

Tin, the most scarce and the most valuable of the base metals, could actually be regarded as a semirare metal. In fact, the availability of tin lies somewhere between that of the precious metals—silver, platinum, and gold—and that of the other nonferrous-based metals—lead, copper, zinc, and aluminum. For comparison, tin measures 1.7 parts per million (ppm) in the earth's crust as compared with lead at 12.0 ppm and silver at 0.075 ppm.

Recoverable tin is highly concentrated in only a few parts of the world. The richest deposits are found in a belt running from Yunnan in southern China, through Laos, Burma, Thailand, and

Malaysia, to three Indonesian islands off the coast of Sumatra and south of Singapore. Approximately two-thirds of the total world production of tin in the twentieth century has come from this Asian belt. The second most important concentration of tin lies in the Bolivian highlands, where most of the major mines are found between 11,500 and 16,000 feet above sea level. In Europe, two tin belts have been of major importance historically—one runs from Cornwall through Brittany and in to the Iberian peninsula, and the other through the Erzgebirge highlands of Saxony and Bohemia in central Europe. Other tin deposits of less significance have been found in the U.S.S.R., Australia, and Brazil, as well as in Africa. Interestingly, no significant deposits of tin have ever been found in the United States, despite extensive prospecting.

Tin became an important metal early in the development of civilization because, when alloyed with copper to form bronze, it created a metal far superior to the stone implements used for millennia by prehistoric man. Copper itself was the first metal to succeed stone as a material for weapons and tools; but copper, being relatively soft, was not the ideal substance. Bronze, on the other hand, could be sharpened to a cutting edge, which led to the development of more effective weapons of war and more efficient hunting implements. When copper and tin were melted together, the mixture was more fluid than molten copper by itself. The resultant casting was much better than one made from copper alone, because the alloy would fill a mold more completely.

This alloying of copper with tin led to a uniquely identifiable stage in the development of almost every culture—the Bronze Age. The Bronze Age is not a distinct period of time in the history of the planet. Rather, it represents a stage of development in the history of a people. Different civilizations have passed through this important stage at widely different periods of time historically, yet every major civilization has experienced a Bronze Age, preceded by a brief Copper Age and followed by an Iron Age.

In parts of Asia and Europe, bronze seems to have been widely used sometime before 3000 B.C. In Egypt, China, and western and northern Europe, the Bronze Age seemed to have occurred between 2500 and 1500 B.C. The Japanese Bronze Age dated from somewhere around 800 B.C., while the Incas in Peru were experiencing a Bronze Age when the Spanish Conquistadors arrived during the sixteenth century. Bronze Age people developed good metallurgical skills through generations of working with alloys of copper/tin, copper/arsenic, and copper/antimony, looking for just the right alloy to give a satisfactory hardness and strength to their bronze. Gradually a ratio of 90 percent copper to 10 percent tin became the favorite mixture, a ratio that has continued in modern times as the preferred alloy.

Initially, the development of bronze seems to have come about by accident. In a few places where copper was mined in ancient times, copper and tin appeared together in certain ores. When smelted, this accidental alloy created a superior "copper," which was actually a crude bronze. Following that, areas where copper and tin ores lay in close proximity to each other led to the deliberate addition of tin to copper by certain societies. As the local source of tin depleted, however, many of these societies were found to have added less and less tin to the copper. It was then that the tin trade developed as civilizations reached out for new sources for this critical alloy. Thus it was that very early civilizations looked for tin in the far reaches of the known world, leading to the development of some of the ancient trade routes linking early societies.

An important early source of tin was Malaysia, where it is still mined to this day. Much of the transportation and communication infrastructure that exists in Malaysia is the result of extensive tin mining in the nineteenth century. Other important sources of early tin mining were Cornwall in England, various parts of Spain, and Brittany in France.

During the past century and a half, the pattern of tin production in the world has changed significantly. In the 1850s the United Kingdom produced abut one-third of the world's tin, but by the 1880s Australian production had exceeded that of the United Kingdom, and Malaysia had become the world's largest producer. Since the turn of the century, Bolivia and Indonesia have increased their production significantly, while the Congo and Nigeria have also risen to an important position among tin-producing countries.

The past two decades have seen continuing changes in patterns of world tin production. In 1970 Malaysia was indisputably the largest tin producer, accounting for 32 percent of the world's tin. At that time Bolivia and the U.S.S.R. were the next two largest producers. In 1980, only ten years later, Malaysia was still number one. But worldwide production had increased in the interim, while production in Malaysia had decreased, with the result that Malaysia in 1980 accounted for only 25 percent of the world's production. In the meantime, the U.S.S.R., Thailand, and Indonesia, as well as Bolivia, had risen to important positions in the world's tin community. By 1988, however, production in Bolivia had declined by over 70 percent, reducing that country's importance as a supplier of the metal.

For the last four years Brazil has been the primary supplier of tin to the United States. Malaysia held that position in the past, but more recently has been sending more and more tin to Japan. Malaysia's tin reserves have been dwindling during recent years. In 1988 six countries—Malaysia, Brazil, Indonesia, Thailand, Bolivia, and China—produced most of the world's tin. The largest producer, Malaysia, accounted for 16 percent. Second was Brazil with just over 15 percent, while Indonesia, with 14 percent, was not far behind. The top six producing countries, together with the U.S.S.R., mine over 80 percent of the tin that is produced worldwide. Other countries, like Australia, the United Kingdom, Peru, Canada, and several African nations, also produce significant quantities of the metal, but nowhere near the level of output from the top seven countries.

Tin Mining

Tin, like gold, is quite heavy, and tends to accumulate in the form of sand and stones in stream beds. The earliest forms of tin mining, therefore, involved recovering tin ore from these alluvial deposits in the beds of rivers and streams. Miners would simply gather tin ore from the stream bed or dig through the more recent silt to uncover the tin that lay in the older stream bed. Much of the alluvial tin could be recovered by simple panning in the stream beds in places like Malaysia and Indonesia. Today, alluvial tin is mined in open cuts and in shallow shafts, or dredged from river beds or low-lying alluvial deposits—some of which lie offshore. Both Malaysia and Indonesia have large alluvial deposits of tin ore, which is primarily recovered by deep dredging. Washing the accumulated gravel carries away the lighter minerals and leaves the tin ore.

As with gold, the tin that lay in the river bottoms often originated in the veins of very rich ore that lay exposed among the higher cliffs and rocks. In Bolivia, in particular, tin ore is found primarily in these veins in the mountains, from which it is excavated under very harsh conditions—coming out as broken stone. This stone must then be crushed to a fine powder and washed with water to recover the tin. Because most Bolivian ore is lode ore, the process of obtaining the tin is difficult and expensive, requiring heavy machinery that can crush the stone in which the veins of tin lie.

Commercial tin is obtained primarily from an ore known as cassiterite—also known as tin stone or tin oxide. When chemically pure, this mineral is 78.6 percent tin in metallic content. As with other minerals, when tin is found in lode ore—typically imbedded in granite rock—it carries numerous impurities that make it difficult to melt and refine. Lode tin mining is hard rock mining at its most difficult.

The secondary, or placer, deposits—where the alluvial ores that have eroded from their original sources have settled—are easier to mine and have historically been a primary source of tin. Secondary ores carry fewer impurities and are easier to smelt than primary ores. Alluvial deposits of tin—like those in Malaysia and Indonesia—are relatively easy to separate from surrounding rock and earth using various washing techniques involving water: the heavier tin remains when the other particles are washed away, leaving an ore that is between 60 percent and 76 percent tin metal. Because of this high concentration, tin smelters can be located at points far away from the mine itself. In fact, much of the world's tin smelting is done in both producing and consuming countries alike.

Uses of Tin

Tin has a number of characteristics that make it economically attractive. It is nontoxic and extremely resistant to corrosion. Thus, it has become popular as a coating for steel and other more corrosive materials, particularly for use in food packaging. Tinplate, which is steel covered with a thin layer of tin, has traditionally been a very inexpensive material. Although tin is quite malleable, with a very low melting point, when it is mixed with other materials it tends to create an alloy that is harder than either of the materials that were joined together. In ancient times, as we have seen, this was important in the manufacture of bronze implements. In more recent times, tin has become popular as part of the alloy that is used to produce bearings. Not only is the alloy quite hard, but the tin imparts a significant antifriction quality to the material.

Tin has worked its way into the common vernacular through two well-known earlier uses of this soft, easily melted metal—tin foil and the tin can. Tin foil, which was in common use a few decades ago, has given way to aluminum foil, although the original name seems to have stuck. The "tin can" is really steel covered with tin, but remains a popular way to keep food fresh over time. Because of the ubiquitous nature of tinplate the words *tin* and *tinny* have grown to be used as synonyms for "cheap" or "of low value."

In recent years, the largest use of tin has been in solder, accounting for approximately one-third of the world's consumption. The second largest use is in tinplate. The low melting point of tin made it popular for use in setting type, although computer technology has virtually replaced metal type in most applications.

Pewter, a popular material for tableware in earlier centuries, but presently more of a curiosity, is the only metal in which tin is the primary ingredient. Pewter, which is more than 90 percent tin, is essentially tin, in the same way that 22-karat gold—which is 87.5 percent gold—is gold, and sterling silver—which is 92.5 percent silver—is silver.

During the Roman occupation of Britain, tin, in the form of pewter, was widely used for dinnerware, jewelry, and other objects. Early pewter was often alloyed with a high proportion of lead, which often had disastrous consequences in the form of lead poisoning. Before Roman times the use of pewter was quite rare, and following the Roman occupation, little is known of the use of pewter.

Pewter objects are easily made by melting tin and pressing it into a metal mold, from which it is withdrawn when it is solid. Enterprising individuals made a living, in fact, from collecting worn-out pewter articles and recasting them for the owners, who saved the cost of a new piece. Thus, from roughly A.D. 1400 to 1800, through four centuries in Europe, pewter was widely used in ordinary households. During the nineteenth century, however, porcelain began to replace pewter. By the 1860s, the manufacture of pewter had essentially ceased. In more recent times, pewter continues to be used in the manufacture of various decorative and useful objects, although it is unlikely that pewter will achieve the ubiquitous status that it enjoyed historically.

Supply and Demand Factors

In 1987, total world consumption of tin was approximately equal to that of 1960. During the intervening 27 years, consumption hit a high of 215,000 metric tons in 1973. The low point was in 1982, when just under 154,000 metric tons was consumed. From 1982 to 1987 there was a steady growth in the volume of tin used worldwide, reflecting the expanding economy during that period. Usage in 1987, however, remained significantly below the high of 1973—at 166,000 metric tons. This fluctuation in consumption reflects the changing nature of tin as an industrial commodity.

Other than its use in pewterware, which has a very limited market, tin is used commercially as a coating or as an alloy. The metals that do contain tin—tinplate, solder, and various alloys—are primarily intermediate products used in the manufacture of other items. This situation, just as with silver, creates a certain inelasticity of demand; that is, the price of tin can fluctuate widely without significantly affecting the price of the end product. Therefore, the price of tin is relatively unrelated to the demand for the many products containing tin.

On the other hand, other materials can easily be substituted for tin in many situations, if the price for tin goes too high. During World War II, for example, when tin was in short supply, the United States developed tin-free cans. In addition, plastic-lined fiber containers have become popular in the packaging of frozen food, while other types of plastic containers threaten to replace the use of tinplate in many applications. Aluminum cans, which are weaker than tin-plated steel, work for some foods, but not all—aluminum is susceptible to corrosion from more chemical sources than tin and also is resistant to coating by tin. Nevertheless, the long-term role of tin as an essential component of food packaging is probably doubtful.

Tin-based solder, on the other hand, seems to be essential to the growing electronics industry, where suitable substitutes have not been found. Because the amount of tin in an individual application of solder is so minuscule compared to the product itself, the high price of tin seems to have no affect on its use. Therefore, we can expect long-term growth in the demand for tin from the electronics industry.

As a component in the alloy that goes into the manufacture of bearings, tin is also virtually irreplaceable. Although extensive research and testing has gone into the search for other materials, only those alloys that contain substantial amounts of tin meet the necessary performance standards for commercial bearings.

Looking into the future, experts predict that the consumption of tin for tinplate will remain fairly stable, reflecting not only a growing use of tinplate in food processing in the developing companies, but also an increase in the use of tin-saving electrolyte plating. The use of tin in soldering materials should expand with the growth in overall industrial activity. The use of solder in plumbing and automobile manufacture—two areas where demand has traditionally been large—will decline, but the use of tin-based solder in the electronics industry should grow. In the electronics field itself, even though the amount of solder used per joint has declined significantly, the number of connections to be soldered has grown substantially. Overall, then, the demand for tin over the next few decades should enjoy modest growth, with the caveat that substantial substitution is possible in the event of a major interruption of supply.

The Role of Tin in International Economics

The primary producers of tin—Malaysia, Brazil, China, Indonesia, the U.S.S.R., Thailand, and Bolivia—are all either developing countries or, in the case of China and the U.S.S.R., undergoing significant political and economic changes. This situation suggests the likelihood of disruptions in tin supplies to the major industrial nations. Otherwise, even though tin is the rarest of the base metals, supplies from the producing nations seem adequate to meet demand for some time to come. Unstable political conditions seem to be the only threat to the interruption of supply in one or more of the producing nations.

In a few producing countries, in fact, tin historically has been their most important source of revenue. In Malaysia, early economic development was dependent on the development of the tin-mining industry. In Bolivia, tin mining supplanted silver mining as that country's chief economic base around the turn of the century, and by 1929, Bolivia was producing 25 percent of the world's total tin output. Unfortunately, however, tin miners in Bolivia amount to less than 2 percent of the population of the country, and whatever wealth is generated by the export of tin is therefore concentrated among a very few.

In many of the other major tin-producing countries, various political events throughout the twentieth century have created major disruptions in the flow of tin from those countries. This, combined with the fact that the post–World War II growth of tin output has been sluggish in comparison to general economic growth in the producing nations, has relegated tin to a less important role in the economies of many of the producing countries.

In the industrialized nations, particularly the United States, tin is almost solely an imported metal. Thus, many of the industrialized nations have stockpiled tin to avert any potential disruption of supplies from the rather vulnerable producing nations. These stockpiles have functioned not only as a buffer against the interruption of supply, but also as an economic tool to exert some control over the price of tin on the international market, ultimately leading to the financial collapse of the International Tin Council (ITC) in 1985.

The ITC was a consortium of tin-producing nations originally formed with the intention of dampening the volatility of worldwide tin prices. To accomplish that task, the ITC drafted a series of International Tin Agreements among producer and consumer nations, establishing quotas for exports and providing for a buffer stockpile of tin to be held by the ITC. This stockpile gave the ITC the ability to support prices during low periods by buying tin on the open market and to sell from its stocks during periods of higher prices. The ITC was forced into default in 1985, however, when it could not meet the financial commitments necessary to take delivery of tin on the London Metals Exchange. This event, in turn, led to the halt of tin trading on the London Metals Exchange.

The Association of Tin Producing Countries (ATPC) has succeeded the ITC with another plan for international price support. The group, which functions as a producers' cartel, includes Malaysia, Indonesia, Thailand, Australia, Nigeria, Zaire, and Bolivia. Brazil and China have been asked to function as observers, and so far both have been cooperating formally with self-imposed export quotas.

The Base Metals as Investment Vehicles

Of the base metals, perhaps the only one that offers a sufficiently liquid market is copper. While tin futures are traded in London, the copper market is a more internationally active and offers investment potential both in stocks and in futures. Copper prices have been highly volatile since the 1950s, as can be seen from the monthly cash price chart shown in Figure 2–1. There have been some large price moves in copper futures since the 1950s as well. Figure 2–2 shows the monthly futures chart for copper and its price cycles.

In addition, there are numerous copper-producing and -mining firms whose stocks are publicly traded on virtually all world exchanges. I recommend caution, particularly if you are considering investments in "penny" copper stocks or in some of the South African or South American producers inasmuch as political problems are always a threat to production and, therefore, earnings.

Another aspect of copper prices is that they have frequently been responded to war or the threat of war by moving sharply

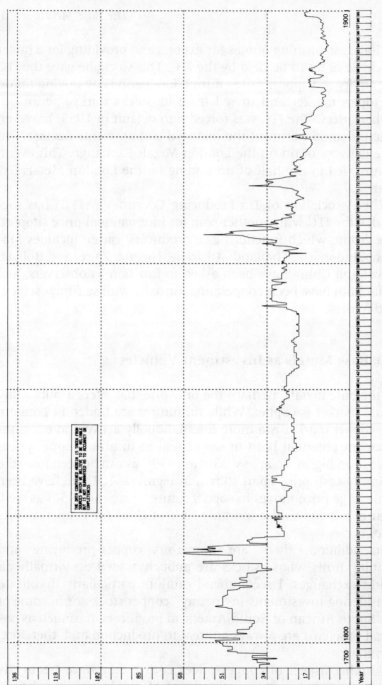

Figure 2-1 Monthly cash average price for copper, 1796–1990 (continued below).

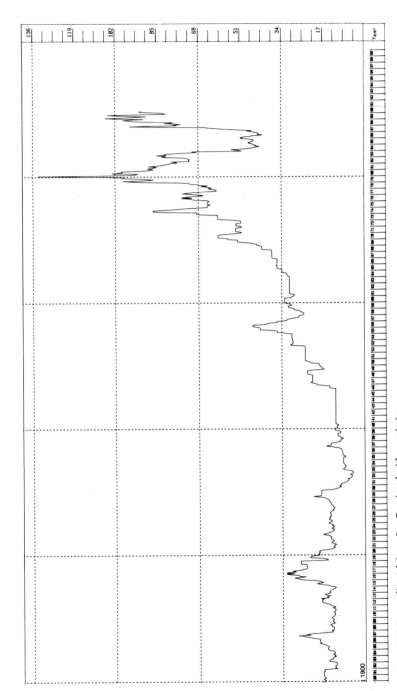

Source: **MBH Commodity Advisors, Inc. Reprinted with permission**

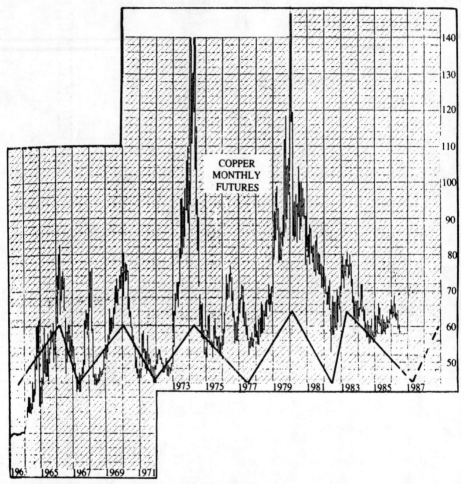

COPPER
MONTHLY
FUTURES

Source: Commodity Price Charts. Reprinted with permission

Figure 2-2 Five- to six-year cycles in copper; monthly futures prices, 1963–1985.

higher. Investors who are concerned about international conflict might consider copper shares as an investment, or futures as a higher-risk speculation.

In addition to copper shares, copper stock options, and copper futures, one can also speculate in copper futures options. These, however, are highly risky, and a majority of investors or speculators who buy futures options lose most if not all of the money they have invested in options. Another word of warning is necessary with regard to futures options, whether copper, silver, gold, or any of the other metals. Since the mid to late 1980s, futures options have become very popular speculative vehicles. The lure of a relatively small investment in futures, combined with virtually unlimited profit potential and predetermined risk has provided a near-perfect vehicle for ruthless brokers. While they stress the upside potential and the fact that one cannot lose more than what is originally invested, they do not advise their would-be clients (victims) that the odds of success are very low (perhaps less than one chance in one hundred) and that these odds are reduced even further by a very large front-end commission charge. While most brokers charge from $25 to as much as $75 per options-round-turn commission, these firms charge as much as 30 percent of the option premium. In other words, an option costing the investor $2,000 would require a commission of as much as $600. The underlying futures contract would need to increase in value substantially before the investor could break even, given the excessive commission. While charging such commissions is not illegal, the unrealistic claims and high-pressure tactics often used by these firms is clearly in violation of the Commodity Futures Trading Commission and National Futures Association rules and regulations. You must be careful to avoid such brokers.

If you have any doubt about a particular options strategy or investment, or a particular brokerage firm, I urge you to consult an experienced, reputable investment counselor and/or the regulatory authorities. If you lose money in copper options because you failed to investigate the program adequately, then you will have no one to blame other than yourself. Remember that futures options are distinctly different from stock options in terms of risk and reward, and in terms of commissions and probability of success.

3 GOLD

ALTHOUGH one of the rarest of minerals, gold can be found in small quantities in most places on earth. More than fifty-four countries around the world produce gold in some quantity, although in many of those countries the amounts produced are so small as to be insignificant. Antarctica is the only continent where gold has not been found.

Geologists tell us that the earth's crust contains gold in the amount of 3.5 parts per billion (ppb). Compared with other minerals such as iron and aluminum—or even copper at 70 parts per *million*—the relative scarcity of gold is readily apparent. Although gold in commercially viable quantities is difficult to find, it is, like most minerals, ubiquitous. Even in sea water, for example, gold is found in minuscule amounts (0.011 ppb).

Gold occurs naturally in three primary forms: as a native metal, as an alloy with other metals, and as tellurides. Through the ages, the process of erosion and weathering has carried much of the free, or metallic, gold from its primary deposits into streams and rivers, there to settle as a placer deposit of small grains (gold dust) and nuggets. These placer, or alluvial, deposits have historically been the source of the most easily found gold and have played a central role in the famous gold rushes of the world.

As we know from the romantic tales of the Forty-niners who flocked to San Francisco after the discovery of gold at Sutter's Mill in 1849, and from the exciting tales of the Yukon Territory during the Klondike gold rush that occurred a few years later, the dream of every miner was to find the fabled "mother lode." These are the small but extremely rich streaks of gold left within the fissure veins of quartz deposits as the earth cooled eons ago, and they are the source of the gold in the placer deposits. The most famous of these was the Comstock lode, discovered near Virginia City, Nevada, in 1859.

Unfortunately, these lodes tend to be exhausted quickly, as do the richest of the placer deposits. Because of this, the typical gold rush of recent history has been rather short-lived, although the present Wild West–type gold rush in the Amazon basin of Brazil shows no sign of subsiding.

After a gold rush, once the easily found gold has been scooped up by the hordes of fortune seeks, it has typically been left to the better-capitalized individuals and corporations to bring in sophisticated mining and processing equipment needed to separate the remaining gold from its ores. Year by year, the ores from which gold is extracted grow poorer, as the more accessible gold is depleted. Fortunately, the technology for retrieving gold has become more and more sophisticated, allowing previously unusable ores to become commercially viable.

Gold ores in the United States are presently running around 0.1 ounce of gold for each ton of ore. In South Africa, the world's largest producer of gold, ores average approximately 0.2 ounce per ton. The larger deposits of gold that are being mined lie several hundred feet below the earth's surface, and are recoverable only with complex and expensive mining techniques. For that reason, gold mining today is primarily in the hands of a few large, wealthy corporations.

Sources of Gold

Although many countries mine a little gold, only a few account for the bulk of the gold that is produced each year. South Africa is by far the largest producer, accounting for over 30 percent of the total world output in 1989. The Soviet Union is firmly in second place, with approximately 15 percent of the world production, with the United States in third place at just under 12 percent. Canada, Australia, Brazil, China, the Philippines, Colombia, and Papua New Guinea each contribute a sizable amount to the world's new supply of gold each year.

South Africa

It is ironic that South Africa dominates the world in the production of gold, because there have been no stirring tales of huge nuggets or spectacularly rich lodes coming out of the gold fields of this controversial country. Those kinds of romantic ventures, commonly associated with the search for gold, have always occurred elsewhere in the world: California, the Klondike in Canada, Australia. In fact, when South African gold was discovered in 1886, the ore was of such low grade that it was not economically feasible to mine it. A few of the wealthy diamond miners attempted it but quit by 1890 after taking a loss. There were never the rich veins or shining placer deposits that fortune seekers found in places like Sutter's Mill or Virginia City, Nevada.

Rather, South African gold is found within a huge "reef" of tightly packed white pebbles, called conglomerate, in which the flecks of gold are, for the most part, not visible without magnification. The reef itself, called the Witwatersrand Reef, varies in thickness from one-tenth of an inch to as thick as one hundred feet. The average thickness is only about one foot, but the reef extends in an arc over three hundred miles long, creating a nearly unlimited supply of this low-grade ore.

At the time of the discovery of gold in South Africa, the old methods of extraction were able to obtain on average only 65 percent of the gold contained in the ore. This process had worked well in the rich veins found in the United States and Australia, but at 65 percent, only a little more than 20 grams of gold was being produced for each ton of South African ore—creating a loss of over $4 per ton. But then in 1887 the MacArthur-Forrest process was patented. The application of this process, which uses cyanide to extract the gold from its ore, allowed up to 96 percent of the gold to be recovered, and the vast reefs of low-grade ore in

South Africa suddenly became very valuable. Whereas in 1887 the total output of gold from South Africa was limited to 1.2 tons, by 1892 South Africa was accounting for over 15 percent of world production, having laboriously gleaned over 30 tons of gold from the reluctant ore fields of the Witwatersrand Reef.

From the start, only well-capitalized individuals or corporations were able to mine this low-grade ore, and as a result, a few wealthy companies have dominated the South African gold-mining industry since its beginning. Because the gold-bearing reef crops out on the surface in only a few locations, and otherwise angles below the surface at an incline of 25 percent, the mines in South Africa go to depths of two miles and beyond. In the 1890s it cost as much as $2 million to start up a mine. In the 1980s, the cost of bringing a new mine into full production was well over $300 million. Only capital from institutional investors could be adequate to fund that kind of large-scale endeavor. The largest mining conglomerate in South Africa is Anglo American, which holds direct sway over nine mines that produce over 40 percent of the gold that comes out of that county.

Since 1980, when gold hit an average price of $614 per ounce, gold production worldwide has increased dramatically, while production in South Africa has remained rather static. Because of the huge capitalization costs involved in expanding production, the country has not raised its output as quickly as the rest of the world. Thus, South Africa's share of world production has declined dramatically. In 1970, two-thirds of the world's gold came from the reliable, yet low-grade, ores of the Witwatersrand Reef, but in 1981, South Africa produced just over half of the world's newly mined gold. Presently, South Africa's share of worldwide production is around one-third of the total, and has been hovering around 20 million ounces for several years. One can only speculate as to how worldwide disfavor for apartheid and the plight of black Africans has contributed to a lack of available capital with which to expand operations.

Regardless of present production, however, the U.S. Bureau of Mines estimates that South Africa sits on approximately one-half of the world's total gold resources, estimated at about 2.4 billion ounces. Barring a major political upheaval, this should ensure South Africa's role as the leader in gold production well into the next century.

The Soviet Union

Like South Africa, the Soviet Union is also experiencing unprecedented political turmoil, which could affect its current position as the second-leading producer of gold in the world.

Nevertheless, in 1989 the Soviet Union produced approximately 9.6 million ounces of gold, well ahead of the United States and Canada, but less than half the output of South Africa. This effort represented approximately 15 percent of the total worldwide production for 1989.

Gold in the U.S.S.R. comes from mines in the Ural Mountains of Siberia. These same alluvial fields produced much of the gold that found its way into ancient civilizations via trade routes to the Black Sea and the Mediterranean. In 1744, the discovery of a quartz outcrop near Ekaterinburg (now Sverdlovsk), on the eastern slopes of the Urals, led to a revival of Russian gold mining. As in the Yukon and Alaska, the conditions under which gold is mined in Siberia are very harsh. Occurring in similar strata, the deposits in both areas are often remote and barely accessible. Nevertheless, between 1804 and 1848, when gold was discovered in California, the bulk of the world's gold production came from the Siberian gold fields.

Production of gold has increased dramatically in the U.S.S.R. as the price of gold has remained relatively high through the 1980s. In 1970, the Soviet Union produced approximately 6.5 million ounces of gold, which represented over 13 percent of the total world output that year. By 1980, Soviet production was up to 8.3 million ounces, representing 21 percent of the world total, which had declined in the meantime from 47.5 million ounces to 39 million. Production continued to climb through the 1980s to a high of approximately 9.6 million ounces in 1989, representing 15 percent of the world total, which had also increased—to 63.4 million ounces.

Of course, the real output of gold from the Soviet Union remains something of an estimate, because of Soviet secrecy about its economic situation. Nevertheless, the amount of gold brought to market by the Soviets through their own bank in Zurich, the Wozchod Handelsbank, is a good indicator. In recent years, the Handelsbank has become a sophisticated trader of gold and is often able to manipulate the gold market to its own advantage on the short term. Once seen as a country that would simply dump gold to pay for poor harvests, the Soviet Union now adeptly anticipates future needs for hard currency and sells gold when the markets are more favorable. At other times, the Handelsbank might be a large buyer of gold, so that market watchers never know for sure whether the Soviets are selling from their own substantial gold stocks or simply selling gold they bought previously on the open market. It remains to be seen whether the current economic changes being attempted by the Soviets will lead to more openness in their gold dealings worldwide.

The United States

The fortuitous discovery of gold not far from San Francisco in 1848—by a carpenter who was building a mill for one John Sutter—very quickly unseated Russia as the leading supplier of European gold. For a few short but exhilarating years, the attention of much of the world was drawn to the California gold rush, as tales of overnight wealth lured thousands of people from their farms and their jobs to the bleak existence of the gold fields. Although the majority of the Forty-niners never got rich, thousands made small fortunes from their claims, and the substantial wages paid in the gold fields allowed many of them to earn much more than they could have back home. Of course, the cost of living in the gold towns was also quite high, so many were able to only eke out a living. Nevertheless, the quantity of gold mined during those few years changed forever the role that gold would play in international economics.

Prior to 1848, the amount of gold held in government coffers worldwide, though substantial, was simply not sufficient to support a gold standard. Although gold coins had been minted for centuries, nothing like a gold standard—where currency could be converted into gold on demand—had ever existed. From 1848 to 1852, for example, the amount of gold reserves in the Bank of England increased from £3.5 million to £23.5 million.

Two later discoveries—the Comstock lode near Virginia City, Nevada, in 1859, and the Klondike in far northern Canada—continued to fuel gold fever in the minds of individual prospectors looking to make a quick fortune. Along with discoveries in Australia, these two finds also helped to supply government storehouses around the world, perpetuating the "absurd waste of human resources," in the words of Robert Triffen, Yale University professor, involved with "digging gold in distant corners of the earth for the sole purpose of transporting it and reburying it immediately afterwards in other deep holes, especially excavated to receive it and heavily guarded to protect it."

According to estimates by the Bureau of Mines, the United States accounts for approximately 12 percent of the world's total 2.4 billion ounces of gold reserves, or over 280 million ounces. As in the Soviet Union, most gold in the United States is found in placer deposits or lode mines, although a significant portion of the gold produced in the United States is a by-product of copper production or the mining of other base metals. In 1988, according to the Bureau of Mines, there were approximately 420 lode mines, mostly in the western states; 12 large placer mines, mostly in Alaska, and many small placer mines. Because of the high costs associated with the production of gold, large corporations and large mines, like the Homestake in South Dakota, tend to dominate the industry, and only a small number of mines account for the bulk of domestic output.

Nevertheless, the relatively high price of gold throughout the decade of the 1980s has led to significant expansion of the gold industry in the United States. At the beginning of the decade, there were only about 250 active mines, compared with well over 425 in 1988. Production in 1980 hit a low of 951,000 ounces, but by 1989, the United States mined nearly 7.5 million ounces of gold, an increase of almost 700 percent during the decade!

High prices have also led to a continuing demand for scrap gold, with old scrap from jewelry and other sources providing nearly 2 million ounces per year in the United States, well over half of the total U.S. consumption of gold. Worldwide, the demand for gold has meant increased exports from the United States during the past decade.

Canada

Most people probably don't even know where the Klondike is. This remote area in far northwestern Canada, the scene of the last great gold rush of the nineteenth century, contributed as much to the lore and romance of that period as the San Francisco rush nearly 50 years earlier. But Dawson City, once the scene of many an adventure story, had faded into a tourist attraction by the mid-1960s, much like Virginia City in the United States.

With the rise in the price of gold in the late 1970s, however, the gold-mining industry in Canada began a new era of productivity. From a low of only 1.5 million ounces in 1980, Canada was projecting over 5.5 million ounces in 1989, an increase of more than 265 percent. Along with the rejuvenation of the older gold fields, newer exploration has uncovered a rich field in northwestern Ontario, the Hemlo field, which promises to maintain Canada's position among the major gold producers in the world.

During the 1970s, Canada outproduced the United States, primarily because the Canadian gold-mining industry had enjoyed state subsidies for over 20 years. This aid was made available mainly to protect communities like Dawson City from becoming ghost towns, but it meant that when mining became profitable again the structure was in place to respond quickly. Consequently, it was not until 1986 that the United States slipped past Canada to take third place in world production of gold.

Most of the gold in Canada lies at a depth of about 1,000 feet, as opposed to South Africa, where the average depth is 10,000 feet or more. This means that new mines in Canada require less capitalization and can be brought into production in a much shorter period of time.

Australia

When San Francisco became the focus of the world in 1848–49, Australia was a little-known South Pacific land that had been used primarily as a penal colony by the British. All of that changed, however, when Edward Hammond Hargraves, an Australian, returned from California in 1850, having experienced very little luck in the gold rush there. From firsthand observation, however, he knew the type of geological formation in California that often produced rich lodes and placer deposits, and he knew where those same kinds of formations were likely to exist in Australia. Immediately upon his return, he headed for New South Wales, where he promptly found gold, just as he knew he would. As soon as word got out, Australia found itself in the midst of a full-fledged gold rush that rivaled California's. Within 10 years, the population of Australia had tripled.

In the 1890s, when Californians were stampeding to Alaska and the Yukon territory, Australians were heading to western Australia and Kalgoorlie, where a second gold rush was in full swing. As with every gold rush, however, the easy-to-find gold was soon depleted, and the race for riches was soon over. As the treasure seekers began to return home or to turn to other pursuits, mining companies were formed, extensive capital was raised, and the job of the individual prospector was taken over by the large mining concerns, who could go deeper for the gold and could profit with lower-grade ores.

From this auspicious beginning, Australia then sank to a relatively unimportant role in the worldwide production of gold. In 1970, a year when Canada produced almost 2.5 million ounces. Australia weighed in with just over 600,000. By 1985, however, Australia was producing nearly 2.5 million ounces to Canada's approximately 3.4 million. By 1987, Australia was at nearly 3.5 million ounces, with Canada at just under 3.7 million ounces.

The recent scenario, of course, has been similar to that in the United States and Canada. As gold prices have risen and remained relatively high, gold fields that were believed to have played out have become profitable, and even the residual gold from some mines can be leached with cyanide through the MacArthur-Forrest process patented back in 1887. Higher prices also encourage new exploration, and a few new mines have been opened.

The People's Republic of China

Little is known about the extent of Chinese gold production. For centuries, the Chinese have mined gold in the eastern provinces of Shandong, Henan, Jiangxi, and Zhejiang, from mines that often are little more than communal enterprises. During the past decade, however, China has increased production significantly through exploration and the discovery of new deposits and the opening of several new, more modern, mines.

As late as 1980, China was not even listed as a separate source of gold in the Commodity Research Bureau (CRB) Commodity Yearbook. By 1985, increased production placed it fifth in order of annual production, with nearly 2 million ounces, and in 1989, it was estimated that China would mine over 3 million ounces of gold.

Brazil

Among all the major players in the gold industry, Brazil—with its current gold rush—comes closest to recapturing the spirit of the individual prospector last seen at the close of the nineteenth century. There in the gold fields of the Amazon River basin, thousands upon thousands of fortune hunters have converged to stake small claims or to work as diggers or carriers for those who hold title to the claims. At Serra Pelada ("gold hill" in Portuguese), a horde of diggers, resembling nothing so much as an army of ants, reduced the hill to a huge pit in a matter of months, at the same time pulling out millions of dollars worth of gold. Prospectors are working jungle claims with high-powered water spray, at the same time destroying thousands of acres of lush foliage. Others work on dredges in the tributaries of the Amazon and on the great river itself, sunctioning up tons and tons of river sediment in search of the bright flecks of yellow metal.

Just as in earlier centuries, the search for gold has led prospectors along untraveled paths, opening up areas that heretofore were inhabited only by native tribes living in relative harmony with their environment. One tribe in particular, the Yanomami in northern Brazil—numbering approximately 9,000 people—has found its way of life seriously threatened by the 45,000 or so gold prospectors who have invaded the 35,000 square miles inhabited by the tribe for centuries in relative tranquility. The search for riches has resulted in denuded forests and fouled rivers, and has brought prostitution, weapons, alcohol, and diseases heretofore unknown by the tribe and against which they have no natural immunity. Nearly 2,000 have already died from maladies brought by the modern-day prospectors, who have used airplanes and helicopters to invade the farthest reaches of the isolated and forbidding region.

Much of the gold being brought out of the Amazon basin is being bought by the government of Brazil, which suffers from a crushing foreign debt. The government has also instituted a program of exploration and development designed to fill its coffers with the yellow metal. Reports by geologists indicate that the total reserves of the region might exceed those of South Africa. Like the Witwatersrand Reef, however, the majority of those reserves are primary deposits—reefs—that require huge amounts of capital and years of development to become profitable.

That capital might come soon, though, in the form of Japanese investment. A group of Japanese industrialists, in fact, have made an offer to assume the total Brazilian foreign debt in exchange for mining rights in the region. At the time of this writing, the Brazilian government was seriously contemplating this rather extraordinary offer. In the meantime, gold production in the Amazon basin continues to rely primarily on essentially the same techniques employed by the Forty-niners almost a century and a half ago: sluicing, panning, digging ore by hand and crushing it, then using mercury to precipitate the gold from the ore. These rather archaic methods, however, have placed Brazil among the leading producers of gold in the world. In 1980, Brazil was listed only among the group of other producers, its output too insignificant to merit a separate listing. In 1985, the *CRB Commodity Year-*

book still did not give Brazil a separate listing. A projected output of nearly 2.9 million ounces in 1989, however, ranked Brazil seventh in worldwide production.

The Philippines, Colombia, and Papua New Guinea

Rounding out the list of major producers of gold are three countries that each contribute over 1 million ounces of gold per year to total world production. In the Philippines, a substantial amount of gold is produced primarily as a by-product of copper mining, although activity in the past decade has increased the proportion of primary gold production. Total output, however, has not varied a great deal for more than 20 years.

In 1970, the Philippines produced 603,000 ounces of gold, nearly as much as produced by Australia. During the 1970s, production slumped slightly to a low of 501,000 ounces. By 1980, however, output was back to just over 700,000 ounces, 200,000 ounces more than Australia produced that year. During the 1980s, however, when Australia and other gold-producing countries responded to unprecedented price increases with significantly expanded output, production in the Philippines rose only incrementally. Granted, the estimated high of 1.4 million ounces for 1989 was double that of 1980, but this seems a weak effort when compared to Australia's more than fivefold increase during the same period. That kind of inability to respond dramatically to increases in the market price of a commodity is typical when a metal is produced in large part as a by-product.

If the price of the primary metal—in this case, copper—does not show a corresponding rise in price, the secondary metal—gold, in this example—will not respond significantly to market conditions. The cost to increase production is too great, and the resulting increase in availability of the primary metal might just depress prices of that commodity even more. This is called inelasticity of supply. With silver, the effect of this phenomenon is even more pronounced, because silver tends to be mined primarily as a by-product.

Papua New Guinea, formerly an Australian colony, rose to prominence as a gold producer in the 1970s. Originally the bulk of the gold produced there was to be a by-product of the Bougainville copper mine. Just as the mine came into production, however, the price of gold started rising. Not only that, but the gold content of the ore was richer than originally thought. These two situations combined to make the Bougainville an important source of newly mined gold. Later development has opened other mines that have replaced the subsequent decline of production from Bougainville and maintained Papua New Guinea's role as a major producer of newly mined gold.

In Colombia, as in Brazil, a certain frontier spirit permeates the gold industry. In Brazil, however, the miners and prospectors adhere to a kind of self-imposed code of ethics. Consequently, relatively few incidents of theft or other crime have occurred. This is not so in Colombia, where criminals have thwarted attempts by organized mining companies to establish formal mining operations. As a result, most of the gold from Colombia derives from the efforts of individual miners or small operations up and down the rivers that run from the Andes—the location of the primary deposits that feed the placer deposits, not only in Brazil and Colombia, but also in Chile, Ecuador, Peru, and throughout much of South America.

Other Countries

The top ten gold-producing countries of the world together accounted for over 90 percent of the total worldwide production of gold in 1989. The remaining 10 percent of the gold was produced by more than 45 other countries, 16 of which each produced more than 100,000 ounces in 1989. That converts to over 3 metric tons each and, at a price of $400 per ounce, more than $40 million worth of gold produced by each of those 16 countries.

Gold Mining

The earliest forms of gold mining centered around stream beds and rivers where centuries of erosion had deposited specks of gold (and a few larger nuggets). These placer deposits were worked (and still are in many places) by various hydraulic techniques. The simplest, of course, is the miner's pan, which is used to separate the denser, heavier gold from the gravel that is scooped up in the pan. The process relies entirely on gravity and the miner's skill in manipulating the pan. More-sophisticated miners use sluice boxes to handle a larger quantity of gravel, but the principle is the same: gravity separates the gold from the lighter gravel.

Sometimes placer deposits are found in locations other than present-day stream beds. One way to get at gold trapped in dry soil or gravel is to use a high-powered stream of water to wash the dirt and gravel into a sluice-box-type apparatus. Otherwise the technique is the same. In parts of Brazil today, workers using sophisticated pumps and high-pressure hoses are washing away huge hillsides in the never-ending quest for gold.

Another technique for separating gold from the soil and rock in which it is trapped is to crush the ore into a fine powder, then use water to wash the powdered ore over a set of copper plates coated with mercury. The gold attaches itself to the mercury and thereby separates itself from the surrounding debris. In Brazil, miners carry small vials of mercury that they use to precipitate the gold. The mercury is then separated from the gold and reused. Unfortunately, some of the mercury is carried away with the debris and finds its way into the streams and rivers of the Amazon basin, and then into the fish that swim in those rivers and are caught for food for the prospectors and natives, thus creating a potential health risk.

Whereas mercury amalgamation captures only about 65 percent of the gold present in ores, a process invented independently by John S. MacArthur and Robert and William Forrest—the MacArthur-Forrest process—uses cyanide to extract up to 96 percent of the gold. The powdered ore is circulated through tanks that contain a weak cyanide solution. The solution dissolves the gold but not the rock particles. Once the rock is filtered off, zinc dust is added to the solution, replacing the gold—which is precipitated out and then refined. It was this discovery that made the huge Witwatersrand Reef in South Africa economically viable for development.

A more recent variation of the MacArthur-Forrest process has been used successfully in very dry areas of Nevada. With this process, called heap-leaching, the ore, which is usually very low grade—sometimes, in fact, the tailings from older mines—is piled in a mound or a heap. A weak cyanide solution is then poured over the top of the mound. As the solution works its way through the ore—a process that takes up to two weeks—it absorbs the gold. The gold-rich solution that drains from the bottom of the mound is then treated to recover the gold. This process, which has converted huge areas of very low-grade ore into economically viable reserves, recovers up to 95 percent of the gold from the ore.

The mining of ore itself takes several forms. In rivers and streams, dredges with huge pumps suction gravel from the river bottom and then separate the gold from the gravel, using gravity systems. Gold mined in this fashion is often quite pure, since it has already been separated from the ore by the process of erosion that has carried it into the river beds. When miners go after the lode, however, a lot of good old-fashioned digging is involved. The mine follows the thin vein of gold until it finally peters out. Naturally, a great deal of rock and other debris comes out with the gold, all of which must be ground into a fine powder and then processed to extract the gold. A young lode mine produces very rich ore, but as the mine proceeds further and further into the mountainside, the ore becomes less and less rich.

In the mines of South Africa, where the gold is dispersed in very small quantities among the amalgam of gravel, huge quantities of ore must be brought to the surface in order to extract very small quantities of gold. In 1983, for example, 100 million tons of rock were reduced to a fine powder and then passed through tanks of cyanide solution to produce only 679.5 tons of gold. This is why mining in South Africa requires such a huge amount of capital.

In Brazil, huge tracts of land have been reduced to small individual claims that lie side by side. As each miner works his claim, digging deeper and deeper into the earth, the land becomes a huge open pit. A similar open-pit process is used in a section of Nevada, where large strata of low-grade gold-bearing ore have been discovered that can be mined, and then the gold extracted using the heap-leach process. Here, of course, the open-pit mining is not done by hand, as in Brazil, but by heavy equipment brought in for the task.

The Marketing of Gold

There are 15 major centers for the trading of gold. London and Zurich, however, remain as the two leading "primary" trading centers. A primary market is a trading center that actually handles physical gold. Whereas New York is a large center for the trading of gold, no physical gold actually flows through that market. Zurich, which handles most of the gold from South Africa and the Soviet Union, is probably the most important primary market for gold trading. London, however, which has the greatest history of handling physical gold, continues to be the most visible to American investors.

Twice every day in London, representatives from five of the old-line elite gold-trading firms meet to establish the price at which they will sell their gold. The youngest of these firms, Samuel Montagu and Company, Ltd., was founded in 1835. The oldest, Mocatta and Goldsmid, Ltd., was founded in 1684. The London gold fix, obviously, holds an elite position based on centuries of tradition. Even though the London fix is only a benchmark by which gold traders around the world establish their prices, it is important as an international price that is clearly posted twice each day.

During the 1980s, gold futures trading established itself as an important element in the trading and marketing of gold. Even London, which for centuries had been an important primary market for gold, was forced to establish a gold futures market in order to maintain a leading role in the buying and selling of gold. The COMEX, in New York, has become an important trading center for gold futures only in the past decade. Other futures markets are located at the Chicago Board of Trade, the International Monetary Market at the Chicago Mercantile Exchange, and in Winnipeg, Sydney, and Hong Kong.

Uses of Gold

In ancient times, the appeal of gold lay primarily in its beauty and its scarcity. Because it was so rare, it could be used as a medium of exchange. Because it was practically indestructible, it could be hoarded. Because it was so beautiful, it could be made into jewelry and worn as a symbol of wealth. Early artisans learned that gold had other desirable characteristics as well. It is the most malleable of all metals, and therefore can be pounded into thin sheets and used to cover articles made from other less valuable metals. And because it is practically indestructible, gold that has been made into jewelry or coins or pounded into gold leaf can be melted down and reused.

Not only was gold extremely rare and extremely beautiful, it also would not tarnish. Treasures of gold that have lain on the bottom of the ocean for centuries following the sinking of a trading vessel have been recovered, shining just as brightly as the day they were submerged in salt water.

Through the ages, gold has traditionally been seen as a storehouse of value. For centuries, nearly all gold found its way into government storage vaults around the world. Since the late 1960s, however, gold has been allowed to function as a free-market commodity, and most of the gold that is produced each year now goes into private investment, jewelry, or industry.

Gold in recent times has taken on a whole new importance as the world has moved into the electronic age. Gold has two characteristics that make it attractive to the electronics industry: it will remain completely free of tarnish, and it is very high in electrical conductivity. Because solid-state electronic devices employ low voltages and currents, and because even a small amount of tarnish would interfere with performance, gold, which will remain chemically and metallurgically stable for the life of the device, is the metal of choice for printed circuit boards, connectors, contacts, and miniaturized circuitry. Thus, gold is found in calculators, computers, telephones, television sets, missiles and spacecraft. In a computer, a microscopic circuit edged with liquid gold can replace miles of conventional wiring. Ordinary equipment like a touch-tone telephone or a Polaroid camera, contains gold contact points, which contribute to the reliability of the product.

As the price of gold increased through the 1980s, the amount of gold used by electronics manufacturers for each device has been significantly reduced. Whereas gold plating had been as thick as 20 microns, it has now gone to as low as 2.5 microns. Nevertheless, the total volume of gold used in electronics continues to grow each year because of the continuing surge in the production of electronic equipment and devices.

Not only is gold unparalleled as an electrical conductor, it surpasses all other metals at conducting heat. Thus, gold has replaced the far-heavier asbestos for use in protecting components from the extreme heat of a jet engine. The lunar module of the Apollo program used gold foil as a radiation shield. When astronauts take their periodic walks in space, the umbilical cord that ties them to their space vehicle is gold-plated.

In architecture, the combination of malleability (an ounce of gold can cover up to 1,000 feet of coated glass) and heat-reflecting ability has made gold both practical and useful. We have all seen the gold-plated domes of the various mosques and monasteries around the world, but few of us are aware of gold's application in modern architecture, which makes extensive use of glass in the construction of high-rise buildings. Glass coated with gold not only is pleasing aesthetically, but it also permits the use of smaller heating and air-conditioning plants. Cooling and heating expenses in a glass-walled building can be reduced by as much as 40 percent by the addition of gold coating on the glass.

When firefighters are called to battle an intense fire, such as that caused by an air crash, the visors on their helmets may be coated with gold to shield them from the intense heat. In airplanes and in some trains used in alpine areas, gold is often used as an electrical heating element on the inner services of laminated glass. This prevents windshields from icing up or misting over. In porcelain and glass dinnerware, gold in the form of an oil solution is often applied as decoration.

In the dental industry, gold again is the metal of choice, because of its nonallergenic properties and its ability to remain free of tarnish. It is also easy to work with because of its malleability and the fact that it softens and melts at low temperatures. Thus, gold is used in inlays, crowns, bridges, and other orthodontic appliances. Although very expensive, gold has the advantage of far outlasting silver in these kinds of applications.

The oldest use for gold is in the creation of jewelry, and the jewelry industry today continues to account for over 55 percent of the total quantity consumed each year. The next-largest group of gold consumers are investors, who hoarded 35 percent of all the gold that was absorbed into the world economy in 1987, in the form of coins, medallions, and bullion. Thus, jewelry and investment together—both of which could be considered hoarding—represented over 90 percent of the total absorption of gold in 1987, while growing industrial and electronic applications consumed less than 10 percent of the year's total.

Supply and Demand Factors

Because gold is practically indestructible, most of the gold ever mined is still in existence. Total world production from the beginning of time is estimated at about 3.3 billion ounces. Because gold is such a dense metal, the total quantity of gold ever mined in the world would form a cube measuring just over 55 feet on each side.

To understand how scarce gold has truly been through the centuries, one must consider that almost two-thirds of the gold ever mined has been extracted during the past 60 years. Gold has been available in any quantity in the world only since the middle of the nineteenth century, when the California gold rush turned a small trickle of gold into a virtual flood that filled the coffers of several of the world's major governments. Prior to 1850, it is estimated that under 10,000 tons of gold had been mined since the beginning of time. During the last half of the nineteenth century, an additional 10,000 tons was mined. In 1847, annual production of gold was approximately 77 tons, but by 1852 annual production had risen to nearly 280 tons. Before the California gold rush, Britain, France, and the United States had minted new gold coins each year worth $8.4 million. By 1851, the average annual value of new gold coins minted in those three countries alone had increased to $75 million.

In any given year, the supply of gold on the market comes from four basic sources: (1) new mine production, which in 1989 was well over 60 million ounces; (2) secondary gold—scrap industrial gold, old jewelry, and other scrap—which in 1989 amounted to just over 15 percent of the total world supply of gold; (3) gold sales from the centrally planned economies, which have been extremely difficult to predict year by year but which should become less so in future years, since the entire bloc of countries within the sphere of influence of the Soviet Union has been moving rapidly toward free-market economies; (4) official sales by free-market governments.

In 1989, the total new-mine production of gold in the world was estimated at 63.4 million ounces. This represented an increase of 5.5 million ounces over 1988—a 9 percent increase. The leading producer in 1989 continued to be South Africa, with just under 20 million ounces. In the United States, the production of newly mined gold continued to increase dramatically in 1989, as the 72 new mines that had opened in 1987 and 1988, along with several other mines that had expanded their capacity, made their presence felt. The Bureau of Mines estimated domestic mine production at 7.5 million ounces for 1989, nearly 1.7 million ounces greater than in 1988 and up from nearly 5 million ounces in 1987. The total increase in only two years: over 2.5 million ounces per year! Around the world, the exploration for new gold has been proceeding at a feverish pace, far exceeding the exploration for other commodities.

The Bureau of Mines estimates that total world resources of gold—identified and unidentified—stand at approximately 2.4 billion ounces. Of that, approximately 50 percent are found in South Africa, while the United States, Brazil, and the Soviet Union each account for approximately 12 percent.

Gold scrap is an important secondary source of gold supply. In 1980, when the price of gold exceeded $800 an ounce, supplies of scrap gold brought to market exploded, as citizens everywhere searched for old jewelry and other items of gold that had been lying around in their dresser drawers or attics. Signs everywhere read "We Buy Gold," and at those prices, people responded. Since then, the amount of secondary gold brought to market has decreased significantly. As industrial users of gold become more and more efficient, that source of scrap gold has dwindled also. With so many individuals now holding gold in the form of jewelry, one cannot help but believe that if the price of gold should again skyrocket, much of that jewelry would be sold by individuals wishing to cash in on an unexpected windfall. In the meantime, most of the gold that ends up in chains, necklaces, bracelets, and other baubles tends to stay off the market.

Approximately one-third of all the gold that has ever been produced in the world lies in government vaults. The U.S. government alone owns approximately 262 million ounces of gold. That number, however, represents a huge decrease from 1950, when the government owned 650 million ounces. By 1960, U.S. government holdings had been reduced to 500 million ounces, and by 1970 to 315 million ounces. Present U.S. government reserves, though depleted, are nevertheless daunting. The closest competitor is Germany, which has only 95.2 million ounces of gold stashed away.

The real story of gold as a free-market commodity, of course, began only in 1968, when the major industrial nations of the world agreed to abstain for a time from additional acquisition of newly mined gold. From that date, gold prices were allowed to adjust to the laws of supply and demand. Then on January 1, 1975, the government of the United States rescinded its ban on private ownership of gold by U.S. citizens. During the next five years, collectors and investors acquired a total of 12 million ounces of gold. Since 1975, the nature of trading in gold has changed significantly. No longer is gold seen as a hedge against losing money, but rather as a commodity with which to make money.

The United States has been moving steadily toward self-sufficiency in gold production. In 1981, U.S. production covered only 17 percent of demand, while in 1988, the United States supplied 43 percent of its needs from new-mine production, according to the Gold Institute.

Worldwide in-ground supplies of gold seem adequate to meet

industrial and investor needs for the foreseeable future. Generally, the demand for gold by investors is such that, when supplies exceed the demand presented by the jewelry industry and industrial users, private investors and central banks can easily make up the difference. For that reason, yearly supply and demand projections for gold are relatively meaningless. Many gold-market veterans, in fact, have stopped trying to interpret the supply/demand statistics for gold.

In a given year, any number of circumstances can upset the supply/demand balance for gold. First, at any time, one or more of the world's governments could resume selling or buying gold on the open market in quantities that would drastically alter market prices. At more than 1.1 billion ounces, central bank reserves, including the International Monetary Fund, represent a huge overhang on the gold market. Second, unexpected gold sales by countries suddenly facing debts they are unable to pay would have a similar affect. Third, unexpected dumping by the Soviet government is always a threat. Fourth, during a run-up in gold prices, large numbers of individuals may bring their personal hoards of gold back to market. Fifth, should someone discover a suitable substitute for gold in industrial applications, however unlikely, the result would be a disruption in the normal supply/demand relationship.

At the end of 1987, total above-ground stocks equaled 2.7 billion ounces. Of that total, approximately 1.4 billion ounces were held as coins, bullion, or jewelry by private individuals. An additional 1.1 billion ounces were held by the world's central banks, including the International Monetary Fund. The annual new-mine production of gold, although expanding in recent years, remains relatively insignificant when compared with the total available supply of gold in the world, both in government reserves and private investments. Therefore, a significant increase in price can produce huge increases in supply practically overnight. Likewise, when the price of gold drops, available supplies tend to dry up rather quickly.

The gold-mining industry itself can only respond slowly, and often somewhat tardily, to escalating prices. The opening of a new mine is both costly and time consuming: it may take more than $200 million in initial capitalization to open a new gold mine, and at least four years are typically required to bring a new mine into production. As a consequence, new-mine production as a source of supply is relatively inelastic. But because it represents such a small percentage of the total supply overhang on the gold market, it has little effect on elasticity of gold supplies.

Demand for gold derives from five sources: (1) Jewelry, which accounts for 55 percent of demand; (2) the electronic industry, which creates just over 5 percent of the yearly demand; (3) dentistry, which accounts for 2.6 percent of annual demand; (4) other industrial uses, which account for just under 2 percent of the annual absorption of gold; and (5) investments, including coins, medallions, and bullion, which absorbed approximately 35 percent of all the gold that was purchased in 1987.

Since the restrictions against private ownership of gold were removed in 1975, the market for gold—particularly on the demand side—has undergone a radical transformation. Prior to 1975, the major participants in the gold market were governments, who bought and sold gold for their central bank reserves, and industry. But during the past 15 years, the most critical factor in determining the price of gold at any given time has become investor demands. Even though each individual investor may buy or sell relatively small quantities of the precious metal, the total pool of investors ready and willing to participate in the gold market has steadily increased to the point where they wield considerable power in the gold market.

Another factor contributing to private investor demand for gold in recent years has been the rather volatile economic conditions worldwide. Individuals with rising personal incomes who wish to hedge their investment portfolio against rising inflation have shown a particular interest in gold. These investors tend to hold gold for the long term as financial insurance. A second group of investors likes to move in and out of the market quickly, hoping to take fast profits. Both categories of investors have been increasing steadily during the past decade, and it is estimated that there are millions more simply waiting for the opportunity to make an investment in gold. In 1987, for example, the first full year of sales of the American Eagle bullion coin, investors snapped up approximately 1.9 million ounces of gold in the form of gold Eagle coins.

In addition to the millions of individual investors, there are also bankers and traders who invest in gold as part of their business, and a growing number of institutional investors who manage investment portfolios and include gold as an integral part of those portfolios.

Experts anticipate that there will be little change in the usage patterns for gold over the next several years. The jewelry industry will probably continue to be the primary user of fabricated gold, and the electronics industry will continue to expand the total amount of gold used, while continuing to find ways to reduce the amount of gold necessary for each application.

Elasticity of demand for gold varies according to its use. In the jewelry industry, demand tends to respond quickly to changes in the price of gold. As the price goes up, many individuals simply don't buy gold jewelry. If the price goes high enough, many of those who own gold jewelry will bring some of that jewelry to market to sell for a profit. Thus, gold in the form of jewelry, which comprises more than 50 percent of the total demand for gold in any given year, is a very elastic segment of the gold market.

In dentistry and electronics, which account for a relatively small part of the demand side of the gold market, demand is much less elastic. In industrial usage, there are few substitutes for gold in most applications, and the amount of gold used in an individual application is ordinarily a small portion of the total value of the product. Thus, the escalating price of gold has little effect on the price of the item itself. In dentistry, there simply is no suitable substitute for gold, except for silver which, although widely used, has several characteristics that make it less attractive than gold for specific applications. In spite of a relative inelasticity of demand in these two segments of the market, total demand for gold in the long run will drop in response to an escalation of prices, as we have observed during the past several years.

The Role of Gold in International Economics

Historically, the measure of a country's relative wealth has always been the size of its gold reserve. Of all the metals throughout history, therefore, gold has played the most important role in international economics. Traditionally, gold has been, and remains today, the only universally recognized medium of exchange. According to Green, "It is the ultimate currency by which one nation settles its debts with another."*

From the Greeks and Romans right up to modern times, both gold and silver were used extensively as coins. Silver, however—and occasionally copper, in the form of bronze—was much more widely accepted as a medium of exchange in individual transactions. Because of gold's relative scarcity and therefore higher value, it was a commodity that had great value for use in ornamentation, and as a store of wealth for kings, merchants, and the church. Although the first gold coins were manufactured as early as 550 B.C. by Croesus, king of Lydia (western Turkey), it wasn't until the California gold rush of 1848, which led the world into a new era of abundance, that gold existed in sufficient quantity to be a practical basis for a monetary standard worldwide.

In 1816, as a result of increasing gold supplies and a steady flow of silver to the Far East, Britain formally adopted a gold standard, having functioned with gold as the de facto basis of her monetary system since 1717. Following the California gold rush and the ensuing discovery of gold in other parts of the world, enough gold existed such that other European nations were able to follow Britain's lead in the 1870s. The United States finally abandoned a bimetallic system and adopted a gold standard in 1900, in spite of the fiery rhetoric of William Jennings Bryan in his famous Cross of Gold speech. But in 1914, with the outbreak of World War I, most of the world effectively abandoned the gold standard when the transport of gold via sea routes became quite dangerous.

With the abandonment of the gold standard by the major world economies, there remained one formal link between gold and currencies, until the late 1960s: the gold exchange standard. By agreement of the major trading countries, gold reserves were supplemented by key currencies—sterling and dollars—that could be exchanged for gold. But in 1971, a flood of dollars

---

*See *References*, Green p. 67.

worldwide—dollars that could ostensibly be exchanged for gold at $35 an ounce—rendered the gold exchange standard obsolete. The United States thereafter no longer allowed the redemption of dollars for gold at the Federal Reserve Bank of New York. With no further link between gold and the major money systems, international currencies were allowed to float on the open market.

Even though the formal relationship between currencies and gold had been severed, however, gold has maintained its informal long-term position as the ultimate medium of exchange between countries as well as the de facto standard of value for other commodities. Through the centuries, a curious relationship has existed between gold and most other goods. Over long periods of time, it has been observed, commodity prices tend to remain more or less in line with the price of gold, even though in the short term there may be little correlation. "Regardless of the dollar price involved, one ounce of gold would purchase a good-quality man's suit at the conclusion of the Revolutionary War, the Civil War, the presidency of Franklin Roosevelt, and today," remarked one public figure. "It is interesting to note that the average earnings of an English worker in 1900 came to half an ounce of gold a week, and that in 1979, after two world wars, a world slump and a world inflation, the British worker has average earnings of half an ounce of gold a week," observed another.*

*See *References*, Green, p. xxvii.

4 THE OTHER PRECIOUS METALS

Silver

IN STORIES AND IN SONGS, silver and gold are closely associated. Particularly when we think about wealth or money, silver comes to mind as often as does gold. From the earliest times, silver met all the criteria for being considered a precious metal. It was virtually indestructible, it was readily transportable, it could easily be divided, it was dense so that a relatively small amount could represent a large store of value. It had beauty, nearly as great as that of gold. It was malleable—it could be made into jewelry and ornaments. It was ductile—it could be made into chains to be worn around the neck. As early as the fourth millennium B.C., silver was being fashioned into ornaments, examples of which have been found in the royal tombs in Chaldea. The Mesopotamians, the Egyptians, the Chinese, the Persians, and the Greeks all treasured silver as an ornamental metal.

Most of the silver in the ancient world came from the area known today as Turkey, as well as from Macedonia and Thrace, now part of Greece and southern Yugoslavia. In the Mediterranean, silver was first produced in significant quantities at a site called Laurium, near Athens. These Athenian silver mines probably contributed significantly to the power and influence of that early city-state. Likewise, the silver mines of Spain greatly added to the wealth and power of the Roman Empire. Both the Romans and the Greeks found that producing silver through the use of slave labor, working under the most inhumane conditions, was a very profitable undertaking.

During the height of the Roman Empire, both gold and silver seem to have been abundant. Silver was adopted by the Romans as the official basis for their monetary system, with gold and bronze both functioning as secondary coins. During the decline of the Roman Empire, a great deal of silver disappeared into hoards in the Far East, particularly in India, where to this day, silver remains a popular store of individual value. As Roman influence deteriorated in the outlying regions, the importance of precious metals as a store of value increased among the natives. As the frontiers were repeatedly invaded by Gothic and Hukkish hordes, the visible supply of silver diminished markedly.

As Europe began to revive following the Dark Ages, stocks of precious metals became ever more abundant. In Europe, silver mines were operating in the Saxon Erzgebirge in the tenth century. Then in the sixteenth century, a silver coin called the *Joachimsthaler*—taking its name from Joachim's valley (*thal*) in Austria, from where the silver was mined—became so popular and its presence so commonplace that it gave its name to the dollar. In England, from the time of the Saxons until the end of the seventeenth century—a period when gold became more readily available and silver supplies were being seriously depleted through trade with the Far East—silver was the sole basis for the coinage of England. Although some gold coins existed during that period, there was nothing close to a bimetallic standard.

When the Spanish conquistadors came to the new world, they first seized most of the gold and silver held by the Aztecs and the Incas; then they opened new mines in the Andes and sent the gold and silver to Spain. In those early days of exploration, 98 percent of the metal taken from the Americas to Europe was silver. Between 1500 and 1660, nearly three-quarters of the silver taken from North and South America ended up in private hands.

Peru was the first silver producer in South America; by the end of the third decade of the twentieth century, mines in that country had contributed nearly 9 percent of the total world production since 1492. Even richer deposits were later found in Bolivia, which consequently became the world's greatest producer for a time. Between 1521 and 1930, however, the country that yielded the largest amount of silver was Mexico, who for the past several years has again been the world's leading silver producer. The United States, which was the world's second largest producer in 1989, contributed almost no silver prior to the discovery of the Comstock lode in 1859.

Silver Mining

Although silver is mined all around the globe, three-quarters of the world's newly mined silver in recent years is being produced by only seven countries: Mexico, the United States, Peru, Canada, the Soviet Union, Australia, and Poland. The top four producing countries alone accounted for over half of all the silver mined in 1989: Mexico, the United States, Peru, and Canada. The majority of the silver mined in the world is taken from the mountain range that extends from Alaska south through the Andes, making silver essentially a product of the Western Hemisphere.

Although not as rare as gold, silver is nevertheless a scarce metal; the abundance of silver in the earth's crust is only 0.075 parts per million (ppm). Silver deposits occur in a unique pattern—a pattern determined when the earth's crust cooled many millennia ago. Superheated solutions from the interior of the earth were thrust upward into the earth's crust in areas of volcanic activity. Pressures and temperatures were such that different minerals collected in different places and at different depths. Silver deposits cooled in what is known by geologists as epithermal lodes and pipes. This means that most silver deposits—where silver is the primary metal—occur within a few thousand feet of the surface of the earth and diminish significantly as the depth increases. The primary exceptions to this rule are the mines in the Coeur d'Alene area of northern Idaho. Here, silver veins have been found to run as deep as 8,000 feet, often increasing in silver content as the vein runs lower. In Ontario, a similar pattern is found at the Siscoe mine. These epithermal patterns seem to indicate that most of the world's primary silver mines will continue to produce less and less silver, while the bulk of the world's silver will be derived more and more as a by-product from mining other base-metal deposits.

Silver is taken from four different types of mines. First there are those that extract pure silver from high-grade ores. The numbers of this type of mine are dwindling worldwide. Second are the mines that extract pure silver from low-grade ores. As technology becomes more sophisticated, this type of silver mine continues to gain in importance. Third are the mines that produce silver as well as other metals, with silver being in roughly equal value proportions with the other metal, and fourth are the mines that produce silver as a minor by-product. As the pure silver mines become less and less productive, new silver increasingly is obtained as a by-product of base metal mining, particularly copper, zinc, lead, and nickel. Presently, only one-third of worldwide silver production actually derives from pure silver mines.

The process for extracting silver from its ore is very similar to that of gold. Originally, the silver-bearing ores were separated from surrounding dirt and debris by simple washing. The ores were then smelted to separate the silver from the ore. Later, the amalgamation process was developed, in which mercury is introduced into the wet ore to form an alloy with the silver, thereby extracting it from the ore. The silver is later separated from the mercury. By 1850, silver ore was being roasted with common salt, a process that converted the silver to chlorides. The mixture was then leached with a hot brine, and metallic copper was introduced to precipitate out the pure silver. More recently, cyanide has been used to extract the silver from its ores. The "heap-leaching" process, in which a cyanide solution is poured through huge mounds of low-grade ore, has made it possible to extract silver from otherwise uneconomical low-grade ores.

Uses of Silver

Silver was first used in Asia Minor for ornamentation and display. As early as 2300 B.C., gold and silver and an alloy called electrum, which is part silver and part gold, were placed in graves of the rich and noble; it was common for rulers of the era to exchange gifts of gold and silver drinking vessels. Throughout the ages, silver has been known primarily as a precious metal because of its beauty and its monetary usage. For ancient craftsmen, it was the most ductile and malleable of metals, next to gold. It was the whitest metal and so exhibited the highest reflectivity. Like gold, it could be melted down and turned to other uses. And when silver was made into coins of high-grade purity, the value of the bullion in the coin roughly equaled the trading price of the coin.

Silver became most popular in ancient times as a currency, more popular than gold, copper, or bronze—the other leading contenders. Sometime after the eighth-century B.C., silver, gold, and bronze were all being circulated as coins and money. Silver became the most popular currency because its value lay somewhere between gold and bronze. Gold, being more valuable and therefore too precious to use in ordinary commerce, was reserved as the "tribute to emperors, the ransom of kings, the indemnity of war, the ornament of princes and the plating of idols."* Bronze, on the other hand, being far more abundant and therefore much less valuable, was used for the daily currency of the marketplace. Then, as villages grew into towns, an expanding middle class used silver coins as a convenient payment for purchases of medium value. Thus, silver became the metal of choice throughout much of the world for settling business transactions.

In the twentieth century, silver has experienced a near-complete transformation—from a precious metal prized for its beauty and its monetary value to a full-fledged industrial commodity. Since the turn of the century, two major occurrences have caused significant repercussions for the industrial consumption of silver. From 1900 to 1910, silver was one of the metals very important to the process of electrification in America. Then the period from 1938 to 1945—World War II—ushered in the electronic age and guaranteed silver's long-term value in industrial

*See *References*, Groseclose, p. 88.

applications. By 1965, 47 percent of worldwide silver consumption was for industrial use. In 1979, 95 percent of the world's silver was going into industry, while only 5 percent was being used for coinage.

During the decade from 1978 to 1988—a period of inordinately high silver prices—industrial consumption of silver was reduced from a high of 160 million ounces to 120 million ounces, yet industrial consumption comprised 93 percent of total silver usage in 1988. During that same decade, silver going into coins declined from 36.3 million ounces in 1978 to as low as 8.7 million ounces in 1984. Recently, as more and more nations have been producing commemorative silver coins and medallions—generally not for use in common currency but designed more for the collector and the investor—the use of silver in coins has rebounded, to just over 30 million ounces in 1988.

During the past several decades, the predominant commercial user of silver has been the photographic industry. In 1979, photographic materials accounted for 39 percent of total industrial consumption. Ten years later, the industry has accounted for nearly 45 percent of total industrial usage—almost 60 million ounces of silver per year—in spite of greatly intensified efforts to conserve and recycle silver. And although millions of dollars have been spent in a search for a suitable substitute, silver remains many times better than the second-best light-sensitive substance available.

The second most important industrial consumer of silver is the electrical and electronics industry. Here silver, because of its high resistance to corrosion, is used as a plating for electrical contacts, relays, and switches; as conductor wire for small electronic components; and in certain critical products like aircraft spark plugs. Such usage accounted for 30 percent of total industrial consumption of silver in 1987.

That same year, approximately 13 percent of all silver that was used in the United States went into sterlingware, silver plate, and jewelry. Other uses include dental fillings, medicinal compounds, coatings for mirrors, photochromic glass, and optical and heat-reflecting surfaces.

Supply and Demand Factors

From 1492 until 1987—nearly five centuries—approximately 29.7 billion ounces of silver were mined in the world. Of that total, nearly 90 percent has been produced during the past two centuries.

Supply and demand patterns for silver are unique among the precious metals. The most important factor governing the supply of silver relates to the geological characteristics of silver deposits. With the two exceptions noted earlier—the Coeur d'Alene area in Idaho and the Siscoe mine in Canada—the richest deposits of silver have been found at the surface of the earth. The deeper the mine, the less silver per ton of ore. Because many of the richest primary silver deposits have thus played out, the majority of silver—75 percent of new silver—is found as a by-product of lead, nickel, copper, and zinc mining. And even there, the yield is declining. In 1962, the average yield of silver per ton of base metal mined was 32 ounces per ton. By 1965, it had fallen to 25 ounces per ton, and by 1971 to 20 ounces per ton. Yield in recent years is even less.

Because of this unique characteristic, newly mined supplies of silver are almost entirely a function of demand for the four base metals—not of the demand for silver itself. As the production of base metals increases, so does the supply of silver, regardless of price. Conversely, the price of silver can increase substantially without a corresponding increase in new mine supplies. Between 1972 and 1979, for instance, silver prices increased by 556 percent, while world production of new silver increased by only 10 percent.

The second source of silver is new scrap silver—industrial silver that has been recycled or recovered. In response to increases in the price of silver over the past two decades, industrial users have focused a great deal of attention on recycling, as well as reducing, the amount of silver used in various applications. In 1980, for example, as the price of silver increased dramatically, Eastman Kodak reprocessed even the tiny scraps left from punching the sprocket holes in the edge of film. This source of secondary supply—approximately 45 million ounces were recovered in 1988—is also rather inelastic. Because the influence of price is steady and persistent, the incentive to recover and recycle new scrap always exists, and any fluctuation in supply depends more on the size of the available pool than on the price of silver itself.

A third source of supply is old scrap—silver jewelry, sterling silverware, and other silver objects—like old coins, for instance. When silver soared toward $50 an ounce in 1980, this rather fickle source of silver responded in spades. Untold numbers of individuals emptied their personal collections of silver coins, which had become many times more precious than the face value of the coins themselves. By its very nature, old scrap is an extremely elastic source of silver supply, responding as it does primarily to high prices.

Of particular interest is the vast quantity of old silver objects supposed to exist in the Far East. Experts who watch the silver market closely refer to this "Asian hoard" as a constant overhang on the silver market. For century upon century, individuals in India and other south Asian nations have prized silver as an individual store of wealth; an ages-old practice in India dictates that only wealth in the form of personal jewelry can be transferred as a female inheritance. As a result, during the seventeenth and eighteenth centuries the East India Company traded huge quantities of silver for the teas, coffees, spices, textiles, and other articles that they brought back from the Far East. Such vast supplies of silver were transported from England to the Far East, in fact, that England was forced to abandon the silver standard it had clung for over a century.

As late as 1933, the bulk of all silver that had been produced since 1492—approximately 15,486 million ounces, of which all but 3,946 million ounces were still accounted for—was thought to be in China and India. Because of the centuries of hoarding, no one can be sure how much silver remains in India today. There are likely immense quantities of personal jewelry, tableware, old coins, religious objects, and art that have been collected through the ages.

Exporting of silver from India is illegal, yet when the world price of silver is high, smugglers manager to sell untold quantities of the illicit metal—during the 1970s, an average of 45 million ounces of silver were brought to market from the Asian hoard. Consequently, the silver from India is extremely responsive to world price. In recent years, however, supplies from India have not responded in the same quantities as before, leading experts to question whether the stores of silver in that country have been seriously depleted.

To summarize, most sources of silver are price-inelastic. Newly mined supplies are practically unrelated to silver prices; new scrap from industrial sources is limited by the amount of scrap produced. Personal hoards of silver—the only silver supply responsive to price—seem to have been significantly depleted during periods of previous price increases.

In the twentieth century, silver has become essentially an industrial metal; over 90 percent of all silver used each year goes into industrial products. As we have seen, silver is in high demand for certain very specific industrial uses—notably photographic supplies and electrical and electronic products. Yet silver remains a precious metal—attractive to speculators and investors alike. Because of these competing interests, silver seems subject to the worst of both worlds: prey to the periodic business cycle as well as vulnerable to the whims of speculative demand.

In its role as an industrial material, the demand for silver is quite inelastic—for two very important reasons. First, no suitable substitutes for silver have been found in the two most important industries where silver is used—electronics and photography—even though millions of dollars have gone into extensive research to locate workable replacement materials. Second, the industrial demand for silver is primarily derived demand; the amount of silver used is such a small part of the cost of a completed product that a large price increase in silver does not appreciably affect the price of the product itself.

Industrial demand for silver has been growing in recent years, even as the principal silver-consuming industries have become skilled at reducing the amount of silver necessary for each application. In the photo industry, in particular, the amount of silver used in film has been slashed, at the same time that the industry has become adept at recovering silver from used film, developing papers, and solutions. In the electronics field, the amount of silver on any individual contact or switch is minuscule compared to the quantity used in similar applications just a decade or so ago. In spite of such drastic efforts to conserve silver, though, the quantity of silver that goes into industry continues to grow, after a small slump following the 1980 surge in prices. The reason: continued growth in both the photographic and electronics industries.

The unknown demand factor for silver is the scope of investor interest. In many respects, silver has become a real battleground of competing interests. Producers, brokers, and dealers alike fuel speculator demand by insisting that prices are going up, while industrial users—the photographic companies, the electronics manufacturers, and the makers of silverware and jewelry, who have an interest in keeping prices low—insist that the speculators are driving prices higher. Many investors, who view silver as a scarce metal subject to ever-increasing demand by industrial consumers, dream of a return to the heady days of 1980.

The reality is, however, that silver today is actually a surplus metal; a review of the production and consumption statistics since 1976 reveal that fact quite clearly. In 1976, total world mine production of silver was 316.4 million ounces, while consumption stood at 467.2 million ounces—a deficit of 150.8 million ounces between new supplies and actual use. By 1981, high silver prices had driven world consumption down to 353 million ounces, while world mine production had escalated to 361 million ounces—a surplus of 8 million ounces. By 1987, world production stood at 429.1 million ounces, while consumption was only 415.7 million ounces—an even greater surplus. But these figures do not take into account the extensive supplies of old silver in existence around the globe—silver waiting to be brought to market when the price is right. When that factor is considered, even in deficit years a de facto surplus exists because of all the elastic supply of old silver hanging over the market.

The factors creating the present surplus in new mine supply seem to be 1) higher prices for silver that have encouraged expansion of mining operations; 2) more efficient recovery and recycling of silver by industrial users; 3) significant reduction in the amount of silver used in individual products; 4) increased investor demand. In recent years, it seems that investors have been very willing to take up the slack in the supply/demand differential in silver, much as they do with gold. With gold, however, growing industrial usage amounts to only 5 percent of the total annual demand, while with silver, industrial use is well over 90 percent annually. Because of this, even though investors are exerting an ever more important role in the price of silver, silver remains very sensitive to the business cycle as well as to the speculative influence. In the short run, however, it is these very speculators and investors, rather than industrial demand, who seem to dictate the price of silver.

The Influence of Gold

Despite the fact that silver is much more abundant than gold and that it is primarily an industrial metal subject to normal business cycles, silver continues to be inextricably intertwined with gold, just as it has been throughout the centuries. All logic to the contrary, where gold prices go, silver prices seem to follow. Since 1970, the price of silver has closely tracked that of gold. In times when silver is plentiful and its price, by all normal laws of supply and demand, should go lower, if the price of gold goes up, silver tends to follow. The reason, of course, is speculative demand. In spite of that effect, silver maintains a mind of its own, displaying greater short-term volatility than gold. This, too, is a characteristic consistent with historical patterns.

The Role of Silver in International Economics

Throughout history, silver has been practically indistinguishable from money. In both the Old and New Testaments of the Bible, there are frequent references to silver as a form of payment or as a measure of value. Thirty pieces of silver was the price, for instance, that Judas Iscariot charged to betray Christ to the Romans. Whereas Genesis first mentions gold by including it in the creation story, silver is first introduced as a medium of payment. Swashbuckling tales of Spanish explorers routinely refer to "pieces of eight," while the British pound refers, of course, to pound sterling. In French, the word *argent*, a term generally used to mean money, translates literally as silver.

Throughout history, along with motivating individual acts of betrayal like that of Judas, silver—along with other precious metals—motivated acts of war and conquest. When Alexander the Great marched upon Persia, he did so not only for the gold but also for the silver that was there. But even though the precious metals—gold and silver—were often the root causes of wars, they also provided the impetus for world exploration; it was the search for precious metals that drew the Spanish across the Atlantic ocean in the fifteenth and sixteenth centuries. Silver and gold, then, are linked inextricably to the history of world economics and politics, and silver, as the most popular medium of exchange throughout much of history, has played a central role.

Although there are references to silver throughout ancient writings, it wasn't until 1273 that the first statistical records were kept. William the Conqueror placed the mint within the walls of the Tower of London in that year and introduced the "Tower pound" as a regulated unit of weight for silver. By the sixteenth century, great quantities of silver were finding their way into England, which was establishing itself as a world power through its international trade. Elizabeth I took it upon herself to straighten out her country's currency mess by establishing a silver standard. Until the seventeenth century, silver was the sole basis for the monetary system of England. Some gold coins circulated during that time, but represented an alternative standard.

As silver began flowing to India in vast quantities via the trading ships of the East India Company, gold at the same time began to arrive in England in ever-increasing quantities from France, through increased trade between the two countries who, after 1713, were at peace. England rapidly began moving toward a de facto gold standard, which led a century later—in 1816—to a de jure gold standard. In the United States, sizable discoveries of silver and gold originally led to a bimetallic standard of currency but, because of the vagaries of international trade, the United States was forced by 1900 to adopt a single gold standard.

As more and more nations switched to gold during the late

nineteenth century, substantial quantities of silver began to flow from official holdings onto the free market, lowering the value of silver. In the United States, citizens had previously been able to freely exchange their silver bullion for legal tender at the mint, a practice that established a fixed price for silver. When the gold standard was adopted, this privilege was removed and the consequence was a severe depression in the price of silver.

As long as silver had been universally monetized, it was incumbent upon the world mints to maintain the price of the metal within relatively narrow limits and to maintain those limits over substantial periods of time. This was necessary if silver was to be a measure of value for other commodities and services. The mints did their job for over 300 years, from the middle of the sixteenth century until the end of the nineteenth century. Once the world moved toward a gold standard, however, silver became increasingly a free-market commodity, a role that was in direct competition with its role as a monetary standard.

From 1873 to 1973, then, silver seemed to hold practically no value to the governments of the world. They sold off their silver stocks and debased their silver coinage and, by 1932, the price of silver had fallen to an all-time low of under $0.25 a ounce. In an attempt to support the price of silver, the Silver Purchase Act of 1934 instructed the treasury to buy silver until the traditional mint price of $1.29 was again reached. This led to wild speculation to accumulate silver on the open market. The Silver Purchase Act, which did raise prices, however artificially, also led to a huge accumulation of silver by the U.S. government such that, by the beginning of World War II, the government held almost 3 billion ounces of silver in its vaults.

During the 1960s, as the world economy grew at a tremendous pace, the demand for silver grew along with it. When the treasury's selling price of $1.29 was broken, suddenly the vast numbers of silver dollars then in circulation became worth more as bullion than for their face value. In order to rectify that situation, the government began selling from its stockpile in an effort to drive the price of silver back down. Finally, in 1968, all silver coinage was removed from circulation. It was this demonetization of silver and the end of government attempts to manipulate its price that ultimately led to the attempt by the Hunt family of Texas to corner the silver market in 1979, resulting in a huge temporary increase in the price of silver—all the way to $50 an ounce.

During the past two decades, silver has played a much-reduced role on the world economic stage. Although the U.S. government continues to hold onto 150 million ounces of silver, less than a third of that amount—43 million ounces—is held by the treasury. The remainder, over 100 million ounces, is held as part of the strategic stockpile, which clearly defines the primarily industrial role played by silver in the 1990s. Of all other foreign governments, only Mexico, with 41.7 million ounces, and India, with 67.5 million ounces, are holding any sizable reserves of silver. In the world of international economics, then, it would seem that the sun has set on silver as a leading participant.

Platinum and Palladium

Although platinum has been found alloyed with other metals in objects dating back as far as the seventh century B.C., the actual discovery of platinum as a separate metal is a relatively recent occurrence. When the Spanish conquered South America, they found platinum in the stream beds of Columbia. The Spanish called it platina—"little silver." In 1823, platinum was discovered in the Ural Mountains in Russia, and in South Africa in 1924.

Today, the Soviet Union and South Africa remain the two largest producers of platinum and the platinum group metals, which include palladium, iridium, osmium, rhodium, and ruthenium. The metals commonly occur together. In 1988, South Africa, where platinum-group metals are found in primary deposits, produced just over 50 percent of the world's supply. The Soviet Union, where platinum-group metals are a by-product of copper and nickel, produced an estimated 44 percent of the world's new supply. In third place was Canada with some 3 percent.

Mining Platinum and Palladium

The United States, which accounts for less than 2% of the world's supply of platinum-group metals, has significantly increased its production in the last few years with the development of the Stillwater Complex in Montana. In 1988, this particular mine produced approximately 36,000 ounces of platinum and 124,000 ounces of palladium, but for 1989, further development at the mine was expected to increase output to as much as 267,000 ounces total. Further plans call for a second mine near Stillwater that would begin production by 1991. In spite of that, the United States continues to rely on imports for over 93 percent of its consumption of platinum-group metals.

Platinum is an extremely rare mineral—much rarer than gold or silver. Whereas an ounce of gold can be produced from approximately four tons of ore, it requires ten tons of ore to produce just one ounce of platinum. In 1988, there were 6.7 million tons of copper produced worldwide, 430 million ounces of silver, 63 million ounces of gold, and only 8.9 million ounces of platinum-group metals.

Palladium was only discovered in 1903 by a British scientist, who was able to separate it from platinum residues. Like platinum, palladium is a silvery-white metal, nearly impervious to oxidation and corrosion. Even though palladium was initially discovered as a by-product of platinum, it is actually more plentiful—although still very rare.

Uses of Platinum and Palladium

Platinum and palladium—the "noble metals"—are extremely strong and durable, much more so than even gold or silver. Twice as dense as lead, platinum has a much higher melting point than gold, yet is still malleable. Both platinum and palladium can be classified as precious metals, industrial metals, and strategic metals. Only a few years ago, nearly all the demand for platinum and palladium was for industrial use. For years, oil companies have used platinum and palladium in the refining process to improve the octane rating of gasoline. More recently, platinum and palladium have both been used in the catalytic converters on all North American cars. In 1986, the average catalytic converter used approximately 0.057 ounce of platinum, 0.015 ounce of palladium, as well 0.006 ounce of rhodium—very small quantities indeed, yet totalling a significant amount when the millions of cars and light trucks that are produced each year are considered. In 1988, in fact, automobile catalysts accounted for 45 percent of the total consumption of platinum group metals in the United States.

In the United States, more than 95 percent of the consumption of platinum group metals is for industrial usage. In addition to the automotive industry, platinum and palladium are widely used in the electronics and electrical industry, as well as for dental and medical applications. Both metals combine the beauty and scarcity of gold with the industrial versatility of silver. Palladium, in fact, is often substituted for the higher-priced platinum and gold in both electronics and auto emissions control.

In the field of agriculture, nitric acid is an essential ingredient in most agriculture fertilizers. Nitric acid, in turn, is produced using catalysts of platinum or palladium alloys. In most industrial applications, platinum seems to be superior to palladium, although each is virtually interchangeable with the other. The determining factor actually seems more to be price. Platinum is rarer but goes twice as far as palladium. Therefore, when the price of palladium reaches half the price of platinum, the net cost in an industrial application is essentially equal. As long as palladium remains below that threshold, there is an economic advantage to substituting palladium for platinum.

Palladium itself is primarily used in electrical applications, but both metals are becoming increasingly popular for use in jewelry, particularly in Japan, where, like gold and silver, platinum jewelry is seen both as a decorative item and an investment. Worldwide, in fact, the investment demand for both platinum and palladium has increased significantly in the past several years. In 1988, investors accounted for more than 50 percent of the total worldwide demand for platinum, third behind auto catalysts and jewelry.

Platinum and palladium both play an important role in the development of the fuel cell, the batterylike device at the heart of future electric cars. As oil-based fuels become scarcer and ever more problematic, this particular application could very well become another important industrial use for the two metals.

Although platinum and palladium have rarely been used to coin money, the recent increase in demand by investors has led to two new platinum coins—the Australian Koala and the Canadian Maple Leaf, both 99.95 percent pure platinum. First produced in 1988, both coins are considered legal tender and are available in one-ounce, half-ounce, quarter-ounce, and one-tenth-ounce weights.

Supply and Demand Factors

The United States is the world's largest consumer of platinum and palladium. Within the United States, the auto industry is the largest user of platinum and palladium for catalytic converters. Because most other nations of the world have not adopted the strict auto emissions standards of the United States, they have not experienced the same growth in demand for platinum and palladium.

That will likely change soon, however, as world leaders become more and more cognizant of the need to reduce emissions. In 1988, Ford Motor Company announced that it was testing a catalytic converter that did not use platinum. This new converter, which would not be ready for larger-scale use for several years, would still rely on palladium, rhodium, and alloys of rare-earth metals to function as the catalyst. Presently, there are no real substitutes for platinum and palladium in auto antipollution devices. Thus, the long-term growth in demand for both metals seems assured.

Platinum and palladium both suffer from a chronic undersupply, even though expansion of production facilities is under way. An important source for secondary platinum and palladium is junked automobiles. It has been over 15 years since catalytic converters were first installed in American vehicles, and many of the cars so equipped have long since ended their useful life and ended up in scrap yards around the country. As demand for platinum and palladium continues to grow, these cars will become an ever more important source of recycled platinum-group metals.

In their industrial applications, particularly in automotive catalytic converters, both platinum and palladium comprise a very small part of the finished product. Therefore, major fluctuations in price of the two metals have little effect on their use. Even more important is the fact that, for the foreseeable future, there are no suitable substitutes for the two metals. These conditions result in very low elasticity of demand for both platinum and palladium.

As with other metals, capitalization involved in expanding production tends to militate against rapid response to increased prices. On the other hand, a significant amount of the supply of platinum and palladium comes from mines in South Africa dedicated primarily to their production. Thus, during periods of lower prices, it becomes feasible to reduce production significantly in response to lower demands. The result is some elasticity of supply, as opposed to silver, which is produced primarily as a by-product of other metals.

The Role of Platinum and Palladium in International Economics

For several reasons, platinum and palladium have not historically played a major role in international economics. The primary reason, of course, is the relative recency of their discovery. Whereas gold and silver had become prized for their beauty and scarcity during earliest antiquity, platinum had to wait for the Spanish invaders in the New World for its discovery. Following that, platinum remained little more than a curiosity until commercially viable deposits were discovered in South Africa in the early part of the twentieth century.

Nevertheless, both platinum and palladium seem destined for a much brighter future. Like gold and silver, platinum and palladium are both rare metals. Likewise, they are essentially imperishable and have great value in both industrial applications and as a store of wealth. Even more dense than gold, a quantity of platinum or palladium of great value can be stored in a small space and transported easily.

The names of platinum and palladium do not ring with the same romance as the names silver and gold. They don't quicken the heart nor cause us to dream. Nevertheless, for very practical reasons, both metals will be occupying ever more important positions on the world economic stage.

5 THE STRATEGIC METALS

THE STRATEGIC METALS, for many years known as the "minor" metals, are considered crucial to defense and industry in the United States under the terms of the Strategic Stockpile Act. All of the metals in this group are essential to the functioning of a complex industrial society, while at the same time being available almost exclusively from countries and areas of the globe that are generally unstable both economically and politically. Because the United States and Europe are almost totally dependent upon uncertain sources of supply for these metals, most of them are stockpiled for reasons of national security.

Not all the metals discussed in this chapter are included in the Strategic Stockpile Act. Some, in fact, are quite plentiful, but for one reason or another, have not achieved widespread use. Magnesium, for example, is the eighth most abundant element in the earth's crust—certainly not scarce, by any measure. As the main alloying element in sheet aluminum—the material used in the production of aluminum cans—its importance in the world economy cannot be underestimated. Other aluminum-magnesium alloys form critical lightweight structural parts for aircraft and missiles—and for myriad consumer goods. Yet in 1988, only 364,000 tons of magnesium were produced worldwide, compared with 17.3 million tons of aluminum and 879 million tons of steel.

Each of the strategic metals is considered minor only in the sense that its annual consumption may be dwarfed by other, more widely used, materials. As a group, the strategic metals are crucial to the growth and continued development of modern technology—in electronics, in aerospace, and in engineering and construction. They may be used in small quantities, but each serves an essential function in the development and production of stronger, more efficient materials vital both to industry and defense.

The title "strategic" is only a recent development. These are metals, after all, that have been traded for over a century in London under the less pretentious designation "minor metals." During recent years, however, they have become increasingly popular with spectators who recognize that the specific conditions of supply and demand for each of the metals can lead to extreme price volatility and therefore an opportunity for profits. As a group they picked up the more exotic appellation "strategic" because marketing and sales people—eager to tap this speculative fervor—felt that investors would be reluctant to risk money on a "minor" metal. They therefore attached the "strategic" moniker to enhance the image of these little-known, but absolutely essential, metals.

Antimony

China, the world's largest producer of antimony, is also the largest foreign supplier to the United States, accounting for more than 50 percent of total imports. Additional U.S. sources include South Africa, Hong Kong, and Mexico. Together, China and the U.S.S.R. produced nearly half of the world's supply in 1987. Bolivia, traditionally a very unstable country in South America, was third with just under 15 percent of world production, while South Africa was fourth-largest producer with approximately 12 percent. The United States produces virtually no antimony, other than as a by-product of domestic lead ore.

Antimony generally occurs in three forms: metallic needles

embedded in ore; as a compact, sooty black sulfide stibnite; or as a secondary yellow-oxide stibconite. It is most commonly found as stibnite—in massive, shallow lodes containing 60 to 70 percent antimony. At times, it is also found in combination with gold, silver, mercury, and arsenic. Methods for the mining and recovery of antimony are fairly conventional. In the mill, the ore is crushed and milled, then concentrated into sulfides of 60 to 65 percent antimony content. These sulfides are then dried, bagged, and shipped. At the refineries, the ore is converted to oxide and then to metal. Antimony is usually delivered in the form of bars, blocks, or pigs weighing 44 to 60 pounds each.

Uses of Antimony

Antimony is a silvery-white, brittle, crystalline metal. Neither malleable nor ductile, it is easily reduced to powder. Antimony exhibits the general physical properties of a metal, but the chemical properties of a nonmetal. It is a poor conductor of electricity and heat.

Because of its extremely high melting point—630 degrees Celsius—antimony, in the form of antimony oxide, is primarily used as a flame retardant in plastics, rubber, and textiles. These uses represent about 65 percent of total consumption. In lead-acid batteries, alloys of antimony and lead are used to make a stronger lead alloy that is more resistant to corrosion; automotive storage batteries account for another 11 percent of total use. An additional 9 percent is consumed by the chemical industry, while a smaller portion—roughly 5 percent of the total—is used as a decolorizing and refining agent in optical glass, as well as in other glass and ceramic products. In addition, antimony compounds are used as stabilizers to retard the degradation of plastics by light and heat.

Supply and Demand Factors

Total world resources of antimony amount to 5.6 million tons. Identified world reserves are approximately 3.5 million tons, of which China controls the largest share—about 2 million tons. At projected rates of consumption, these supplies should be adequate to meet demand for the foreseeable future. All of the domestic antimony deposits in the United States are small and uneconomical when compared with foreign operations; reserves in the United States were estimated at 90,000 tons in 1988. The U.S. government's stockpile target for antimony—36,000 tons—was reached in 1987.

Because antimony is obtained as primary metal, rather than a by-product of other metals, worldwide production responds directly to the price of antimony on the international market. For the past ten years, for example, the price has remained fairly constant and, because of relatively low prices, total world production of antimony declined from 69,534 tons in 1979 to just under 62,000 tons in 1987.

Substitutions for antimony, in most of its applications, are available, leading to broad elasticity of demand. In paint, pigments, and enamels, a number of different compounds of titanium, zinc, chromium, tin, and zirconium can be substituted. For hardening lead in lead-acid batteries, combinations of calcium, strontium, tin, copper, selenium, sulfur, and cadmium can replace antimony. Finally, selected organic compounds and hydrated oxide are widely accepted alternative materials in flame-retardant systems. Although these other materials can be substituted, however, long-term availability and cost tends to favor increased demand for antimony.

Beryllium

Although beryllium ore is produced throughout the world, the three largest producers in 1988 were the United States (64 percent), the U.S.S.R. (23 percent), and Brazil (just under 11 percent). In 1988, the United States imported just under 15 percent of total consumption, according to the Bureau of Mines. Brazil is the largest source for imported beryllium (56 percent), while China provides 25 percent, and France 13 percent. South Africa accounts for only 3 percent of U.S.–imported beryllium.

Uses of Beryllium

Beryllium is a gray metal, the third-lightest metal after magnesium and lithium. Though brittle, beryllium is also very hard. Its primary end use is as an alloy with copper in electronics, electrical equipment, and aerospace applications. Beryllium is also used in nuclear weaponry and reactors. The beryllium-copper alloy has a much greater strength and resistance to stress than copper alone. Beryllium is used in aircraft components, springs, and electrical contacts. Beryllium-copper is also used to make non-spark-producing tools for use in coal mines and oil refineries, where there is a danger from flammable gasses. New applications for beryllium include use as sensors in air-bag systems and as sensors to regulate transmission performance in automotive transmissions.

Supply and Demand Factors

The U.S. Bureau of Mines has no quantitative information regarding foreign resources of beryllium-bearing minerals and rocks. Known domestic deposits in the United States are estimated at 66,000 tons; recent consumption of beryllium has been running just over 300 tons per year. The national defense stockpile goal is 400 tons of beryllium. In 1988, the total stockpile of beryllium metal amounted to 290 tons.

Beryllium is produced as a primary metal, and supply therefore responds to market prices, which have remained rather high for the past several years. An important contributor to the high price of beryllium recently is the high cost of environmental-regulation compliance. Because beryllium is extremely toxic, workers handling the metal must be very careful. Since the 1970s, occupational health experts and union leaders have been trying to tighten standards for beryllium exposure levels—cancer and chronic lung disease being the major concerns. It is possible that up to 800,000 workers in the United States involved with the manufacture of nuclear missiles, reactor parts, spacecraft, jets, electrical contacts, and synthetic gemstones have been exposed to beryllium. As a consequence, the only mine in the United States, located in Delta, Utah, is under fire from environmental groups because of the toxic nature of beryllium.

On the demand side, there are a number of suitable substitutes for beryllium. These include steel, titanium, or graphite composites for beryllium metal, and phosphor-bronze for beryllium-copper alloys. Even though a significant loss of performance is noted with these substitutes, the high price of beryllium in recent years has encouraged the use of substitutes. Beryllium has thus been restricted principally to applications that require light weight, high strength and high thermal conductivity.

Cadmium

Cadmium is obtained as a by-product when zinc is refined from concentrates, and also from zinc flue dusts. Because cadmium has a lower melting point than zinc, it is more easily recoverable in the smelting process, which uses electrolytic and electromotive systems. In electrolytic processing, cadmium is recovered by electrolyzing purified solutions. In the electromotive system, a metallic sponge is displaced from purified solutions by zinc dust. The sponge may be formed into the shape of a briquette, and charged, then distillated and remelted and cast into shapes.

Although produced by a number of countries around the world, the four largest producers are the U.S.S.R. (12.9 percent), Japan (12 percent), the United States (10.7 percent), and Canada (7.8 percent). Resources of cadmium are linked directly to those of zinc and amount to 0.3 percent of zinc resources. It is estimated that from 5 million to 50 million tons of cadmium are contained in undiscovered cadmium reserves, depending upon the ore occurrence model used. The largest known reerves are located in Canada, the United States, Australia, and the U.S.S.R.

In the United States, the Bureau of Mines estimates a large potential reserve of cadmium contained in zinc-bearing coals in the midsection of the continent. It is also possible that cadmium is contained in carboniferous coal in other countries. An important secondary source of cadmium is the recycling of nickel-cadmium batteries, a procedure that is heavily utilized in Europe but not in the United States.

Uses of Cadmium

Cadmium is a bluish-white metal, soft enough to be cut with a knife. With a very low melting point, it is an extremely malleable metal. It was discovered in 1817 in Germany, as an impurity in pharmaceutical zinc carbonate. Nickel-cadmium batteries have been the largest consumer of cadmium in recent years, accounting for 32 percent of total use. Twenty-nine per cent of total consumption of cadmium presently goes into electroplating and coating, and 15 percent into vinyl plastics, where cadmium is used as a stabilizer. Cadmium is an important component in the production of low-melting-point alloys, and some cadmium is used as pigments. Recently, research has identified a new application for cadmium in the form of cadmium sulfide and cadmium telluride in solar photo-voltaic cells.

Supply and Demand Factors

The supply of cadmium is dependent upon the supply of zinc ore. Because of that, the production of new cadmium is rather heavily insulated against steep price increases or decreases. Even further than that, much of the research that focuses on the discovery, mining, refining, and processing of cadmium is incidental to zinc research. As with many of the minor metals, nevertheless, the price of cadmium can be very volatile. The largest growth potential for cadmium seems to be in the use of nickel-cadmium batteries. In other applications, substitute materials are available. Zinc coatings or vapor-deposited aluminum can be substituted for some cadmium-plating applications. For plastic stabilizers, tin may be used in place of cadmium compounds. Zinc and iron pigments can be used in place of cadmium pigments, albeit at the cost of durability and performance.

Chromium

Nearly 60 percent of the world's chromium is produced by two countries: South Africa and the U.S.S.R. Other smaller but important sources include Albania, Finland, India, Turkey, Zimbabwe, Iran, and the Philippines. Total world resources of chromite, which is a compound consisting of chromium, oxygen, and iron, are estimated at 33 billion metric tons. More than 95 percent of that amount is found in southern Africa. Of the total chromite resources, the U.S. Bureau of Mines estimates minable reserves at 1.03 billion tons, of which 828 million tons—80 percent—are in South Africa, and 17 million tons are in Zimbabwe. There is some chromite found in the United States, although until recently the cost of mining it was generally too high. The United States, which is the world's largest consumer of chromium, presently produces no chromium but meets about 10 percent of its needs through recycling.

To recover chromite ore, both surface mining and underground mining techniques are used; in the major producing countries of South Africa and Zimbabwe, underground mining is the more common technique. To produce chrome from chromite, the ore is melted in arc furnaces along with iron to produce ferrochrome—the chief chromium product. To produce pure chromium, aluminothermic reduction or electrolysis of chromium solution is utilized.

Uses of Chromium

Chromium is a lustrous, hard, brittle steel-grey metallic element. Resistant to tarnish and corrosion, it can take a high polish. It is most commonly used to harden steel alloys and to produce stainless steel. Refined chromium is also used as a corrosion-resistant decorative plating, often on the bumpers and trim of automobiles. Chromium is also used as a pigment in glass.

Chromium is indispensable in the production of stainless steel, which in turn is essential for the production of jet aircraft, armaments, automobiles, mining and drilling machinery, hospital equipment, and surgical instruments. In the manufacturing of magnets, pure chrome is alloyed with several nonferrous metals. Chromium metal is used as a catalyst for many purposes, and chromite ore is used as a refractory in iron and steel processing.

Supply and Demand Factors

Although world reserves seem adequate to meet demands, the uninterrupted supply of chromium is threatened by the fact that the two primary producers—South Africa and the Soviet Union—are experiencing rather turbulent political and economic changes. This situation is not improved by the fact that the second-largest supplier of chromium to the United States, Zimbabwe, has experienced its own internal upheavals during the past two decades. In South Africa, major cutbacks in the supply of chromium during 1988 left many U.S. importers scrambling to meet their demands. Whereas South Africa accounted for 69 percent of all imports during 1987, its percentage of total chromium imports had fallen nearly 35 percent in 1988. Tight supplies during 1987 and 1988 led to extensive plans by numerous countries in various parts of the world to develop or expand their ferrochrome capacity.

In recent years, the nearly total dependence of the United States on imported supplies of chromite and ferrocarbon steels, plus the primacy of South Africa in refining and metals production, has focused a great deal of legislative interest toward encouraging domestic production of chromium. In response, the Chrome Corporation in the United States in 1988 developed the chromium resources in Montana's Stillwater Complex, using a new kiln-roast prereduction refining process developed by Germany's Krupp Industrie.

Because chromium is produced as a primary metal, not as a by-product, increased production of chromium responds rather quickly to higher prices and increased demand, as occurred in 1987 and 1988. Stainless steel production continues to be the major consumer of chromium, and all indications are that demand for stainless steel will continue to grow. Because there is no known substitute for chromium in the manufacture of stainless steel, there is little elasticity of demand based upon volatility of price. A trend toward smaller automobiles and the replacement of chrome-plated steel bumpers with plastic has led to a reduced demand for chromium from the automotive industry. It is expected, however, that increasing demand for industrialization of Third World countries, as well as a growing demand in China, will lead to long-term growth in the demand for chromium.

Cobalt

Of all the minor metals, cobalt is perhaps the most representative of the potential problems that exist with the so-called strategic metals. Cobalt is vital to the aerospace and electrical products industries. Jet engines cannot be built without cobalt. Yet the United States is totally dependent upon imports to supply its need for cobalt, and the primary sources for those imports are in politically unstable countries in southern Africa. Zaire is, by far, the world's largest producer of cobalt, with 63 percent of the total output in 1988. The next largest producer, Zambia, accounted for 12 percent of production in 1988. Together, these two developing nations produced three-quarters of the world's cobalt in 1988. The third largest source, the U.S.S.R., produced 6 percent of the world's total in 1988, followed by Canada with 5.6 percent.

Cobalt was last mined in the United States in 1971. Because of the vulnerability of cobalt supplies internationally, there is some movement to reopen domestic mines. Most of the resources in the United States—estimated to be 1.4 million tons—are found in only minor concentrations, which makes their use rather doubtful, although new leaching processes have made cobalt mining in the United States more economically feasible. The U.S. Bureau of Mines anticipates that new mine and refinery production in the United States will be in place within two years. Small amounts of cobalt are recovered in the United States from recycling.

Identified worldwide cobalt reserves total approximately 12

million tons, most occurring in nickel-bearing laterite deposits. Most of the remaining reserves occur in nickel-sulfide deposits and in the sedimentary copper deposits of Zaire and Zambia. Moreover, it is widely hypothesized that millions of tons of cobalt resources exist in the manganese nodules and crusts on the floor of the ocean. A large nickel-copper-cobalt deposit, believed to be the second-largest nickel reserve in China and estimated to contain 40,000 tons of cobalt, has recently been discovered by geologists in western China.

Most of the world's cobalt is recovered as a by-product of either copper or nickel mining; the only mines in which cobalt is the primary ore occur in Morocco. In the United States, lead ores are being considered as a commercial source of cobalt. The method employed in the recovery of cobalt depends upon its source: concentrations from copper-cobalt ores are leached in sulfuric acid, while concentrates from nickel-ferrous laterites are treated by ammonia or acid leaching.

Uses of Cobalt

Cobalt is a tough metal, resembling iron and nickel in appearance. Similar to iron, it is much harder and is magnetic below 1,075 degrees centigrade. Egyptians used cobalt in the fifteenth century B.C., but little indication of its use from then until A.D. 300 has been found. In the sixteenth century, German miners, believing that goblins had substituted "kobald"—meaning goblin, or demon of the mines—for silver in the copper-nickel mines of that era, gave the metal its name. Cobalt, which appeared similar to silver, was at that time a worthless metal. In 1735, a Swedish scientist isolated metallic cobalt, and in 1780 cobalt was established as an element.

Because cobalt is such a tough metal, it is used in a number of high-temperature alloys, magnetic alloys, and hard-facing alloys resistant to abrasion. In 1988, superalloys, used mainly in industrial and aircraft gas turbine engines, accounted for nearly 38 percent of total consumption. Other uses include paint dryers (15 percent), magnetic alloys (12 percent), and catalysts (9 percent).

Supply and Demand Factors

Although total cobalt reserves worldwide seem adequate to meet growing needs in the foreseeable future, the unstable economic and political conditions of the countries primarily responsible for that supply leave those reserves somewhat vulnerable. Because of the essential nature of cobalt, demand will likely continue to grow in the foreseeable future. In addition, there are virtually no substitutes for cobalt in most of its essential uses. In the super-alloys, nickel may be substituted without adverse affects, but in all other cases, performance suffers when substitutions are made.

In recent years, the civil war that has raged in Angola has created major disruptions in the supply of cobalt. Zaire and Zambia, the world's largest suppliers, depended for years on the Benguela railroad, originally built when the Belgian Congo was a European colony, for the transport of cobalt and copper exports. Throughout 1988, however, this railroad was completely closed because of the Angolan civil war. Plans are in place among the countries of southern Africa to redevelop the railway during the next ten years. It is a modern-day irony, however, that the closing of one isolated railway into the interior of Africa can jeopardize the entire aerospace industry of the United States.

Columbium

Columbium is primarily found in Brazil, where over 80 percent of the world's reserves are located. Brazil accounted for 73 percent of total columbium exports between 1984 and 1987. Most of the remaining known reserves are located in Canada, Zaire, Nigeria, Uganda, and the Soviet Union. The United States has approximately 800 million pounds of columbium resources in identified deposits, but which were considered uneconomic to mine at 1988 prices.

Columbium is found in the minerals columbite, pyrochlore, uexenite, and columbium-tantalite; the most common of these is pyrochlore. To produce columbium from its ores, various methods are used. Pyrochlore can be decomposed with the use of hydrofluoric acid. Low grade ores are commonly smelted and the columbite then separated by fractional distillation, while ferrocolumbium for steel is produced using the aluminothermic process.

Uses of Columbium

Columbium, also known as niobium, has been used since the 1930s as an ingredient in high-strength, low-alloy steel—steel that is very desirable to the aerospace industry. Other ingredients often include titanium and zirconium.

Columbium is primarily used in the manufacture of alloy steels, in the form of ferrocolumbium and—to a much lesser degree—pentoxide. These specialty alloy steels are often used in a wide variety of applications, such as for beams and girders in buildings and in offshore drilling towers, and for railroad equipment, ship plating, automobiles, and oil and gas pipelines. The use of columbium continues to grow as the demand for oil and gas pipelines increases and through its use in the nuclear and electronic industries. Columbium is one of the metals found in the superalloys used in turbine engines and jet engines. Alloyed with carbide as columbium-carbide, it becomes one of the hardest substances available and is used in machine cutting tools.

Supply and Demand Factors

Worldwide resources of columbium are more than adequate to meet growing demand for the foreseeable future. On the other hand, because the United States is the primary consumer of columbium yet produces none of its own, supplies—many of which come from developing counties—are vulnerable to political and economic disruptions. Because columbium is mined as a primary metal, worldwide supplies are very responsive to price and are therefore quite elastic.

On the demand side, steadily increasing demand for high-strength alloys—especially in the manufacture of oil and gas pipelines—points to a long-term increase in demand for columbium. Replacements are available, however, should prices rise too high. Vanadium and molybdenum can be substituted for columbium in high-strength low-alloy steels, while tantalum and titanium are viable substitutes in stainless and high-strength steel and superalloys. In high temperature applications, molybdenum, tungsten, tantalum, and ceramics may substitute for columbium. Thus, elasticity of demand in relation to price volatility is somewhat limited. As prices go up, substitutes become more economically feasible and will likely be used.

Gallium

Gallium is a little-known metal that occurs primarily as a by-product of aluminum and zinc. Recovered from bauxite-processing fluids and zinc-processing wastes, only a small percentage of available gallium is actually extracted from aluminum or zinc ore because of the high cost of the process and the present low demand for gallium. Gallium producers include Canada, Czechoslovakia, Germany, the United States, Hungary, the U.S.S.R., and Switzerland. Swiss Aluminum, Ltd., is the largest producer in the world.

Uses of Gallium

Gallium is primarily used in semiconductors, laser diodes, light-emitting diodes (LEDs), and integrated circuits. These applications, in turn, are used in calculators, radios, television receivers, stereo equipment, and other electronic devices. Gallium is also used in various measuring devices. Gallium has the potential of replacing silicon chips in some electronic devices, and is also finding expanded use in the manufacture of photo-voltaic cells, for the generation of energy directly from sunlight. Silicon, which is ore commonly used in photo-voltaic cells, has a theoretical efficiency of 17 to 18 percent, while gallium's theoretical efficiency, in this particular use, is around 25 percent.

Supply and Demand Factors

Gallium exists in sufficient quantities worldwide to meet any future projected need. In fact, gallium is not held in the U.S. strategic stockpile, and the only limitations on its availability seem to be the high cost of production. In addition, alternative materials may be substituted for gallium in most of its commercial applications. When used in semiconductors, silicon, germanium, and indium compounds are less costly than gallium arsenide. In one particular application, however—LEDs—the superior performance of gallium offsets its higher price when substitutes are considered.

Several factors contribute to the high cost of gallium—its low concentration in source materials, the need for extremely close quality control in the production process, the relatively slow reaction, and the small scale of its production. All indications are for continued growth in the demand for gallium, as new technology develops in the conversion of solar energy and in the application of fiber optics in the communications industry.

Germanium

The annual production of germanium is very small compared with other metals, even other minor metals. Germanium is obtained commercially as a by-product of copper or zinc refining; one of the largest sources of germanium is the Tsumeb mine in southwest Africa. A second major source is the Kipushi mine in Zaire. In the United States, lead-zinc-fluorspar ore found in the Mississippi Valley is the principal source of germanium domestically, but a rich potential source of germanium is in the ash and flue dust that result from burning certain coals for power generation. The U.S. Bureau of Mines predicts that if germanium were obtained in this way, the potential worldwide germanium resource would become several billion kilograms.

Uses of Germanium

Germanium is a very brittle and hard metal, grayish-white in color, and only exhibits the characteristic properties of metals under certain circumstances. It is a semiconductor that embodies characteristics that fall between metal and insulator. Of all the germanium produced, 90 percent is used in the electronics industry for various forms of semiconductors, such as diodes used in pocket calculators and digital watches. Germanium is also used in the manufacture of specialized glass and in the production of certain solders. Germanium functions as a stabilizer for zirconium against phase changes and, as such, is used in the fabrication of fuel elements in atomic reactors. In 1988, total U.S. consumption of germanium was an estimated 40,000 kilograms. Sixty-seven percent of this amount was used in infrared optics, 8 percent in fiber-optics systems, 7 percent in detectors, 6 percent in semiconductors, including transistors and rectifiers, and 12 percent in other applications.

Supply and Demand Factors

Supplies for the foreseeable future remain adequate to meet demand, except that the primary sources of germanium—Zaire and southwest Africa—remain economically and politically unstable. The commercial availability of germanium is established by the rate at which zinc or other germanium-bearing ores are processed and refined. Thus, the supply of germanium is relatively inelastic.

Demand remains strong for germanium because of its use in infrared optics. In such applications, zinc selenide or germanium glass can substitute for intrinsic germanium metal, but performance suffers as a result. In other electronic applications, silicon, which is less expensive, is increasingly used as a substitute. Other minor metals can also be used as a substitute for germanium. In some high-frequency and high-power requirements, germanium is more reliable and is more economical as a substrate for some light-emitting diode applications.

The U.S. government's established stockpile goal for germanium was set at 146,000 kilograms in 1987. By the end of 1988,

11,729 kilograms of germanium were in the government's stockpile. In 1988, the United States produced approximately 50 percent of its consumption.

Hafnium

Approximately one-third of the world's known reserves of hafnium lie within the borders of the United States. Even so, very little hafnium is mined in the United States. Rather, South Africa and Australia are the world's largest producers. Hafnium is extracted from the mineral zircon, which contains about 1 percent hafnium metal; consequently, production of hafnium from ore is expensive and very complicated.

Uses of Hafnium

Hafnium is a gray metallic element closely resembling zirconium, but with an important difference: hafnium possesses the important property of neutron absorption. Thus, it is used in neutron-absorbing reactor control rods to slow down nuclear chain reactions and quench atomic fires. Increasingly, hafnium is also being used as an alloying agent in high-temperature refractory metals. And a hafnium-columbium carbide alloy can be used as a less expensive substitute for tantalum-carbide for the coating of tool bits.

Supply and Demand Factors

Even though hafnium is very difficult and expensive to produce, supplies seem adequate to meet demand for the foreseeable future. Because hafnium is an essential metal in the nuclear industry, demand is expected to increase for this important strategic metal. In its primary application in nuclear-reactor control rods and refractory alloys, there are few substitutes for hafnium, leading to high elasticity of demand. In some refractories and ceramics, though, zirconium oxide or metal can be used as an alternative.

Indium

Indium is not mined in its natural state; it is a by-product of ores that have been mined primarily for their value in other metals, principally zinc. Indium is produced in the United States by treating smelter flue dusts, slags, and bullions, and residues from zinc and other base-metal concentrates. Canada and Japan are the two major producers of indium, but the United States remains an important source for this metal.

Uses of Indium

Indium is a soft, grayish-white metal capable of marking paper like lead. Softer than lead, indium is malleable and ductile, yet crystalline. Indium is used for electronic components, low-melting-point alloys, solders, coatings on electrical contacts, dental alloys, nuclear-reactor control rods, and infrared detectors. Recent research has led to indium's being used as a coating on automotive windshields to prevent fogging. Indium also has potential for use in solar-energy devices and is used as a thin alloy layer in high-performance bearings in sports cars. Some of the low-melting-point alloys are used in glass lens grinding and polishing and as plugs for fire sprinkler systems. Indium is further used in catalysts and in the purification systems for the manufacture of man-made fibers, and as a coating on aluminum wire and connectors.

Supply and Demand Factors

Because indium is a by-product of other metals, its availability depends entirely on the production of those metals. Supply is therefore extremely inelastic; the supply of indium as a by-product is not responsive to indium prices but to zinc prices. Consequently, the availability of indium depends on the economics and growth of the zinc industry; as long as the price of indium remains high enough to make its recovery from zinc residues attractive, the supply will be adequate.

Demand for indium is expected to increase as aluminum wire continues to replace copper in electrical circuits and as infrared detectors, solar cells, and nuclear-reactor control rods demand more indium. In some applications, other metals can replace indium. In transistors, silicon can replace germanium-indium, and gallium can substitute for indium in dental alloys and in sealing glass joints. Boron-carbide can replace indium in reactor control rods.

Lithium

Lithium is found in three different types of ore: pentolite, lepidolite, and spodumene. It is also found in, and produced from, certain brines. Recovery from ores is by an acid or an alkaline treatment, but when produced from brine, recovery is accomplished by leaching and concentration. Approximately 60 percent of the total world reserves of lithium are found in Chile, although very little lithium is produced there. The United States is second, with 17 percent of total world reserves, while the U.S.S.R. and Zaire each contain 7 percent. Other important sources are Canada (6 percent), Zimbabwe (2 percent), and Brazil (2 percent). The United States produces approximately 80 percent of the total lithium produced worldwide. In the United States, lithium comes mostly from subsurface brines in Nevada.

Uses of Lithium

Lithium is the lightest metal known to man. It is soft and ductile and can readily be made into various shapes. A highly reactive metal, especially to water, lithium burns spontaneously at 176 degrees centigrade. Because of these highly reactive properties, lithium enjoys only limited uses, and then in compound form. Lithium is used primarily in one of two forms: lithium carbonate or lithium hydroxide. Lithium carbonate has historically been used mostly in the production of ceramics and enamels. More recently, lithium has become an important component in the aluminum-smelting industry—its presence greatly increases the production yield. Lithium is also used in the manufacturing of small quantities of lightweight alloys, as well as in the manufacture of steel as a degassifier and a scavenger. Lithium serves as a deoxidizer in the melting of copper and copper alloys.

Lithium hydroxide is used primarily in the manufacture of greases and lubricants. Compounds of lithium hydroxide are also used the manufacture of bleaches, disinfectants, synthetic rubber, welding, brazing, and glass manufacture. Lithium is under experimentation for use in the batteries employed to power short-range passenger vehicles. More recently lithium is being used in medical and psychiatric drug applications.

Supply and Demand Factors

Available resources of lithium seem adequate to meet demand in the foreseeable future. To better meet long-term demand, both of the major United States producers have been expanding their operations into Chile and the United Kingdom. The primary problems involved with the supply of lithium relate to its toxicity. A large capital outlay is required to contain problems of contamination and pollution of the environment, as well as in the protection of the work force from contamination.

Because lithium continues to be important in the aluminum industry, growth in demand should continue, but is related to world economic conditions. In the ceramics and glass industries, as well as in greases and batteries, substitutes are available. Calcium and aluminum soaps can be used as substitutes for lithium stearates in greases, while zinc, magnesium, calcium, and mercury can be used as an anode material for most primary batteries. At present, however, no suitable substitute exists for lithium's role in the production of aluminum.

Magnesium

Of all the minor, or strategic, metals, magnesium is the most abundant. It forms about 2.5 percent of the earth's crust. It is the eighth most abundant element and the third most abundant element dissolved in sea water, which is the primary source for magnesium. Magnesium is also recovered from dolomite and forsterite ores and from concentrated brines in salt lakes and salt wells. The United States is the world's largest producer of magnesium, accounting for over 40 percent of the world's population. Close behind is the U.S.S.R., with 27 percent. Dow Chemical Company is currently the world's largest primary magnesium producer, using sea water as its raw material. Magnesium reserves are considered to be unlimited.

Uses of Magnesium

Magnesium is a silvery-white chemical element, the lightest of all structural metals. In its pure state, magnesium is highly reactive; polished metal gradually assumes a gray film on exposure to air. When alloyed with aluminum or zinc, magnesium, which has little structural strength on its own, can be made into machine parts or structural shapes that are very strong in relation to their weight. When alloyed with manganese, magnesium is highly resistant to salt-water corrosion. Magnesium, which is a poor conductor of heat and electricity, is a malleable and ductile metal.

Magnesium is the primary alloying element in aluminum sheet used in the production of aluminum cans, which accounts for slightly more than half of the magnesium consumption in the free world. Magnesium is also used in steel desulfurization and in the production of ductile iron. Aluminum-magnesium alloys are used extensively in aircraft, automotive, and machinery applications.

When reduced to a fine powder, magnesium burns brightly and rapidly, making it useful for pyrotechnics, for photographic flash powder, and for incendiary bombs. Epsom salt, which is hydrated magnesium sulphate, is used as a cathartic and also in dyeing, leather tanning, and in fertilizers. Magnesium alloys are used to construct lightweight military equipment for jungle warfare, as well as for consumer goods such as vacuum cleaners, luggage, lawn mowers, portable tools, and sporting equipment. Oxide of magnesium is used as a heat-resistant material in refractory bricks and glass-making crucibles.

Supply and Demand Factors

Because of its abundance in nature, magnesium is unlikely to be in short supply. The only conditions potentially affecting supplies are environmental pollution considerations. For example, a major European producer of magnesium, Norsk Hydro A.S., was forced to shut down its plant in Norway in 1988 as a result of the Norway State Pollution Board's plan to impose fines totaling $237,000 per month for failure to meet mandated pollution levels.

Because magnesium is a primary product—not a by-product— the supply of magnesium as a commodity is highly elastic. Production will respond quickly to the price of magnesium. On the other hand, aluminum and zinc are potential substitutes for magnesium casting and wrought products. Because the principal application is as an alloy with aluminum, long-term demand for magnesium is closely related to the demand for aluminum as well as to an increased capacity to recycle aluminum cans. At present, aluminum cans are becoming more and more popular overseas, where recycling is not as widespread as in the United States. This situation results in a short-term projection of increased demand for magnesium.

Manganese

The largest reserves of manganese are located in South Africa. Total worldwide recoverable manganese reserves are approximately 1 billion tons, 407 million of which are located in South Africa. Second is the Soviet Union, with 325 million tons of manganese, followed by Gabon, with 110 million tons, and Australia, with 75 million tons. The United States has no significant manganese reserves. Fully 40 percent of the world's production of manganese ore in 1988 was attributed to the U.S.S.R. South Africa, with 13.6 percent of worldwide production, was second, followed by Brazil and Gabon, at just over 10 percent each, and by Australia, with just under 8 percent.

In its natural state, manganese is found most commonly in the form of oxides of manganese in ores known as pyrolusite, psilomelane, and wad. Manganese dioxide, the most common form of the metal, is a black or brownish-black crystalline material or powder. Large amounts of manganese are known to exist in the form of nodules on the floor of the Atlantic and Pacific oceans, but commercial recovery of these ores is still in the future.

Uses of Manganese

Manganese is a gray-white, hard, brittle metal, essential to the production of steel. Manganese ores are first converted to ferromanganese and then added to iron ore; the function of the manganese is to remove oxygen and sulfur from the steel during production. Without manganese, it would be nearly impossible to produce the quality of steel required for most industrial steel alloys.

Smaller amounts of manganese are used in the manufacture of dry-cell batteries, as an alloy for aluminum, as a fertilizer, and in various minor chemical applications.

Supply and Demand Factors

Worldwide reserves of manganese seem adequate to meet steel-making demand for many years to come. The problem, of course, is where the manganese is located. South Africa and the Soviet Union together account for nearly three-quarters of the world's recoverable manganese reserves. The implications there are obvious. In 1986, the government acknowledged the critical role of manganese in the U.S. economy by placing South African ferromanganese on the list of ten strategic materials that are allowed entry into the U.S. under the anti-apartheid act. United States fabricators have been developing relationships with other countries, such as Brazil and Australia, to take care of long-term manganese needs.

Because approximately 95 percent of all manganese produced

is consumed by the steel- and iron-making industries, continued healthy demand for the metal seems assured. Demand, of course, is tied directly to the demand for steel. With advances in metallurgy, steel makers have reduced the amount of manganese they use. Because manganese neutralizes the hardening affects of sulfur in steel, as companies produce products with lower sulfur levels, less manganese is required. Otherwise, there are no known substitutes for manganese in the steel-making process.

Because of its critical strategic role, manganese is included in the national defense stockpile. The goal is to stockpile 2.7 million tons of manganese ore, and the current inventory is over 2 million tons. For high-carbon ferromanganese, the goal is 439,000 tons, and current stocks are approximately 757,000 tons.

Mercury

The U.S.S.R. was the largest producer of mercury in 1987, with 37.4 percent to total world production. Spain was second with 24 percent, followed by Algeria with 12.3 percent, and China with 11.2 percent. The United States, which produces a significant amount of mercury, has withheld production figures since 1986. In the United States, mercury is produced as the primary product at only one mine, and as a by-product of gold at six other mines. Some secondary mercury is obtained from obsolete items and waste products such as dental amalgam, batteries, and instruments. Chlorine and caustic soda plants as well as department of energy stocks provide another secondary source for mercury. Spain, with the world's largest mine, is the primary source of mercury for the United States, followed by China in the past few years. Together, the U.S.S.R. and Spain provide more than half the world's output.

Mercury, which rarely occurs in its native state, is recovered mainly from cinnabar ores, but is also refined from corderite and other mercury ores and minerals. It is found in small quantities as a by-product of gold refining. Mercury is commonly found among red sulfide, limestone, sandstone, and calciferous shales. To extract mercury from these ores, the ore is heated in furnaces, collected as a vapor, then cooled into a condensed, liquefied metal. Even though recovery technology produces a yield of around 90 to 95 percent of the recoverable mercury, huge energy costs are incurred in the process of recovery.

Uses of Mercury

Mercury, also known as quicksilver, is the only common metal in a liquid state at ordinary temperatures. It is a fair conductor of electricity and a poor conductor of heat. First mentioned by Aristotle in the fourth century B.C., mercury at that time was used in religious ceremonies. The best-known use for mercury is in thermometers, barometers, and pressure gauges, but such uses account for only about 10 percent of total consumption. The metal is used in the manufacture of alkalis and in various electronic applications. In 1988, the electrical industry utilized 43 percent of total mercury production. The electrolytic production of chlorine and caustic soda accounted for an additional 20 percent, with 11 percent being used in the manufacture of paint, and 6 percent in the manufacture of industrial and control instruments.

Supply and Demand Factors

Available supplies seem adequate to meet worldwide demand, which has been declining during the past decade. Mercury is a very toxic metal and has an adverse effect on the environment. Because of this, demand for mercury in paints and batteries has been dropping steadily. Some small gains in electrical applications have failed to offset this overall decline in demand. In other industrial applications, such as the manufacture of chlorine and caustic soda, efforts are under way to phase out the use of mercury. Japan, in fact, eliminated the use of mercury in the manufacture of these chemicals by the mid-1980s. There are few adequate substitutes for mercury in its principal use in electrical equipment and industrial and control instruments. In other applications, some satisfactory substitutes do exist. Mercury is held as part of the national defense stockpile, but recently supplies of excess mercury have been sold from Department of Energy stocks.

Molybdenum

The primary producer of molybdenum is the United States, with 40 percent of total production in 1987. The second-largest producer was Chile, with just under 20 percent, followed by Canada and the U.S.S.R—each of which produced just over 13 percent of the total world mine production. Molybdenum is produced from molybdenite, which is mined by the open-pit method. From the molybdenite, a molybdenum sulfide is concentrated by flotation. An oxide is then produced by heating the sulfide in air. A significant amount of the world's molybdenum—between a quarter and a third—is produced as a by-product of copper production. Molybdenum is also found as a by-product of tungsten mining.

Uses of Molybdenum

Molybdenum is a silvery-gray metal, occurring in thin tubular plates—usually hexagonal. The plates have a basal cleavage and may split into thin flakes. Molybdenum, which resembles graphite, has a greasy feel to it. First used extensively during World War I to toughen armor plating, when alloyed with steel, molybdenum is stronger and less susceptible to rust and corrosion. Full-alloy molybdenum-steel accounts for approximately one-fourth of total consumption in the United States. The next largest use is in the production of stainless and heat-resistant steel. Mill products made from molybdenum powder also account for a large percentage of molybdenum consumption. Recent research has discovered that lumber treated with molybdenum is an environmentally acceptable method of combating termites. Tough molybdenum steel is extremely important to the military as an alloy for the hulls of submarines, military combat vehicles, and aircraft carriers. Other applications are found in the production of mining equipment and machine components, as well as oil pipelines. The pure metal molybdenum has a small but increasing application in highly technical industries such as nuclear energy, aerospace, and electronics.

Supply and Demand Factors

Identified molybdenum resources worldwide amount to approximately 46 billion pounds with approximately 19 billion pounds in the United States. Supplies, which remain rather stable, seem adequate to meet demand for the foreseeable future. Supply of molybdenum is quite elastic, responding rather quickly to fluctuations in price. In 1987, for instance, oversupply resulted in U.S. producers' mining at dramatically reduced levels. Into 1988, however, as stockpiles diminished and demand remained strong, the major mining companies began boosting their operating rates once again. Demand for molybdenum depends, to a great extent, on the demand for steel; there are few substitutes for molybdenum in steel alloy making. Because of its usefulness and availability, the industry is looking for more ways to utilize this metal.

Platinum-Group Metals

Platinum and palladium, the two best-known metals of the platinum group, are both considered precious metals, although their use as industrial metals is extensive. Both have been reviewed previously in the chapter on previous metals. The lesser-known members of the group, however—iridium, osmium, rhodium, and ruthenium—serve an equally important role in industry and defense.

Iridium

Iridium, one of the platinum-group metals, is the most corrosion-resistant metal known. It is usually alloyed with platinum to make crucibles and high-temperature tools, and is also used in pen tips and compass bearings.

Osmium

Osmium, the hardest and rarest of the platinum-group metals, is bluish-white in color and very difficult to fabricate. It is most commonly used as an alloy with other metals to make long-life phonograph needles and instrument pivots.

Rhodium

Rhodium, a third platinum-group metal, is a silver-white metal often found with nickel. It is produced from ores in South Africa, roughly 1 part rhodium to 19 parts platinum. Rhodium is used in jewelry and mirrors, and is alloyed with platinum and palladium for use in furnace windings, catalysts, thermocouple elements, and electrodes in aircraft spark plugs. After platinum is removed from its ore with aqua regia, the residues are treated chemically to produce rhodium powder, which is then converted to solid bars by sintering. Unlike other platinum-group metals, rhodium is also recovered in smaller quantities from nickel and copper ores. Like platinum, the primary producers of rhodium are South Africa and the U.S.S.R.

Rhodium has a very high resistance to corrosion. It is used to plate steel and brass and other metals in order to prevent corrosion by sea water and other elements. The rhodium coating is extremely thin in this application and is used only when the cost is justified. Rhodium-platinum alloy has several important catalytic uses, the most important of which are in automotive emission systems and in the production of nitric acid from ammonia. Rhodium has a very high optical reflectivity, which makes it almost untarnishable. The metal, therefore, has many optical equipment applications, where it is deposited in extremely thin layers on optically ground surfaces. Rhodium is occasionally alloyed with gold, platinum, and other metals for use in jewelry.

Ruthenium

Ruthenium, the last of the platinum-group metals, is a hard white metal. When alloyed with platinum and palladium, it creates an even harder compound that is used in jewelry and in such applications as aircraft magneto contacts.

Selenium

Selenium occurs in the sulfide ores of copper, iron, and other heavy metals. It is recovered from electrolytic copper refining and from the slimes and flue dusts in metallurgical smelters. Approximately one pound of selenium is obtained from one ton of blister copper refining. Some secondary recovery of selenium occurs from scraps that are generated during the manufacturing of electronics and from chemical processing. During smelting, approximately 40 percent of the selenium contained in copper ores is lost, while an average of 48 percent of the remainder is lost during refining. Principal sources of selenium are Japan and Canada. Neither Chile nor Peru, which have substantial reserves of selenium in connection with their copper deposits, are major producers of selenium.

Uses of Selenium

A versatile metal, selenium is used as a decolorizer in glass manufacturing, as well as in electronics, transformers, rectifiers, conductors, photoelectric cells, and in photocopying and xerographic applications. In combination with cadmium, selenium produces an orange-red pigment that is widely incorporated in paints, enamels, ceramics, and plastics. In the manufacture of steel, the addition of selenium improves the forging characteristics of the steel. In addition, selenium is used in the pharmaceutical, rubber, and explosives industries.

Supply and Demand Factors

The supply of selenium seems adequate to meet projected demand but is highly inelastic, given the fact that it occurs as a by-product in the production of base metals. Demand for selenium will likely remain strong, given its versatility and wide range of uses. Dark-colored selenium glass is finding an increasing application for energy conservation because of its glare resistance and heat-transfer properties. In electronics manufacturing—and in photovoltaics—growth in demand for the products promises to provide a parallel increase in the demand for selenium.

Silicon

Silicon is produced from high-grade sands and pebbles. Although silicon, a relatively light, stable metalloid, does not occur freely in nature, when combined with oxygen to form silicon dioxide, it is second only to oxygen as the most abundant element in the earth's crust. The United States is the largest producer of silicon, followed by the U.S.S.R., Norway, Japan, France, and South Africa. The cost of producing silicon is essentially the cost of the electrical energy. Production plants are therefore often linked to large hydroelectric plants.

Uses of Silicon

Ferrosilicon, which is used as an alloying agent in the iron industries, accounts for approximately 90 percent of all silicon consumption. The remaining 10 percent is produced as silicon metal; 75 percent of that is used in the aluminum industry. High-purity silicon metal is used extensively in the electronics industry, particularly in computers, calculators, and communications equipment to control and amplify electrical signals. Silicon rectifiers are more reliable than other types because their performance does not diminish at high temperatures.

Supply and Demand Factors

World reserves of silicon are essentially unlimited. The only problems with supply have to do with environmental pollution. Pollution-control equipment accounts for approximately 20 percent of capital costs and 10 percent of operating costs of new plants. Any increase in the cost of energy significantly affects the price of silicon. Because the vast majority of all silicon is used in the production of iron, steel, and aluminum, demand for silicon mirrors that of these metals, and is governed by the general state of the world economy. Metals and alloys that can be substituted for ferrosilicon in some of its applications do so at a much greater cost. In semiconductors and in infrared technology, germanium is the main substitute for silicon.

Tantalum

Tantalum, along with columbium, is one of the refractory metals. Tantalum is produced from tin slag and concentrates; it occurs chiefly in the ore columbite-tantalite. Tantalum is removed from its ore by dissolution in hydrofluoric-acid magnetic separation, then precipitated by electrolytic processes. Sponge is produced by carbon reduction of the oxide or by reducing tantalum penta-chloride with magnesium or sodium. The sponge is converted into ingot by compaction and melting in a consumable electrode furnace in an inert atmosphere, or by electron-beam melting. The largest reserves of tantalum are found in Zaire, where over 60 percent of total worldwide reserves are found. Nigeria, Thailand, Malaysia, and the Soviet Union all have significant reserves of tantalum. The United States mines virtually no tantalum. Between 1984 and 1987, the largest producer of tantalum was Thailand, with an estimated 32 percent.

Uses of Tantalum

Until the early 1970s, tantalum was primarily used in the steel industry. During the past two decades, however, it has been virtually replaced by columbium, which is lighter and more plentiful. The principal application of tantalum is as a barrier to corrosion in chemical-processing equipment and carbide-cutting tools. Even more important, however, is tantalum's use in the electronics industry in capacitors and filaments. In the electronics industry, tantalum is also used in the manufacture of valves, contact points, and electrodes, and it is used in the chemicals industry to make retorts and pipes. The electronics industry accounted for 60 percent of all tantalum used in 1988, while transportation accounted for 15 percent, and machinery, 11 percent.

Supply and Demand Factors

With the availability of columbium as a substitute, supplies of tantalum are adequate to meet long-range demands. The major sources of tantalum are Third World countries and the U.S.S.R., with all that that implies. There are substitutes for tantalum, although they may present a significant loss in performance. Columbium can be substituted in superalloys and carbides, while aluminum and ceramics are potential substitutes in electronic capacitors. In corrosion-resistant equipment, glass, titanium, zirconium, columbium, or platinum can replace tantalum. In high-temperature applications, tantalum can be replaced by tungsten, rhenium, molybdenum, iridium, hafnium, and columbium. Tungsten-carbide and columbium-carbide are suitable replacements for cutting-tool applications. Because tantalum is primarily used in the electronics industry, increased demand is likely to occur as the electronics industry continues to expand.

Tellurium

Tellurium is generally recovered as a by-product of the electrolytic refining of copper. Tellurium is also found in small quantities in zinc, lead, and gold telluride ores. The major producing countries are Canada, Japan, Peru, the United States, and the U.S.S.R.

Uses of Tellurium

In its elemental form, tellurium is used in copper and steel alloys and as a curing agent and accelerator in rubber compounding, which increases the rubber's resistance to heat and abrasion. Tellurium is also used in the chilling of malleable cast iron. High-purity tellurium is used as a control alloy in selenium photoreceptors—it improves the range of color spectrum sensitivity.

Bismuth and lead telluride alloys are used in semiconductor and thermoelectric applications. Tellurium is increasingly used as a catalyst in synthetic fibers and petrochemical products.

Supply and Demand Factors

Tellurium is a rare metal, but supplies seem adequate to meet demand. In iron and steel production, the use of tellurium is declining while its use as a catalyst is expanding. A growth in demand is also expected from the application of cadmium telluride in the making of photovoltaic solar cells.

Titanium

Titanium is not a rare metal. In fact, in its pure form it is the ninth most abundant element in the earth's crust. Titanium is obtained from rutile, ilmenite, and sphene. Geologically, titanium is found in three types of deposits: beach and stream placers, massive deposits of titaniferous iron ore and igneous complexes in which rutile occurs in association with anorthosites and similar rock. Titanium is also found in vitanites and many iron ores.

Major producers of titanium include Australia, Canada, Norway, the United States, Finland, India, Malaysia, the U.S.S.R., Japan, and Germany. The United States is one of the larger producers of titanium sponge metal in the world, yet at full capacity the United States can produce a little over half the capacity of the Soviet Union. Japanese titanium sponge capacity is approximately equal to that of the United States. Australia is by far the largest producer of titanium concentrates, with over 25 percent of titanium ilmenite concentrates and more than 55 percent of titanium rutile concentrates. Other major producers of ilmenite are Canada (17 percent), Norway (16.2 percent), South Africa (12.3 percent), and the U.S.S.R. (8.6 percent). Major producers of titanium rutile concentrates, in addition to Australia, are Sierra Leone (25 percent) and South Africa (12.3 percent).

When rutile is mined, a form of dredge is usually employed to obtain the rutile from sand deposits. When dredging is not practical, the heavier materials are separated from the lighter quartz, feldspar, and mica through rough concentration accomplished by wet gravity methods. Mining in titanium is a capital-intensive operation that requires a great deal of energy. Years are required to produce the special equipment necessary to mine the titanium, which requires 500 kilowatts of energy per ton that is mined. To avoid the high risk of ground-water contamination, a great deal of cost goes into antipollution devices.

Uses of Titanium

Titanium is lighter than steel, but equally strong. For that reason, titanium is in wide demand for the aerospace industry. Titanium can be alloyed with aluminum, vanadium, molybdenum, iron, and manganese. Titanium is produced in three different forms: titanium sponge metal, titanium ingots, and titanium dioxide pigment.

Titanium sponge metal is produced commercially by the "Kroll process," in which purified titanium tetrachloride is reduced with magnesium or sodium in an inert atmosphere. Residual chlorides are removed by leaching or, less frequently, by vacuum distillation. The sponge is compacted, usually with some scrap additions, and made into ingots by two or more successive vacuum operations by the arc melting process.

Titanium dioxide is used for pigment manufacture, ceramics, and glass formulations. Half the titanium dioxide consumed in 1988 was used in paint, varnishes, and lacquer. The remainder was used in paper, plastics, rubber, and other industries. Seventy-eight percent of the titanium produced in 1988 was used in the manufacture of jet engines, air frames, and space and missile components. The rest was used by the chemical-processing industry, medical-equipment manufacturers, and other non-aerospace industries.

Supply and Demand Factors

Although there is no shortage of titanium in the earth's crust, the high costs associated with producing titanium tend to limit demand for the material to specific applications. As the aerospace industry continues to expand, so does the demand for titanium, for which there is no substitute. In general industrial uses, high-nickel steel can be used to a limited extent as a substitute for titanium, as can the expensive superalloy metals. For titanium dioxide pigment, there is no cost-effective substitute.

Tungsten

More than 90 percent of the world's estimated reserves of tungsten are outside the United States; approximately 50 percent of the world's reserves are located in China. Sizable tungsten reserves are also found in Australia, Austria, Bolivia, Brazil, Burma, Canada, North Korea, Portugal, the Republic of Korea, Thailand, Turkey, and the Soviet Union. China is by far the largest producer and exporter of tungsten, with 44 percent of total world production in 1987. The Soviet Union was second with nearly 23 percent. Most other countries produced significantly less than that amount. Tungsten, from the old Norse "thungr-steinn"—meaning "heavy stone"—is a very heavy, gray-white metallic element that is derived from wolframite, scheelite, huebernite or felberite. All these ores contain tungsten as an oxide. Tungsten mines range from open-cast surface mining to placer operations and underground mining, but most of the world's output comes from underground operations. Ferrotungsten is produced by aluminothermic methods or by reduction in an electric arc furnace.

Uses of Tungsten

Tungsten and tungsten carbide, because of their high-temperature strength, are widely used in the production of machine tools and drilling bits. Alloyed with nickel, and sometimes molybdenum, tungsten is used in the manufacture of a number of high-temperature and high-stress-resistant alloys. Tungsten is used in the manufacture of ammunition, and tungsten wire is extensively used in electric lamp filaments. Additionally, tungsten is used as an alloy agent in steel making and in lubricants, pigments, and catalysts.

Supply and Demand Factors

Worldwide reserves are adequate to meet demand for tungsten for the near future. The fact, however, that China and the U.S.S.R. together produce over 65 percent of the world's tungsten is reason for concern. Demand for tungsten seems to be slackening in the metal-machining industries, while at the same time increasing in the heavy-construction-equipment industry. In 1988, the International Tungsten Industry Association was established, with a mandate to "compile and publish international tungsten statistics, promote tungsten use, monitor ecological issues, and organize seminars."

Vanadium

Vanadium is found in 65 different minerals, phosphate rock, iron ores, and crude oils. It is also found in deposits of titaniferous magnetite, phosphate ores, uraniferous sandstones and siltstones, bauxite, and carboniferous materials including crude oil, oil shale, and tar sands. Vanadium is recovered as a by-product or co-product and is extracted from ores, residues, and slags left from the production of other metals. One important source of vanadium is the flue dust from power stations using vanadium-rich cokes and coals. Ores and slags containing vanadium are converted to vanadium oxide or directly into ferrovanadium. The raw material is then concentrated, leached, and salt-roasted to obtain the oxide. Ferrovanadium is produced aluminothermically from the oxide. Certain vanadium-based alloys and briquettes are made in vacuum electric-arc melting furnaces.

Vanadium is a scarce metal. South Africa, China, and the Soviet Union are the world's largest suppliers of vanadium. South Africa, with nearly 50 percent of the world's reserves, has by far the largest deposits. The U.S.S.R. accounts for nearly 46 percent of world reserves. Australia, Chile, and the United States each have relatively small vanadium reserves, with the U.S. total weighing in at something like 0.6 percent of total world reserves. In 1988, South Africa produced approximately 57 percent of the world's total vanadium, while the Soviet Union produced approximately 29 percent, and China, approximately 13.4 percent. The United States total vanadium-production figures have been withheld since 1984.

Uses of Vanadium

Vanadium is a gray metal, both malleable and ductile. Its primary use is as an alloying agent for iron and steel, and as a strengthener for titanium-based alloys. Vanadium is also a catalyst in sulfuric-acid production. In the production of structural steels, vanadium is used in the form of ferrovanadium. The aerospace industry ranks second to the steel industry in the use of vanadium, particularly in the nonferrous alloy 90/6/4 titanium. Vanadium is also used in the manufacture of synthetic rubber.

Supply and Demand Factors

Vanadium is in short supply worldwide. As evidence, the Soviet Union—which has always been considered self-sufficient—bought vanadium pentoxide on the open market in 1988, and thereby became a net importer rather than a net exporter. The primary source of vanadium in the United States is, of course, South Africa. Because of that, vanadium has been placed on the list of metals that are exempted from sanctions enacted as part of the Anti-Apartheid Act of 1986.

Demand for vanadium remains strong, primarily because of a healthy world economy that has created a strong demand for steel. Major developments in gas- and oil-pipeline construction have placed increased demand on vanadium. Growth in the aircraft industry also has created significant demand. In 1988, the domestic vanadium industry suffered a setback when the Supreme Court overturned a Tenth Circuit Court of Appeals ruling stating that the uranium industry was entitled to protection from foreign-enriched uranium. Because a number of U.S. uranium mills employ vanadium recovery circuits, this decision was of significance to vanadium producers in the United States. In most applications, other metals are interchangeable with vanadium;

e.g., columbium, molybdenum, manganese, titanium, and tungsten. In some chemical processes, platinum may be used. In aerospace titanium alloys, however, there is at this time no substitute for vanadium.

Yttrium

The largest producer of yttrium is Malaysia, with nearly 29 percent of world production in 1988. Second was China, with nearly 23 percent, and third was Australia, with 17 percent. Figures for the United States have been withheld for several years. Yttrium, a metal used in electronics, color televisions, and nuclear equipment, is a very rare metal. Only 750 metric tons were produced in 1988.

Zirconium

Zirconium is a gray, metallic element that occurs in the earth's crust in the form of zircon and baddeleyite. Australia is the world's largest producer of zircon, accounting for nearly 60 percent of total world production in 1988. The closest competitor was South Africa, with 21 percent, followed by the Soviet Union with just over 11 percent. Other important producers are China, India, Brazil, and Malaysia. Zirconium is produced from its ore by a fairly complicated process involving the use of magnesium metal, which makes production of the metal very expensive. The raw material, however, is quite plentiful.

Uses of Zirconium

Ferrozirconium is used in the steel industry. Pure zirconium, because of its high corrosion resistance, is used along with zirconium alloy as fuel sheaths in nuclear engineering. Zirconium is also used to construct valves and thermocouple pockets, where resistance to corrosion is a significant consideration. Zirconium compounds have been used also for making waxes, tanning agents, rust and water repellants, and deodorants.

Supply and Demand Factors

Although supplies of the raw material are plentiful, producing zirconium is quite expensive, leading to reduced demand except for essential applications. Demand is most likely to increase only if there is a major expansion in nuclear-plant construction. Substitutes are available in the steel industry in the form of ferro-titanium, and in certain foundry applications, chromite and aluminum silicate are viable substitutes. Although zirconium is not on the United States' stockpile inventory, the Bureau of Mining does withhold publication of U.S. production figures and import dependence.

Investment Opportunities in Strategic Metals

The key word here is caution. While these markets can respond dramatically to shortages, increases in demand, and disruption of supplies, they are difficult to store and perhaps even more difficult to sell. In many cases the markets are very thin, dominated by only a few individuals or firms, and, therefore, not recommended for the average investor. Should the markets become more liquid, or should a professionally managed fund which is run by experienced and respected managers become available, this may be an excellent area for the metals investor.

6

INVESTING IN METALS THROUGH THE STOCK AND FUTURES MARKETS

THERE ARE MANY DIFFERENT vehicles for investing in the metals. Since the day-to-day prices of precious metals are more commonly followed, there are numerous investment opportunities in gold, silver, platinum, and palladium. While there are also opportunities to invest in the strategic metals and the base metals, there are fewer choices available to the average investor.

While I can't fully discuss every available option, what follows will help you achieve a working overview of what is available, as well as some of the pros and cons of each approach. Should you wish additional information, I suggest you contact either a reputable broker and/or up-to-date reference sources. The world of investment alternatives is not static. Every day brings new and exciting opportunities; however, opportunity also brings risk, and the risks are not only financial. There are always unscrupulous promoters, dishonest brokers, and illegal schemes, all of which are designed to defraud investors of their funds. Fortunately, there are in the minority, but you should still thoroughly investigate the credentials of every promoter, broker, or manager of any program or plan you intend to follow. Some of the potential pitfalls will be pointed out to you along the way.

Investing in Metals Shares

The single most popular way to invest in metals is through the shares market, but there are so many different mining companies, so many choices facing the investor, that knowing which to buy, when, and why is a task of significant complexity and proportion. While it is often assumed that rising metals prices will be reflected in the rising price of mining-company shares, this is not always the case. Nor is it true that falling metals prices will be reflected in the declining price of shares. The production costs, ore reserves, debt structure, and operating expenses of every producer are distinctly different. The cost of mining gold in Canada, for example, is substantially different from that in South Africa. And the location of ore reserves for each producer varies significantly, making it more or less costly for some producers to extract their metals than it is for others.

There are also such considerations as long-term reserves, the grade of ore being mined, the experience of corporate management, and competitive producers. The importance of such factors can be ascertained only by study and analysis. This is where patience, research, and a knowledge of financial analysis can be very helpful. On the other hand, you could ignore the fundamentals and analyze stocks strictly on a technical basis, using charts and price and/or trading-volume data.

In addition, there are numerous investment advisory services that provide specific recommendations on mining shares. In selecting a service that might help you analyze mining stocks, you should consider both the amount of funds you have available as well as the nature of the service. In other words, is it a conservative or an aggressive service? Is it a service geared to penny mining shares, other highly speculative stocks, or some of the better-known stocks?

Consider also whether you want to invest in American, Canadian, South African, or Australian shares, or a combination of the above. Although it is true that some of the more speculative stocks can appreciate dramatically in a bull market, it is also true that these shares often decline in price and your money will be wasted. A mix of shares is often best; however, I suggest you concentrate primarily upon the more-established producers, particularly those listed on the New York Stock Exchange, the American Stock Exchange, some OTC issues, and some of the Toronto Stock Exchange Shares. For more speculative issues, consider the South African mines, but again, try to stay with those that have well-established operations. While it is not my intention to recommend specific mining concerns, you will find a listing of some of the better-known producers in the Appendix.

For those who do not wish to deal with the analysis, study, and selection of mining shares, I recommend some of the mutual funds. Although there are fees involved, the portfolios of these funds are highly diversified, and your return could be very good with little or no effort on your part in terms of selecting the individual stocks to buy or sell. The only thing you'll need to concern yourself about is timing. But there are ways in which this issue can be dealt with very effectively, as you'll learn in later chapters of this book.

Using Dollar-Cost Averaging

One of the most sensible approaches to dealing with the issue of timing purchases and sales is to use a dollar-cost-averaging technique. While this approach is not recommended for futures or other margin-type accounts, it can be very effective in stocks. Dollar-cost averaging is the technique we use to compensate for the fact that our timing in buying metals stocks may be too early, too late, or otherwise incorrect. None of us can know exactly when bull markets will begin or when bear markets will end. Although such methods as technical and/or fundamental analysis can help, they're far from perfect.

Dollar-cost averaging is really a simple technique that can be applied to many different types of investments. There are several methods of cost averaging. The simplest is to invest a predetermined amount in stocks, coins, etc., on a regular schedule. The interval could be monthly, bimonthly, semiannually, or otherwise. In a falling market, each purchase brings the average cost of your investment closer to the mean, or average, price, which will decline steadily in a falling market. Hence, you will be slowly but surely lowering your average price. When prices begin to turn higher, your average cost will be low compared to current prices, and you will have accumulated a large investment (relative to your finances and needs) at what is, hopefully, a reasonably low price.

As you can see, a lot of the decision making is avoided by the use of such a regular purchasing program. Naturally, when the market begins its upswing, you would cease your buying in order not to raise your cost too high and thereby defeat the purpose of your cost-averaging program. However, you may not be able to tell that the market has started its major upswing and, as a result, you may not know whether to stop your program of accumulation.

This problem can be resolved by using a modified program, one that I prefer. Rather than purchase blindly every month, you could purchase selectively based upon price level. Say, for example, that you are interested in accumulating a position in silver-mining shares, but only when the price of the stock you are looking to buy is low in comparison to its historical movements. You examine the price of the stock and observe that since the 1950s it has made several important bottoms in the $8–$11 price range. Currently the price is at $14 per share, and silver prices are falling, along with the price of most mining shares. Your program might, therefore, be to buy 20 shares every month (although I'd recommend at least 100-share blocks in order to save on commission charges) as long as the price of the stock is at $11 or lower. Or you might give yourself a little leeway and buy only if the price is at $12 or lower. If the price is not in your target range one month, you might save the funds and double or triple your purchase the next time the price does enter your predetermined range. This type of selective dollar-cost averaging is, I feel, a sensible long-term approach to investing in metals shares. And it can also be used with metals mutual funds.

You might decide to cost-average on the sell side as well. In other words, you might establish your target range for liquidating shares or mutual funds. This is not necessarily a bad approach; however, you must remember that declining markets fall much more quickly than rising markets rise. In other words, a bull market of several years duration can be erased in a matter of several weeks, or even less. Your liquidation program will, in view of this well-established fact of life, need to be much more aggressive and shorter term. You might modify your program to take advantage of positive news in a given stock or in the general market, liquidating fairly large portions of your holdings on price strength.

Dividends or Capital Gains

There are at least two schools of thought with regard to metals investments. On the one hand, there are those who will tell you that you ought to consider dividends in deciding which stocks to buy, sell, or hold. I say that if you want dividends, you ought to put your money into vehicles that will give you dividends. I regard metals investments as primarily speculative. While there are reasonable dividends to be had from the larger, more-established gold and copper producers, and from some of the more conservative mutual funds, precious-metals investing is primarily a game of capital appreciation. Your decision as to which shares to buy, or which metals vehicles to invest in, should be based on the idea that capital appreciation is your primary goal. Although the stability and fundamentals of the investments you ultimately choose are important considerations, your decision should not take into account dividends. The overwhelming percentage of your profits or losses will occur as a function of price swings and not as a result of dividends.

Futures Trading in Metals

While it is true that futures trading is one of the most speculative ways to participate in the markets, it is also one of the most potentially rewarding. Furthermore, futures trading requires a relatively small amount of investment, inasmuch as margin requirements are in the area of 1–5 percent as compared to the approximate 50-percent margin requirement in stocks. I suggest you read this chapter thoroughly before you attempt to speculate in metals futures. Those who are already familiar with futures trading may wish to pass over the rest of this chapter; however, I suggest that you read the section in Chapter 9 on seasonal price tendencies in metals.

How Does Futures Trading Work?

The futures market is, in many respects, similar to the stock market. There are, however, a number of significant differences. While the stock investor or speculator who purchases shares has a virtually unlimited amount of time to hold those shares, the futures trader does not. This is because futures transactions involve specific delivery times, after which the actual tangible commodity must be purchased by the contract buyer unless the contract has been sold to another trader. This is, of course, where the stereotype of futures trading comes into play. We've all heard of the mythical futures trader who forgot that he had bought live cattle futures (as an example) and awoke one morning to find that 40,000 pounds of live beef steers had been delivered to his home. Naturally this is a complete fiction. In reality this does not occur. While speculators are "called for delivery," the actual commodity is not delivered until the balance of it has been paid for, and when it is delivered, it is sent to a predetermined location such as a feed lot, storage vault, grain elevator, etc., depending upon the commodity.

Here's how the process works. Assume that you felt that gold prices were going to increase. Assume also that your capital was limited to $5,000. You would have several choices regarding allocation of your resources. You could buy 200 shares of a moderately priced gold stock and spend, perhaps, $2,400. Assuming 50 percent margin, you might only spend $1,200. You might decide to take more risk and buy several thousand shares of a "penny mining stock," knowing that the probability of success would be low, but that if you were right in your stock selection, you could increase your funds by as much as several thousand percent. Of course, you would also know that the probability of such profits' actually being made in penny mining shares was rather low. I am not suggesting here that you cannot be successful in penny mining shares. I am merely reaffirming the fact that the odds of profitable penny-stock investing are low and that the mines could easily go out of business. You could decide to place some funds in coins; however, you cannot do so on margin, and you would, therefore, not have any leverage.

Assume, however, that you were interested in buying gold futures in order to maximize your available capital. Before doing this you would need to make sure that all funds used for futures trading were strictly risk capital and that your lifestyle would not be adversely affected if it was all lost. You would also need to know that in futures trading you can lose more than you invest. This is so because at 1–5 percent margin you are controlling a large amount of a commodity with a small amount of capital. Should the market move against you (i.e., down if you have bought, or up if you have sold short), then you might lose more than what you have invested. I'll explain this more thoroughly later on.

Now that you've understood the risks, you decide to go ahead with your trading. Since you have concluded that gold prices are likely to rise, you decide to buy gold futures. Although gold futures are traded at a number of futures exchanges throughout the world, the primary market is in New York at the COMEX exchange. The gold-futures contract at the COMEX has particular specifications, as do all futures contracts. It calls for the delivery of 100 troy ounces of gold, and there are specific delivery months in gold, just as there are in all futures contracts. A delivery month specifies an exact date at which the contract buyer will pay the contract seller the balance of the funds due. If, for example, you buy gold futures at $300 per ounce, the total contract value would be $300 times 100 ounces, or $30,000. The margin on this transaction would be approximately $1,500, although this amount would vary from one brokerage firm to another. As prices rose, your firm might require more margin money, since the contract value would increase. Remember that the $1,500 margin is not your only risk. You could lose more. Here's how. At 100 ounces per contract, a one-dollar decline in gold prices equals a $100 decline in the contract value. A $15 drop in gold prices below your purchase price would equal a $1,500 decline in your funds. Your margin money would be gone if you sold your contract at the $15-lower price. However, if the market declined $25 from your entry price, which could happen quickly, you would not only lose your $1,500, but you'd owe the broker an additional $1,000 if you sold your contract. If you did not send the additional funds, usually within 48 hours, your broker would sell your position at whatever price could be had, and you'd still owe the additional money.

Remember, however, that things could also work the other way. A $25 rise in gold prices from your purchase price would translate into a $2,500 paper profit for you. A $30 rise in gold prices from your entry price would mean that you have doubled your original capital, provided, of course, that you sold your contract.

There are various "delivery months" in all futures markets. In COMEX gold futures, the delivery months are February, April, June, August, October, and December. The contract specifications for each futures market define the exact delivery date, delivery location, and details of the product to be delivered (such as grade, purity, etc.). At the end of the month prior to the delivery month, speculators who do not intend to complete the transaction by actually accepting delivery of the underlying commodity must close out their positions. If they do not, then their broker will receive a "delivery notice" and will then inform the customer. The contract must then be sold immediately or delivery will be made and the additional amount due will be debited to the customer's account.

Since a completed futures transaction costs the speculator a commission, it is in the best interest of the speculator to buy the contract month that will conform most closely to the anticipated length of the market move. Because commissions are relatively low in futures, however, it is best to trade during the nearby delivery months, as opposed to the distant, or "deferred," months, since trading activity is larger in the nearby months, and as a consequence, it is easier to buy or sell because of the substantially larger volume of trading (called liquidity).

As you can see, the leverage in futures trading is exceptionally large. This leverage can be used to your advantage, but it can also work against you. By using leverage effectively, by cutting losses, by fine-tuning your timing to pinpoint accuracy, and by riding profits, you can be extremely successful in futures trading. Yet the risks, as you know, are substantial. A well-planned investment program should include a portion of funds dedicated to futures trading, but I urge all metals investors to diversify their funds among a variety of investment vehicles.

Futures Markets in Metals

Gold futures, as noted earlier, are traded at the COMEX exchange in New York. The COMEX contract calls for a minimum of 100 troy ounces of gold. A 50-troy-ounce contract is traded in Chicago at the Mid-America Commodity Exchange, and gold futures are traded at numerous other exchanges the world over. Delivery months for COMEX gold have been noted above. The COMEX contract is the major gold futures market and is the one that should be traded, unless your funds are limited and the 50-ounce contract is more suited to your pocketbook.

Silver futures are traded in New York at the COMEX exchange. The contract size is 5,000 ounces. This translates to $50 per one-cent move in silver prices. In other words, if you buy COMEX silver futures at $4.75 per ounce, and the price increases to $4.76 per ounce, then you have a $50 paper profit. A $1 increase in silver prices amounts to a $5,000 profit. While there is also a 1,000-ounce contract traded in Chicago at the Chicago Board of Trade, the most active silver-futures market is at the COMEX. Silver futures are also traded throughout the world at various exchanges.

Platinum futures are traded in New York at the New York Mercantile Exchange. The contract calls for delivery of 50 troy ounces of platinum. A $1 move in the price of platinum, therefore, is equivalent to a $50 move in the futures contract. Delivery months for platinum futures are January, April, July, and October. Although platinum futures are also traded in London, trading volume at all exchanges is considerably less in platinum than in either silver or gold.

Because of the relatively low trading activity in platinum futures, and the volatile nature of this market, I advise considerable caution, unless you are an experienced futures trader. While this may change as interest in platinum increases, you should be aware that this market has had a history of considerable volatility characterized by wide price swings.

Palladium futures are traded in New York at the New York Mercantile Exchange. The contract calls for delivery of 100 troy ounces of palladium. A $1 move in palladium prices is equivalent, therefore, to a $100 move in the futures contract. Palladium is the most thinly traded of the precious metals. In fact, the market is so thin (i.e., inactive) that I do not advise novice traders to speculate in palladium futures. If, however, you do, then make certain that you understand the types of orders to give your broker to ensure the best price executions. As investors the world over begin to recognize the importance and explosive price potential of palladium, due both to its supply characteristics and growing demand, the futures market is likely to become considerably more active.

Copper futures are traded at the COMEX Exchange in New York and at the LME in London. There are several other markets throughout the world. Contract size at the COMEX is 25,000 pounds. Hence, a move of 1 cent in copper prices is equivalent to a move of $250 in futures-contract value. Since copper prices are actively traded and since the market is fairly predictable both technically and fundamentally, I recommend it as a good starting point for those interested in metals speculating.

Aluminum futures are traded at the COMEX in New York. At present, the market is essentially illiquid, and I do not recommend trading it.

Analyzing the Metals Markets

The futures speculator has a number of alternatives when it comes to making decisions about the markets. There are, as in stocks, two distinct approaches to market selection and timing. The fundamental approach, in its purest sense, involves studying the basics of supply and demand. The statistics used by fundamental analysts include such things as production data, consumption data, warehouse stocks, consumer demand, industrial consumption, exports, imports, mining statistics, and a host of other significant variables. In addition, the fundamentalist must also consider such things as international and domestic political events, relationships to other markets, and even such things as natural catastrophes and weather.

The purely technical trader, on the other hand, has little or no interest in the fundamental data. Market technicians study price trends, trading activity, futures-contract open interest, and a host of mathematical manipulations of this data. Technicians also study price-chart patterns according to principles and techniques discussed in the classic text on chart analysis by Edwards and McGee.*

While there are many strictly fundamental traders and possibly even more technical traders, most futures traders apply a hybrid approach to their trade selection. They are not entirely committed to one extreme or another, rather, they use their knowledge of technical patterns in order to improve market timing when the fundamentals suggest that a significant price move is likely to develop.

Still other traders will not align themselves with either camp. Rather they'll subscribe to one or more of the many newsletters and advisory services, following their recommendations instead of doing their own research. There is nothing wrong with this approach as long as you take note of the following caveats:

1. Carefully research the performance history of the newsletter or trading advisor whose recommendations you plan to follow.

2. Look for consistency of performance, rather than exceptionally higher percentage returns alternating with large downswings in performance. You are much better off taking the recommendations of a service or advisor who has had average, but consistent, performance as opposed to a service or trading advisor who has had large up and down swings. Con-

*Edwards, Robert D. and John Magee, *Technical Analysis of Stock Trends*. Boston, MA: John Magee Inc. (1981).

sistency of performance will help ensure that you are not entering the program prior to one of the large drawdowns in performance.

3. You are better off taking the advice of a service that specializes in precious metals as opposed to one that gives recommendations in all futures markets.

4. While it is natural to seek as much input and advice as you can possibly get, there are some pitfalls in listening to too many advisors. The most obvious of these is confusion. My best advice is to find several advisors whose work you are pleased with and then follow their advice, or else formulate your own plan based on your analysis of their advice.

5. If you decide to follow the recommendations of just one advisory service, then don't pick and choose from among the recommendations of that service. Many investors find that they pick and choose the recommendations that don't work more often than they pick the ones that do work. Exactly why this is so I'm not sure, however, it seems to be a fact of market life.

6. Try to get started with a service when it has had a losing streak. All too often investors are attracted to a trading advisor or an advisory service when the results of the service have been exceptionally good. Frequently this is about the same time that the service begins to give back some of its profits. Therefore, you are far better off to track a service for an extended period of time and then begin following its recommendations when its results have been on the downswing for a while.

7. Decide whether your approach to the markets will be long term, short term, or intermediate term. Try not to switch time frames; instead, segregate your trades into categories, and then follow them up accordingly.

Do It Yourself or Hire a Money Manager?

While many investors hope to achieve success in metals futures independently, this is not a realistic ambition. Success in futures, metals or otherwise, is difficult to achieve. A vast majority of futures traders lose their risk capital, and they tend to lose it rather quickly. The few who do achieve success are often very successful, and therein lies the attraction for those who decide to invest in futures. In the long run, you may be better off by selecting a money manager or trading advisor to handle your precious-metals futures trading for you. While there are not many money managers who trade in precious metals only, there are some who do, and you can find them by doing a little research. There are two alternatives:

1. You can place funds with a professionally managed futures fund. The publicly offered funds and/or limited partnerships are reviewed regularly either in *Futures Magazine* (219 Parkade, Cedar Falls, Iowa 50613), and by Managed Account Reports (224 Joseph Square, Columbia, Maryland 21044). If you plan to take this approach, then do your homework and find a program with the following characteristics:
   a. *Longevity*—Try to find a fund that has been in operation for at least 10 years.
   b. *Steady growth*—Preferred to large up and down years.
   c. *No more than 50-percent drawdown*—"Maximum drawdown" is the amount of dollar decline from a high point. A fund may show net asset value of $5,000 per unit and then drop to $2,000 per unit, before moving to $10,000. In the interim the investor may lose faith and drop out of the program. Large drawdowns are difficult for most investors to accept, and they tend to drop out of programs when the drawdown becomes large, often at the bottom of the decline. Large drawdowns are also dangerous, since as most funds have a provision that requires them to stop trading once a certain percentage of funds has been lost. The more frequent the large drawdown, the greater the danger that the program will not recover at some time in the future.
   d. *Reasonable management fees*—Some funds have built in a host of management fees, profit incentives, and commission charges which are bottom-line losses to the investor. Carefully study the charges of each fund or program and compare them to other programs. Make certain that the

commission charges are reasonable, preferably discount commissions. Commission charges can add up to a major charge against fund performance.

2. Another approach is to place funds with an individual account manager. The caveats are the same as those given above. Managed Account Reports (MAR) can help you evaluate some of these programs, however, many of them are not examined by MAR. In such cases you must carefully examine the disclosure document of each program. This is a document required by the Commodity Futures Trading Commission and the National Futures Association. Before you place a single penny with an account manager, study the disclosure document carefully and ask questions about anything you don't understand. The same general guidelines as given above are applicable to individually managed accounts.

Other Considerations in Futures Trading

In addition to the guidelines and caveats provided earlier, there are numerous other precautionary considerations for successful trading which must be mentioned in regard to futures and futures options:

1. If you plan to trade for yourself using a technical trading approach, then find or develop a trading system that has a real-time performance record (or computer-tested record if real time is not available) of at least 60-percent profitable trades, with a ratio of approximately 2 to 1 in terms of dollars made versus dollars lost per trade, including commissions as losses). These criteria could also apply to individually managed futures accounts or futures funds. In the absence of real-time results, computer results are acceptable, if you have made provisions for the limitations as discussed earlier in this chapter (i.e., drawdown). Although the figures just given need not be adhered to exactly, they should be used as minimum guidelines in evaluating both the performance of a technical trading system as well as the performance of a managed account or futures fund.

2. The system you find or develop should be one that fits the limits of your available time (with or without a computer system). If the trading signals you plan to use are provided by an advisory service, then familiarize yourself with the trading system, its general principles, performance statistics, historical results, and other details described previously in this chapter.

3. Choose a brokerage firm that will be compatible with your needs. If you are an independent trader who requires no trading advice whatsoever, then select a discount firm that gives prompt order executions. If, however, you are a novice trader, you may prefer to do business with a full-service firm where you will pay higher commissions in order to get the assistance you need.

4. When choosing a particular broker within the brokerage firm, both you and the broker should be aware of each other's needs. The broker cannot serve you well unless he or she knows what you will require in the way of advice, price quotations, assistance with order placement, procedures, etc. Keep the lines of communication open.

5. Make certain you have sufficient risk capital to trade the system you have selected. Your risk capital should be truly risk capital and not funds that you have borrowed or that had been allocated to a different program or need. I cannot overemphasize the importance of this point!

6. Formulate a coherent trading philosophy. As you know, your perceptions of trading, your expectations, your goals, and your market orientation (i.e., long-term, short-term, etc.) are all factors that contribute either to success or to failure. Futures trading in the metals markets is often affected by strong emotions and volatile economic events. If you consider these events within the framework of a consistent and logical trading philosophy, you can integrate and understand these events and emotions more productively and more profitably.

7. Plan your trades, and carry out your plans consistently. Avoid the temptation to make emotional decisions not based on your particular system or method.

8. Do your work in isolation. Some of the most successful traders do their work alone. The value in being an isolationist when it comes to speculation is that it forces you to make decisions based almost exclusively upon your opinions. You don't necessarily want anyone else's input or opinions. With experience and the confidence it brings, you will soon realize that your own opinions are just as valuable as the opinions of any other traders or market analysts.

9. Treat futures trading as a serious business. Before you begin, formulate rules, organizational procedures, goals, and expectations. Delineate these carefully, within the limits of your abilities and expectations, both financial and personal.

10. Don't procrastinate once your trading decisions have been made (whether the decision is to get into a trade or to get out of a trade). It matters not whether you are taking a profit or exiting at a loss. Act as soon as your system dictates action; no sooner, no later.

11. Limit your risk exposure and preserve capital. The best way to limit risk is to trade in only three to six markets at once and to avoid trading markets that have swings too large for your account size. Since there are only four to five major futures markets in the metals, you will not need to worry about trading too many futures markets. Remember also that the precious metals tend to move together. Once you have decided to limit risk to a certain dollar amount or to limit risk using specific techniques, make sure you take your losses as soon as they should be taken. Riding losses is the single most common and costly error made by futures traders.

12. Avoid anticipation. Far too many traders go astray when they try to anticipate signals from their trading system. You cannot tell the market what to do. It will always move in the direction of least resistance, and your task is to follow the

market through its endless twists and turns. If prices are trending higher, then you must trade from the long side. If prices are trending lower, then you must trade from the short side.

13. Evaluate your progress and results regularly. Feedback is important to the futures trader. While the feedback will be obvious when you tally your profits and losses, the reasons for your profits or losses may not be clear if you wait too long to evaluate them. Study your results and, particularly, the specific behaviors that led to those results, good or bad!

14. Do your market work. Whether you are a novice or a seasoned veteran, with or without a computer, you must keep up-to-date in your market studies. Futures markets move quickly, and there is often little time to update your trading signals once a move has occurred. If you have a computer, then you can program it to automatically update your signals or system every day at a set time. If you do not use a computer for your system, then you must set aside a certain time for your market work. You must keep your market analyses current.

15. The chief enemy of the speculator is emotion; however, the greatest friend of the speculator is the emotion of others. In futures trading, emotions must be kept under control. The consequences of emotionally based decisions can be very costly to the speculator since they often (but not always) result in unwarranted actions.

16. Don't take tips, and don't give tips. Trading futures is a lonely task. "Sure things," insider information, and rumor are not consistent with trading systematically. We are all tempted to find the easy way, but the easy way is rarely the best way. Avoid the temptation to take tips, to seek out inside information, to listen to the opinions of other traders or to believe that the people you are listening to knows more than you do. Sometimes they do, but most of the time they don't. Collective opinions are, of course, helpful in the case of contrary

opinion studies, but individual opinions or tips are most often counterproductive to the trader.

17. When you have enjoyed a particularly successful period, it is a good idea to remove money from your account. Whether you do this on a profitable-trade basis or on a time basis (i.e., daily, weekly, monthly) is not important. What's important is to siphon money from your account so that you are in a position to trade with your winnings after having taken your start-up capital out of the markets. Futures traders have winning and losing streaks. During the winning streaks, profits often accumulate rapidly. You may become overly impressed with your own success, and you may then seek to expand your trading. While there will be a time to expand your trading and to increase the size of your position, it is usually not wise to do so when you are feeling euphoric about your performance. I recommend that you withdraw funds monthly. Your broker might not take kindly to your removing profits following every profitable trade.

18. You can develop winning attitudes and behaviors by studying the lives and works of great traders. The essential variable in successful trading is the trader, not the system. A good trader can make virtually any system work.

19. It has been said that "the trend is your friend." This wise old bit of market wisdom is known to many, but understood and used by few. Be cautious when your trades are not consistent with the existing trend. There will be times when your signals will be contrary to the trend; however, you must always be careful about trades and signals that go against the primary trend, since they will most often be wrong.

The rules I have given you are based upon my experiences and observations in futures trading since 1968. While these rules are applicable to all traders, they may be more important to those involved in the metals markets than to other futures traders. The emotion, volatility, patience, and pertinacity required in trading metals futures is considerable. Though some rules may be more important to some individuals than to others, I know that at one time or another, all of the rules I have given you will be important to all traders.

The most effective way to put these rules into action and to internalize them is to study them, to keep them carefully, and to review them frequently. They are intended to keep you on the right track, and they will help keep you honest with yourself. You must never forget that one of the most serious blunders a speculator can commit is self-deception. To refuse to accept a loss is to invite failure with open arms. It is impossible to trade futures without taking losses. No trader or speculator is immune to losses. Ultimately what separates the winners from the losers in futures trading and in most investment areas is the ability to be honest with oneself. From a clear perception of market reality grows the skill to recognize what is important and valuable in the markets and to discard what is useless and meaningless.

Finally, I urge all who wish to trade metals futures to remember the risks at all times. As you achieve success, as you see your positions proven correct, as you watch your profits grow, there will be an ever-increasing urge to pyramid your trading, to add more and more positions to the paper profits you have accumulated. This is not good practice. More often than not such practices will erase all of your profits as soon as the market turns against you. Your pyramid must be largest at the start of a move so that it will have a strong base of support.

7 INVESTING IN COINS

INVESTORS CAN PARTICIPATE in the metals markets through the purchase and sale of coins. There are several ways to do this. Here is a synopsis of your options:

1. *Bullion coins* can be bought and sold through thousands of dealers the world over. The value of these coins is determined by the value of the bullion and a broker's commission charge when bought and sold. Since commission charges can vary considerably, no specific percentage markup for commission can be given; however, 6 percent of the coin bullion value is common.

   In the case of special-issue coins, limited-production coins, or medals, there may be an additional premium above and beyond the bullion value of the coin itself. In such cases there are special considerations that the investor should take into account when making a decision about purchase. These will be discussed later on.

2. *Numismatics,* or coin collecting, is a highly specialized field with literally thousands of coin issues. There are numerous considerations relating to the condition of coins which dramatically affect prices.

3. Since the mid 1980s various firms have organized *coin partner-ships* that manage investor funds in numismatic coins. The in-fluence of such partnerships has grown steadily as a function of the large amounts of money they control. Their effect on the market will continue to grow. Those who invest in num-ismatics should carefully consider the role of such large funds in affecting prices.

Now let's examine each of the alternatives in detail.

Bullion Coins

There are many different types of bullion coins to choose from. Although they are all essentially similar in terms of metal content, the differences among them are essentially aesthetic and price re-lated. Coins such as South African Krugerrands, Canadian Maple Leafs, and Chinese Pandas are popular, but the primary reason for owning bullion coins is for their bullion value. While you may see many advertisements touting the rarity of certain bullion coins, you must decide for yourself whether you are interested in numismatics or in bullion. If you are indeed interested in bullion, then virtually any bullion coin will do the job. Since there are so many different gold, silver, palladium, and platinum bullion coins, and since there are so many more coming to market every year, it would be useless to discuss with you the various types of bullion coins you could buy. By the time this information has reached you it will be outdated. I will give you some guidelines later on how to purchase bullion coins.

Gold and Silver Bullion Coins

These are among the most popular and plentiful of the bullion coins. Remember that when you buy these you will be paying for the metal content and broker commission as well as sales tax, in some cases. You are advised, therefore, to shop around and com-pare prices before you buy, since commissions will vary consid-erably. You must also make certain that you are dealing with a reputable coin dealer. Be sure that you take possession of the coins you are buying. Through the years many investors have been cheated by various schemes, all of which have involved delayed delivery to the buyer and/or holding coins for the customer.

Another factor to consider in buying gold bullion coins is liquidity. Eventually there will come a time for you to sell your coins. You must be prepared to sell quickly, since market tops develop rapidly and since there can be substantial price swings when a top is reached. You should, therefore, accumulate the most popular issues, since these will be the ones in greatest demand when the top is at hand.

It has been my experience that prices from one dealer to another can vary considerably during the time of a market top. I urge you to compare prices when selling. You'll be surprised at the different prices you'll be quoted. You may also be surprised at the different prices you'll get for different quantities of coins. You may be quoted a better price for a larger quantity of coins.

Furthermore, I suggest that you do some research before selecting a coin dealer. There have been instances of forged bullion coins, and you are, therefore, better off dealing with larger firms that will stand behind the authenticity of the coins they sell. Don't be afraid to ask questions about their policies. That's the only way you'll find out what you need to know.

In buying silver bullion coins, remember that a much larger quantity of silver bullion will need to be purchased, since the price of silver as compared to gold is considerably smaller. A bag of so-called junk silver, which consists of U.S.-circulated silver coins, weighs about 45 pounds. For the same amount of money you can have about eight to ten one-troy-ounce gold coins. This, or course, raises the issue of storage for bullion coins, which will be discussed later on in this chapter.

Platinum and Palladium Bullion Coins

These coins are, in my opinion, the most interesting and often most attractive to collect, however, they are considerably less liquid and, therefore, more difficult to sell. There are not too many platinum coin issues and even fewer palladium issues. While you can accumulate these, you should make certain that there will be a dealer who will buy them back from you when the time comes. While prices could move dramatically higher, the lack of a liquid market will result in your not getting a good price when you want to sell. This is an important consideration if you plan to profit from your investment.

Storing Bullion Coins

If you plan to accumulate a sizable position in bullion coins, then you should be concerned about storage. While some investors choose to keep their coins at home, perhaps under the floor-boards, in a mattress, in the freezer, or buried in their backyard, there are other ways to store your coins. The most common of these is to rent bank safe-deposit boxes and store your coins there until you are ready to sell. Since these coins can be quite heavy, and since they can take a large amount of space (particularly in the case of silver), you will need considerable space for a large quantity of bullion. I suggest that you keep boxes at a number of different banks.

Through the years there has been much talk about the safety of items stored in bank safe-deposit boxes. Some feel that in the event of an emergency or banking crisis you may not be given access to your vault. If you are concerned about this, then I suggest you store your bullion coins in a private vault not run by a bank or other financial institution. There are many such firms throughout the country, primarily in larger urban centers.

When to Buy Bullion Coins

Since bullion coins must be purchased for 100 percent cash (i.e., they cannot be bought on margin as you can do with stocks and futures), you will want to accumulate your position slowly over a period of time. The best way to do this is by dollar-cost averaging. In other words, make regular purchases over an extended period of time well before the bottom of the market has been reached. By buying at lower and lower prices you will slowly but surely average your cost down, and when the market begins its upswing, you will have accumulated a substantial position at a relatively low average cost. You could follow any of the strategies discussed below:

1. Buy bullion coins monthly or weekly regardless of price, but make sure you do so when prices are relatively low or following a longer period of declines.
2. Buy bullion coins only when prices are below a predetermined level.
3. Buy coins on a scale-down basis only. In other words, buy only if the price is lower this time than it was the last time you bought.
4. Buy more when prices are lower than they were the last time you bought. In other words, assume you bought one gold bullion coin at $397 last month and that the price this month is $347. You might decide to buy two coins. You could also determine a scale for every $25 or $50 increment below your original purchase price.

How to Shop for the Best Price

While bullion coin prices are tied closely to the value of bullion, you'll be able to save money if you shop for your coins. Not only will you find the lowest commissions, but you may also find lower base prices for the coins. I suggest that you have between four to six sources each month and that you contact them when you are ready to buy. Learn the price and then make your transactions.

Selling your coins is, however, a different matter. You will want to sell your coins when prices are shooting ever higher. It is *always easiest to sell on the way up*, and it is *always easiest to buy on the way down*. If you check with your dealers several times a day when prices are rising sharply, you'll see that prices can vary considerably. Accept the fact that you're not going to get the very top of a move, nor will you get the very bottom of a move. Be prepared to sell out your holdings more quickly than you accumulated them. While market bottoms can take weeks, often months, to develop, market tops can happen in a matter of days. You will need to adjust your buying and selling strategies accordingly.

Numismatics and Numismatic Coin Funds

While numismatics offers tremendous potential to the skilled and patient investor, it is a subject entirely unto itself. Some feel that this market offers the best of all worlds since it combines rarity with the value of bullion. A study of the performance history of numismatics confirms this opinion, but investing profitably in numismatic coins is not a simple matter. I feel that all investors should own some numismatic coins, but the best way to do this is by enlisting the services of a professional dealer or expert unless, of course, you have the time and skill necessary to make informed decisions.

As an alternative to collecting rare coins, you may turn your capital over to professional managers who will buy coins for you. While the returns from some of these programs have been good, there are factors you should consider before you commit funds, such as commissions, management fees, experience of the managers, condition of the markets, and the details of the programs themselves. Here are some things to evaluate before putting your money with a professionally managed coin fund:

1. Are the commission charges reasonable?
2. What are the management fees and/or incentive fees? Are they reasonable?
3. What are the credentials of the program managers? Are they experienced numismatists?
4. Has the firm had previous coin programs, and if so, what have been the results?
6. Can you sell your interest at any time? If so, what are the details and charges? Are you locked in for a certain minimum length of time?
7. How are the coins acquired? Are they bought at auction, or are they bought from the affiliated companies of the firm or

from its directors? It is preferable that they be bought from sources other than the firm's managers or affiliated companies, since this would create a conflict of interest.

8. How will the coins be sold? Will they be sold at auction or privately placed? Coins sold at auction usually get better prices.
9. Is there a loss-cutoff provision? In other words, will the program cease operations if net asset value drops below a given amount?
10. Are there any other provisions for the protection of the investors?
11. Is the fund registered properly with the appropriate state and/or federal agencies?

Consider carefully the above points, and before you take any action, consult with your attorney. Always ask for referrals from the firm, and don't do business with any individual or firm that you have not carefully checked first.

Guidelines for Investing in Coins

Here is a synopsis of my guidelines and considerations regarding coins:

1. Buying bullion coins is an excellent way to get started in metals investing.
2. Locate several coin dealers in your area and check prices regularly. You will come to know whose prices are the best and whose commissions are the lowest.
3. Be sure to check the credentials of numismatists, should you decide to enter this area of metals investing.
4. Before you send funds to anyone for any program, investment plan, coins, or coin-related plans, check with your attorney or advisor.
5. When you buy coins, do so on a dollar-cost-average basis. It is the most reasonable and sensible way of buying coins, and it will often help you get the best average purchase price.

6. When you sell your bullion coins, be prepared to act much more quickly than when you bought the coins.

7. Remember that market peaks come quickly and that you will need to respond much more quickly than you did when you accumulated your position.

8. Don't forget that liquidity is very important. If you have accumulated, or if you plan to accumulate, a large position in bullion coins, then you must do so in coins that are easily liquidated.

9. You can often save money by shopping for the best prices and the best commissions. Don't be afraid to negotiate with dealers, particularly if you are buying or selling larger quantities or if you have been a good customer.

10. There is no need for you to pay a premium for special bullion-coin issues. If you want to collect coins, then do so as part of your numismatic portfolio; however, do not get this mixed up with your bullion-coin strategy.

11. Such things as medals, commemoratives, proof coin sets, special issue coins, etc., are all items that will require you to pay a premium, and often a healthy one. Do not confuse these with your bullion-coin purchase plan. Unless the market for these specialty items turns sharply higher, you will probably not recoup your original purchase price when you sell, particularly if you do not hold these items for a long time.

12. The bullion-coin strategy is a slow and steady one. You may accumulate coins for up to several years while watching your dollars return either no profits or even shrink. This is normal, since market bottoms take a long time to develop. But keep in mind that your plan is designed to take advantage of the up market that will surely follow.

13. There are many excellent coin dealers and coin advisory services that can be helpful as you make important investment decisions. Do a little research and find a service or advisor who can help you.

14. Don't forget that storage is a significant problem, particularly in silver bullion coins. Make arrangements for storage that is both safe and accessible.

15. When you see prices turn sharply higher and when the situation appears to be incredibly positive, be prepared to liquidate some of your holdings, if not all of them, and be prepared to do so rather quickly.

While the information in this chapter has given you a general introduction to bullion coins as metals investments, it is by no means a complete coverage of the topic. Should you decide to put some of your funds into bullion and/or numismatic coins, then I strongly suggest you do additional research along the guidelines provided in this chapter.

8 A PRECIOUS-METALS STRATEGY FOR OUR TIMES

IT WOULD BE an understatement to say that we live in an uncertain world. It would be more appropriate to say that disorder, volatility, political unrest, and conflict are the rule, rather than the exception. While some say that there are better places to invest your money than in the metals markets, others claim that there is no safer place for your money. I do not recommend either extreme. I suggest that serious investors make metals investments a permanent part of their portfolio. However, I also caution that at no time should all of your funds be committed to metals-related investments. While the exact allocation of assets should vary depending on the technical condition and price of the metals, metals should occupy an important role in every well-rounded investment strategy. This strategy is subject to numerous variables:

1. Domestic economic stability is an important consideration. In particular, such variables as stability of the banking system, inflation, disinflation, civil unrest, and government fiscal policy are important considerations. Traditionally, inflation tends to bring higher metals prices, while recession and disinflation tend to bring lower metals prices. This is not, however, a hard and fast rule. Deflation or disinflation, if accompanied by cur-

rency uncertainty and/or political unrest, can also affect metals prices in a positive fashion.

2. International conflict has been a major factor in the past, but it does not always guarantee a higher metals market. Much depends on concomitant world events, as well as on the current trend of metals prices. In a higher-trending market, virtually all news is seen as bullish, while in a lower-trending market, major conflict will often fail to move the markets higher.

3. Petroleum prices have occupied a more dominant role since the 1970s than ever before. Instability in the Middle East and its potential to disrupt world petroleum supplies tend to have a significant effect on precious-metals prices.

4. Instability in South Africa has, for many years, been an important factor for all metals. The possibilities of conflict, nationalization of gold and copper mines, and worker revolts have affected prices on many occasions.

5. Copper prices are affected at least several times annually by copper-mining strikes, particularly in Latin America.

6. All of the metals markets have exhibited distinct seasonal price tendencies. These are important virtually every year regardless of the underlying price trend.

7. With the passage of time, there will undoubtedly be new influences that affect prices dramatically, perhaps more so than ever before.

8. International conflict will have a major impact on the strategic metals.

Because of the many variables that can affect the metals markets, it behooves every investor to use the metals markets both as a vehicle for profit and as a hedge against uncertainty. However, there are so many different opinions as to how this might be achieved that the average investor is often confused about the best strategy. While it would add more confusion to the already-confused picture if I gave you yet another strategy, I can offer suggestions from which you may structure your own program. Remember that the needs and abilities of every investor are distinctly different. They cannot be pigeonholed into a prefabricated program that will be right for everyone.

Furthermore, metals investments should be adapted to the times and to the status of long-term gold trends and other metals cycles. Some investors can afford to have positions in metals at all times. Others may not be so well off. They might need to be selective, not only about the types of metals investments they make, but also about when they invest. With this in mind, I will offer some general considerations as part of my metals strategy for our troubled times, but first you'll need to make a few important decisions.

Evaluate Your Financial Condition

How much risk capital do you have? Are you in a situation that will allow you to speculate in the metals markets? Can you commit your capital to a program that may not return any yield for several years? Are you able and willing to hold your positions for several years with little or no movement in a positive direction? Do you have enough capital to average down your purchase prices? These are all important questions. No matter how much you may want to be involved in the metals markets, the degree to which you can participate is limited by your available capital.

If you are among those who lack the necessary funds, then don't make the mistake of borrowing money or of redirecting funds from a more pressing or immediate need. Remember, above all else, that investing in the metals markets, whether futures, options, stocks, bullion, coins, or otherwise, is a risky proposition, but, moreover, it is a proposition that requires patience and time. You may sit on your stocks or coins for several years and see little or no return. In fact, you might even watch your investment turn lower and stay there. Should you need to liquidate your holdings when they are lower in price, you will lose money and have nothing but the loss to show for your efforts and patience.

On the other hand, the investor with risk capital can afford to let it sit idle as he or she continues to average costs in preparation for the eventual bull market. When the reward comes, it will be a big one and it will make the wait well worthwhile. But this goal can become a reality only if you have the staying power and the adding power. Consider this the single most important point of this chapter.

Determine the Optimum Allocation of Funds

I do not recommend the same level of allocation in metals at all times. Rather, I feel that investors should slowly increase their commitment in metals as prices fall and that their percentage investment in metals should decrease at or near the top of a market. While a small base position can be maintained at all times, it is important to change with changing market conditions. To do this, you will need to know a little about the history of metals prices and about the role of cyclical and technical patterns in metals. While information is readily available about the seasonal and cyclical and technical tendencies in the more popular and actively traded metals, such data is not available on the strategic metals. Let's digress to a discussion of the metals cycles since they will be important in determining the percentage allocation.

Historical Cycles in Metals Prices

For many years, gold has been the preeminent precious metal, capturing the attention and interest of investors and speculators alike. Consequently, there has been much research and study concerning the fundamentals and politics of gold. However, few studies have examined in any detail the cyclical price tendencies of gold. In this section, we'll examine the cycles in gold prices in some detail, providing both historical perspective and trend projections.

Gold

Approximate 6.71-year cycle: Figure 8-1 shows the gold shares index and gold bullion combined in one chart. I evaluate the cycle length as having been approximately 6.71 years on the average. In 1986 I made the following forecast for gold prices: "The next major low is projected for 1988–1989. . . ." As you can see from the cash and futures charts, a low was reached in 1989, completing what should be the 6.71-year-cycle low. A rally through 1992–1993 should follow with an upside projection of approximately 460 as the first long-term resistance level (marked by line A-B). Strong support is likely in the area of line A-B. A monthly average price above A-B should bring a move to the long-term resistance level of 510.

Approximate 33-month cycle: There has also been an approximate 33-month cycle in the past; however, I am not impressed with its reliability, and suggest you not consider it in your analyses.

Because gold prices have not had a sufficiently lengthy history free from prices fixed by government manipulation, it is difficult to arrive at reliable long-term cyclical forecasts. The Foundation for the Study of Cycles is an excellent source for information on gold cycles that are longer term than those discussed herein. As a point of information, various researchers have found cycles of 31, 15.36, 9.26, and 5.58 years in gold prices. The 5.58-year cycle likely corresponds to what I see as an approximate 6.71-year cycle. I refer you to the Foundation for the Study of Cycles for more information on these cycles.

Silver

Approximate 10-year cycle: The major cycle in silver prices has been approximately 10 years, from low to low. Since the price of silver made such a large jump in 1979–1980, the early history of

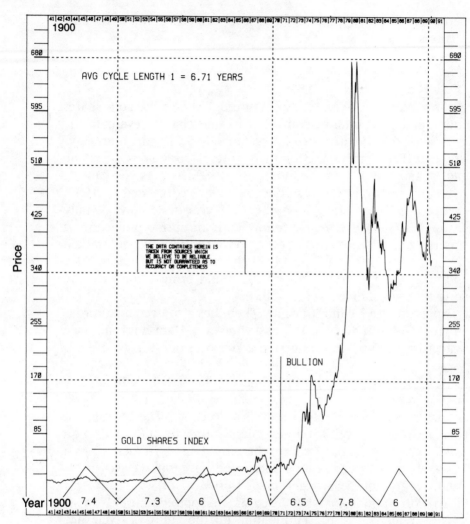

Source: MBH Commodity Advisors, Inc. Reprinted with permission

Figure 8-1 Monthly cash average price for gold, 1941–1990.

prices appears rather limited in terms of range, hence, the approximate 10-year-cycle lows have been numbered 1–7 (see Figure 8-2). Note that these lows have usually occurred early in each decade, most often in the years numbered one or two. The next 10-year low is due in 1991 (point L), but it could come early because of the likelihood of an approximate 5-year-cycle low in

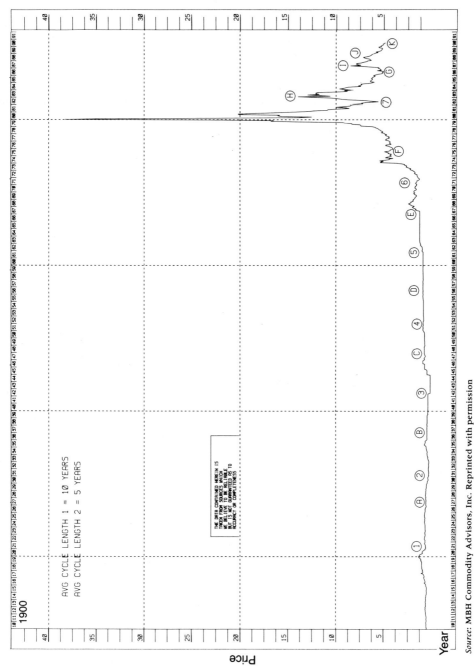

AVG CYCLE LENGTH 1 = 10 YEARS

AVG CYCLE LENGTH 2 = 5 YEARS

THE DATA CONTAINED HEREIN IS
TAKEN FROM SOURCES WHICH
WE BELIEVE TO BE RELIABLE
BUT IS NOT GUARANTEED AS TO
ACCURACY OR COMPLETENESS

1900

Price

Year

Source: MBH Commodity Advisors, Inc. Reprinted with permission

Figure 8-2 Monthly cash average price for silver, 1910–1990.

mid-1990 to early 1991. The 10-year cycle suggests a major top in 1994–1995. During the coming 5- and 10-year uptrends, tops I and J are likely to be penetrated, with the 1980 top in the $20 area as a potential target.

Approximate 5-year cycle: Figure 8-3 also shows the approximate 5-year cycle. A mid-1991 low would be ideal; however, with an approximate 15 percent margin of error, the time window for this low could be as early as mid-1990. A strong bull market top should come in 1994. Note that the confluence of projected cycle lows K and L of the 5- and 10-year cycles suggests that a major bull market is not too far from beginning. Don't place too much faith in the predictive validity of the 5-year projection (dashed line) since it has not had an especially good history of forecasting highs.

Finally, you will note that silver prices based on the monthly cash-average chart, as well as on the futures chart, are in 1990, at an important support level that dates all the way back to the mid-1970s. Note the well-defined support and resistance shown on the monthly futures chart. I see a wave-pattern low developing, with the current leg (from the 1987 top to the recent low) as the last leg of the five-wave pattern. A new bull market may begin soon with $8–9 as the first major target, and $20 as the subsequent target!

Copper

Approximate 12.8-year cycle: Copper has shown an approximate 12.8-year cycle since prior to 1900. The chart in Figure 8-4 shows the last six repetitions of this cycle. It has been fairly regular, forecasting an early 1991 top and a 1997 bottom. The dashed line shows projections through 2010. The next approximate 5.3-year-cycle high, discussed below, is due in 1992–1993, and this may lengthen the next top of the 12.8-year cycle. You will observe that when both cycles top together, there has often been a price spike (see 1980, 1969–1970, and 1956 tops as examples). It should also be noted that the 1986 bottom was an approximate 54-year-cycle low (last low, 1932), which suggests that between now and 2010, the 1980 top of near 136 monthly average price

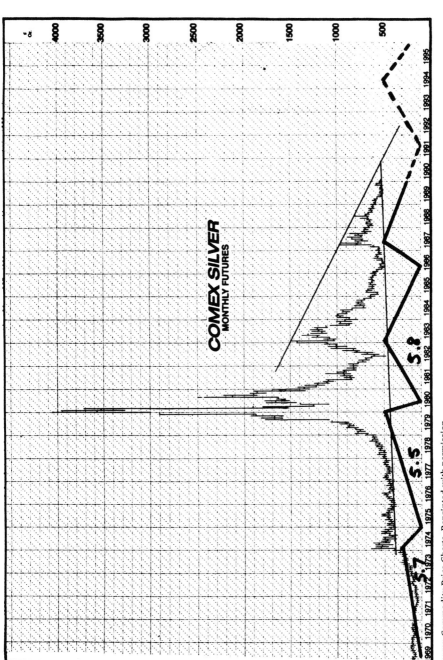

Source: Commodity Price Charts. Reprinted with permission

Figure 8-3 The approximate 5-year cycle in silver; monthly futures prices, 1969–90.

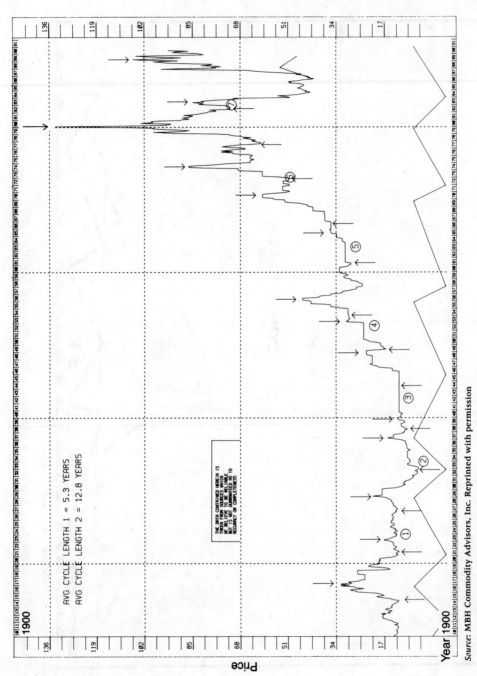

Source: MBH Commodity Advisors, Inc. Reprinted with permission

Figure 8-4 The 12.8-year cycle in copper; monthly cash average price, 1910–1990.

is likely to be eclipsed. It is likely that prices began a new secular bull market in 1985, and therefore, the next 12.8-year cyclical top in 1991 could very well be higher than the 1989 top of the 5.3-year cycle. The futures chart on this page shows the most recent 12.8-year cycles. Long-term resistance is in the approximate 124 area, which, if surpassed on a monthly closing basis in nearby futures, could yield all-time highs by the time the 12.8-year cycle tops in about 1991. Expect long-term support in the $0.80 area.

Approximate 5.3-year cycle: Copper has also shown a reliable 5.3-year cycle. It is shown on Figure 8-5, the long-term cash chart (arrows point out cycle tops and bottoms). The dashed line projects this cycle through 2010. It is entirely possible that early to mid-1990 will witness an approximate 5.3-year low (last low in 1985). The 12.8- and 5.3-year trends will then both be up through 1991–1992. This confluence of cyclical patterns could yield a major bull move, particularly when combined with the early-decade low pattern discussed below.

Early-Decade Low Pattern: I have numbered lows 1–7 as the early-decade low pattern. Years numbered 2 or 3 have often witnessed either a low point or a level from which prices move higher. Combine this with the 5.3- and 12.8-year cycle uptrends, and a delayed top could occur in the early 1990s. Copper prices could "explode" in the 1990s!

Technical Factors in Metals Prices

In addition to the cyclical indicators in precious metals and copper discussed above, there are also long-term technical factors that should be considered by investors in stocks, bullion, or futures. The following discussion is basic and I urge you to consult more advanced texts for additional details on technical analysis of the markets.

In evaluating technical factors, I will be referring primarily to support and resistance levels. In order to avoid taking too long an excursion into technical analysis, I will give you a brief definition of support and resistance.

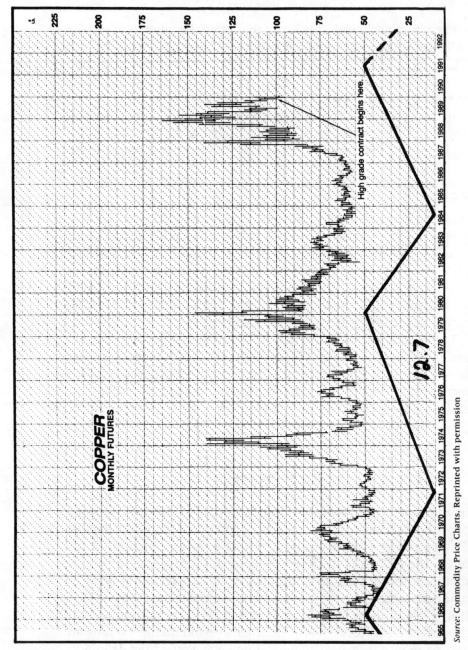

Source: Commodity Price Charts. Reprinted with permission

Figure 8-5 The 5.3-year cycle in copper; monthly futures prices, 1965–1990.

Support is defined as a price level that has, in the past, served as the base or bottoming point for prices, following a period of decline. There are usually numerous technical support levels for a given market. Not all analysts agree on all support levels. Determining support is, to a large extent, a subjective matter; however, it is based on experience as well as on a number of objective rules. *Resistance* is defined as a level that has, in the past, served to turn prices back, following a period of increasing prices.

Silver

As you can see from Figure 8-6, silver prices since 1910 have formed several important support and resistance levels. Major support, that is, support that dates back to the earliest date, is shown as line A-B. The status of support A-B suggests that a decline in prices to the approximate $3.25 area should result in considerable long-term support. At these prices, silver would be considered very low in price from a historical perspective.

As you can also see, there is support at line C-D which is, at the time of this writing, being "tested." Initially there should be a positive move from this level. Both support A-B and C-D are areas that should interest the long-term investor. Accumulation of positions on the buy side could begin when prices are in either of these areas.

Resistance line E-F is the level at about which prices should encounter selling pressure. In other words, this is about where the market is likely to stop a rally. On the other hand, a move above this level for a period of several months could indicate that a new bull market has started, and you would need to consult your charts again in order to project the next resistance and support levels.

Gold

Chart resistance and support points are not as reliable in gold as they are in silver, because gold prices in the United States have been free to fluctuate only since 1971. My chart (Figure 8-7) shows long-term support at line A-B. As this book is being writ-

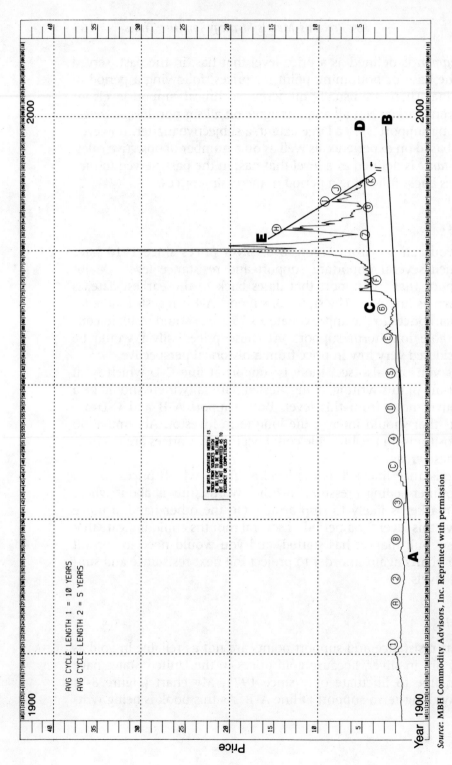

Source: MBH Commodity Advisors, Inc. Reprinted with permission

Figure 8-6 Monthly cash average silver prices, 1910–1990, showing support and resistance levels.

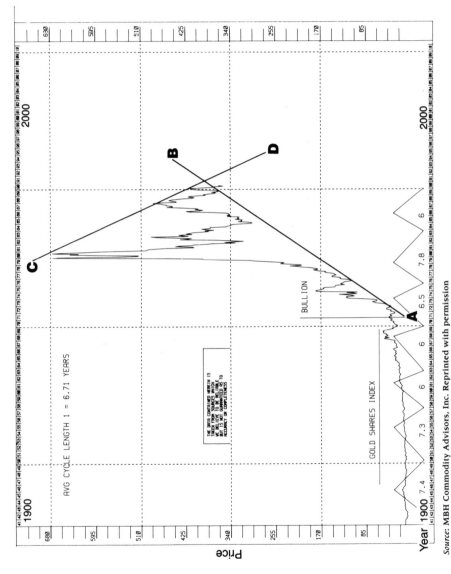

Source: MBH Commodity Advisors, Inc. Reprinted with permission

Figure 8-7 Monthly cash average gold prices, 1941–1990, showing long-term support levels.

ten, this level has been penetrated. However, a considerable rally has taken place, and the market may soon move to long-term resistance line C-D, and if C-D is penetrated, then a new bull market could be born.

The long-term investor could take advantage of the drop to long-term support A-B by beginning a buying program. Should this drop to support be consistent with an anticipated cyclical low, then the program could be even more aggressive in terms of position size.

Copper

Copper prices have enjoyed a long and very predictable history cyclically, seasonally, and technically. Figure 8-8 shows long-term support A-B as having been tested, with a substantial rally developing thereafter. The rally took prices to long-term resistance C-D, which currently stands as the major resistance level. There are many other support and resistance levels in copper prices. They can be found by analyzing the charts in greater depth and/or by using weekly price charts as opposed to the monthly chart shown.

In addition to the traditional methods of chart analysis, I advise investors to become acquainted with the theories of R. N. Elliott, or Elliott Wave. As with most technical indicators, there are many analysts and interpretations. Unfortunately, there are no final answers with Elliott Wave analysis, and it is important for every investor to find an analyst or advisor who has experience, credibility, and a good track record. I have always respected the work of Robert Prechter, the preeminent follower of Elliott's work. Prechter is a serious and dedicated student, and his work should be considered carefully by all metals investors. Bob won't be right 100 percent of the time any more than I or any other analyst will be; however, he has achieved an admirable record through the years and he is dedicated to his work.*

*You can contact Robert Prechter by writing Robert Prechter, Elliott Wave. P.O. Box 1618, Gainesville, GA 30503. Or call 404-536-0309.

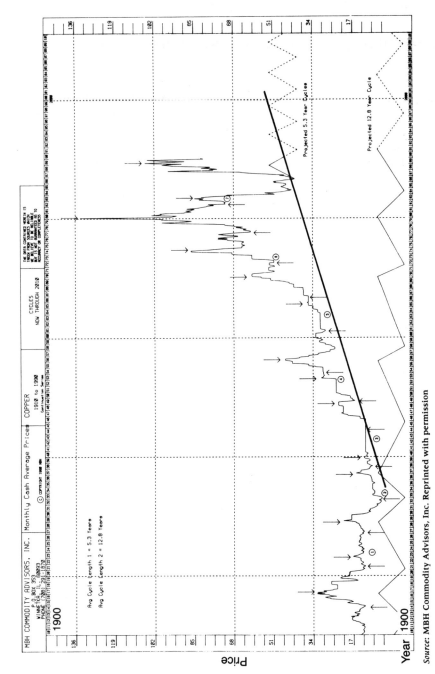

Source: MBH Commodity Advisors, Inc. Reprinted with permission

Figure 8-8 Monthly cash average copper prices, 1910–1990, showing long-term support.

Developing a Precious-Metals Strategy

I have already stressed the importance of precious-metals holdings as part of an overall long-term investment portfolio. For
many years many market analysts and "gold bugs" advanced the
fallacious concept that "precious metals could do no wrong."
Their assertions were based on a limited slice of history and, in
general, arose from the stellar performance of metals during the
1968-to-1980 bull markets. In my writings, seminar appear-
ances, and advisory publications, I warned persistently that the
metals markets were, in most respects, not substantially different
from other markets and that they should not, therefore, be af-
forded any special treatment.

Even in the 1990s the pervasive attitude regarding precious
metals can best be summarized as follows: "We will buy metals,
precious and otherwise, in the cash market or in the form of
stocks or bullion coins with the intention of keeping them indefinitely. Should prices move substantially lower, we will add more
to our positions, knowing that sooner or later we will be right
and that prices will explode." This reasoning was quite prevalent
in the late 1970s and the early 1980s. Unfortunately it is still
commonplace in the 1990s. Apparently the lessons of the bear
markets from 1980 to 1990 have not been learned too well.

There is nothing basically wrong with this approach. Sooner or
later almost everyone will be right on almost any issue or with
almost any investment. The major drawback of this reasoning,
however, is that capital is tied up for a considerable period of
time, not earning any interest and not appreciating in any significant way unless prices rise. Furthermore, there is a high probability that the investor will need his or her capital for other more
important investments, and that this may eventually force liquidation of the metals position at prices much lower than one
would want. Hence, the old adage "eventually we will be right"
may be wise, but it may not necessarily produce profits. For those
who can truly buy, hold, and add, without dipping into needed
resources, or without being forced to liquidate for other reasons,
the buy-and-hold strategy is effective, since it requires virtually
no thought.

Clearly, then the "buy, hold, and add" strategy is not necessarily the best strategy for most investors. Nevertheless, the "buy, hold, and add" strategy, under the appropriate technical conditions and/or cyclical phases, and the liquidation strategy, during cycle top periods, are certainly viable and profitable strategies for most investors. The suggestions I will give you in this chapter are part of an ideal program, and they can vary considerably according to individual investment needs. Nonetheless, the basic principles have underlying validity as well as historical precedent. Therefore, I propose the following general guidelines for the precious metals investors:

1. Precious metals should constitute no more than 20 percent of your total investment portfolio; however, during the bottoming phase of the long-term cyclical patterns, this can be increased to as high as 40 percent. The metals sector of your investment portfolio should ideally include stocks, futures, bullion coins, and, in some cases, future options.

2. The preferred allocation of the above is, of course, based on specific characteristics of the individual cycle; however, I generally recommend that of your maximum 40 percent position in the precious metals, the following breakdown should serve you well:
   a. 10 percent copper-mining stocks.
   b. 15 percent silver bullion.
   c. 20 percent gold bullion coins and futures.
   d. 15 percent platinum bullion coins and futures
   e. 15 percent palladium bullion coins
   f. The balance in mining shares

Highly leveraged investments such as futures are recommended for the investor who can afford and benefit (taxwise) from the inherent risk. Since living standards, as well as the rate of inflation and salary scales, change, it is difficult to state categorically an income level that should serve as a cutoff point for higher-risk traders. I would recommend in this respect that you consult your financial advisor or accountant.

Futures-options trading is not recommended for any investors other than the most financially secure. The probability of success as an options buyer is very low. The major disadvantage of options is that they have a limited life span and could expire before the move one expected has take place. Be particularly careful about futures options programs that offer tremendous potential with high up-front commission charges.

Timing with Cyclical and Technical Factors

While the guidelines I've given are general, there are other things you may wish to consider within the framework of the technical and/or cyclical factors discussed earlier. I am assuming in what follows that a majority of investors will be interested purchases as opposed to short sales. If you are interested in a considerably more aggressive approach to trading in the metals then you can reverse your positions to the short side when the cyclical and technical indicators turn to the downside. For the purposes of this analysis, I've divided the market cycles into stages as shown in Figure 8-9.

Anatomy of a Cycle

Cyclical trends are well known to many investors. They have existed for literally thousands of years and are found in virtually all markets and economic data. Edward R. Dewey, who is frequently called the "Father of Cycles," was the first person to popularize the notion that economic trends, securities, and commodity prices move in predictable, fairly regular, cyclic patterns. This does not mean that all cycles are symmetrical, nor does it mean that cycles are not subject to considerable variation and interpretation. Yet in spite of its limitations, the understanding and use of cyclical price movement is very important. It can prove particularly valuable to the metals investor, since it can facilitate market timing. Examples of cycles in the metals have been given earlier. Now that we've seen some of the cycles, let's examine their anatomy in order to see how they may be used as a tool for investing.

Perhaps the single most important thing to learn about price

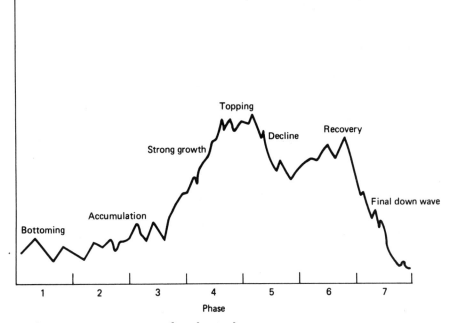

Figure 8-9 Seven stages of market cycles.

cycles is that they usually consist of several specific phases, each phase having its own characteristic price behavior, and each phase capable of being fairly readily identified on price charts. Knowing the different cyclical phases will allow the metals investor to determine where the cycle stands at any given time, and thus to make well-timed investment decisions.

Additionally, each cyclical phase has its own behavioral characteristics, both in terms of price and in terms of fundamentals. A knowledge of these characteristics further assists the investor in making appropriate investment decisions, both on the long side and on the short side. I must warn you that employing cycles as part of an investment program does not automatically mean that we are attempting to predict prices. We are seeking rather to follow trends when we have good reason to believe that they are beginning. Although the distinction between trend following and forecasting is subtle, it is important.

Forecasting prices is a difficult task, as well as a risky one. Frequently we attempt to forecast prices rather than trends. This is where we make our first mistake. Forecasting prices is difficult because it requires being exact. It is far easier to forecast trends than to forecast prices. The cycle allows one to forecast trends and/or to identify trends once they have started. However, trend forecasting can also be a dangerous undertaking.

In the West we have been raised with the underlying belief that life must follow a predetermined course and that certain milestones will appear on schedule. Few of us realize that life must follow whatever course it takes. We have very little control over the future, and we have virtually no control over the future of the market. Consequently, anticipation is not necessarily a worthwhile goal in the marketplace. The most effective approach is simply to follow the markets, since to follow the markets is to accept the fact that you do not know for certain where they are going, but that you want to go wherever they take you. Cycles will allow you to determine the most probable direction of the markets and the manner in which they should be entered. In other words, the job of the investor is to follow the cycles through their twists and turns. In order to do this it is necessary to understand the phases of a cycle.

Most cycles have seven phases:

1. The bottoming phase, during which cycles establish a low following a lengthy period of decline.
2. The accumulation phase, during which knowledgeable investors or insiders begin to accumulate positions.
3. The growth phase, during which prices move higher, finally accelerating sharply as they approach their peak.
4. The topping phase, during which prices peak and begin to give indications that lower prices are imminent.
5. The initial decline phase, during which prices begin their down trend.
6. The recovery phase, a period of brief recovery after an initial move to the down side.
7. The final down wave, during which prices move down sharply prior to establishing their low and returning to the first phase of the cycle.

The following discussion will make extensive use of Figure 8-9, which is a paradigm of the ideal cyclical phases as described above. By learning the general characteristics of each phase, you will be able to examine a price chart of virtually any market and then be able to determine your investment strategy.

Phase 1: Bottoming During this portion, the cycle prices attempt to establish a low after having trended lower for a fairly lengthy period of time as part of the previous downward cycle. This bottoming behavior can take several months, possibly longer, to develop. Typically, the bottoming phase can take one of two distinct forms. The first form is characterized by panic selling or liquidation, during which prices decline sharply and consistently over a brief period of time. The selling prompts further selling, and the market experiences wave after wave of liquidation, often prompted by negative news. Typically, the news backdrop of the bottoming phase is characterized by bearish investor sentiment, extremely negative fundamentals, a lack of interest among professionals, and no obvious or well-known fundamental reasons for a change in trend. Also called a climax bottom, panic liquidations usually correlate closely with extremely negative news.

On the other hand, the second type of bottom, or extended bottom, tends to see bottom over a fairly lengthy period of time with negative news scattered throughout a period of several months. The price range during an extended bottom is characterized by narrow movement.

Examples of extended bottoms are shown in Figures 8-10, 8-11, and 8-12. "Climax" or panic liquidation bottoms are shown in Figures 8-13, 8-14, and 8-15. Various timing signals may be used to confirm the low. Inasmuch as this discussion is designed merely to provide an overview of the various cyclical phases, giving characteristics of each, I will not elaborate on specific timing indicators.

Phase 2: Accumulation During this phase informed investors begin aggressive accumulation of metals positions. While it is impossible to ascertain the precise reasons for their accumulation, it is most likely related to a number of factors, among the most

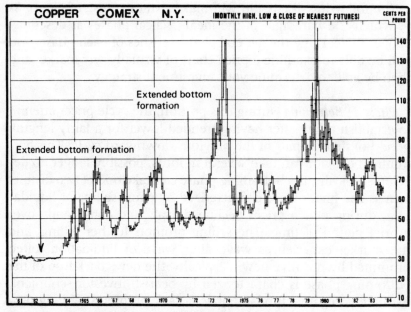

Source: Commodity Research Bureau. Reprinted with permission

Figure 8-10 Examples of extended bottom formations.

important of which are both the relatively low price of metals and the fact that prices have been trending lower for many months.

Frankly, however, it is not actually necessary to know exactly why insiders or informed investors begin to buy during this phase. Perhaps the greatest reasons are those of relative value and price. Typically, informed investors buy low and sell high. After prices have dropped considerably and for a lengthy period of time, forming a base of support, experienced investors are drawn to such markets. Furthermore, after considerable study and analysis of trends, relative value, and economic conditions, they can make decisions regarding market entry and act accordingly. They are aware of the tendency for metals prices to move higher following extended bear markets, and although such investors may not actually be conscious of the cycles, seasonals and technicals, they have often developed a "sixth sense" about the markets.

Another identifying characteristic of the phase-two buying is that it is "accumulation buying"; buying primarily for the long term, by investors who are willing to add to their positions during

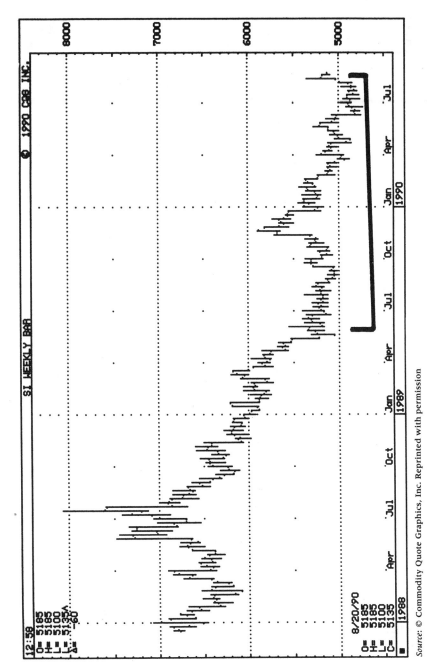

Source: © Commodity Quote Graphics, Inc. Reprinted with permission

Figure 8-11 Example of extended bottom.

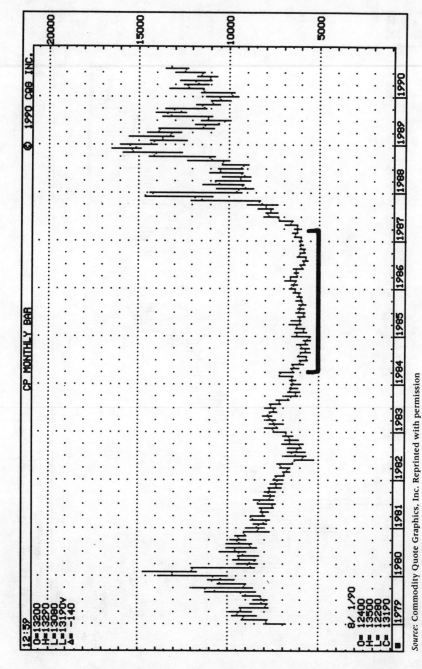

Source: Commodity Quote Graphics, Inc. Reprinted with permission

Figure 8-12 Example of extended bottom.

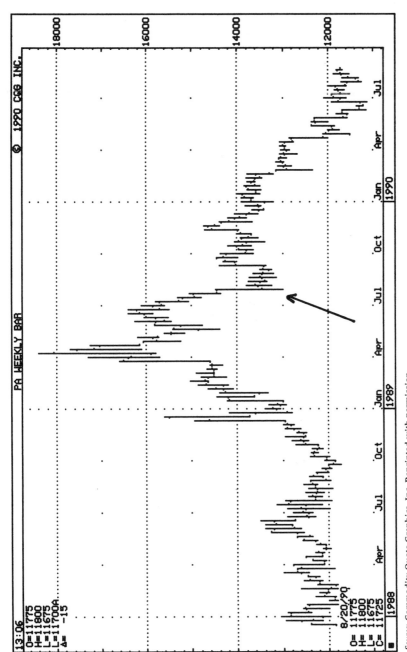

Source: Commodity Quote Graphics, Inc. Reprinted with permission

Figure 8-13 "Climax" or panic liquidation bottoms.

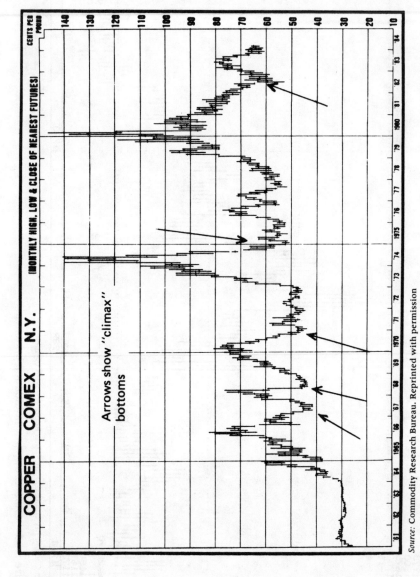

Source: Commodity Research Bureau. Reprinted with permission

Figure 8-14 "Climax" or panic liquidation bottoms.

Source: Commodity Research Bureau. Reprinted with permission

Figure 8-15 "Climax" or panic liquidation bottoms.

the bottoming phase and well into the accumulation phase. Most of their buying, however, is restricted to the accumulation phase, during which prices are not accelerating upward at a high rate. They are accumulating a position at relatively low prices, building an excellent base of support. Figures 8-16, 8-17, and 8-18 show typical chart patterns during the accumulation phase.

Characteristically, the accumulation phase is also marked by specific developments, technically, fundamentally, and behaviorally. The news backdrop still tends to be rather neutral, although some early "bulls" can advance a variety of credible arguments for buying. Typically, public and professional sentiment are still relatively negative for the longer term, since memories of the previous decline still prevent them from considering purchases.

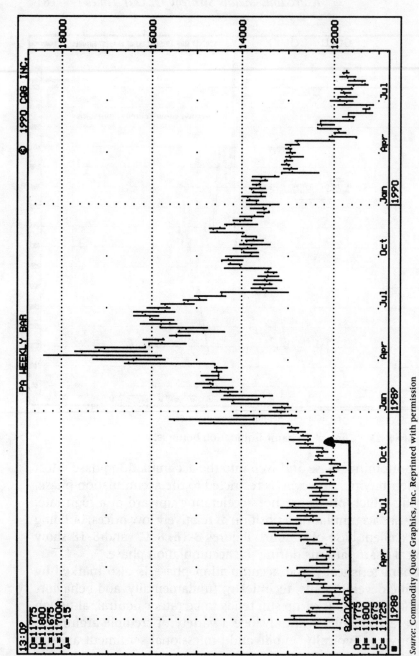

Source: Commodity Quote Graphics, Inc. Reprinted with permission

Figure 8-16 Typical chart patterns during the accumulation phase.

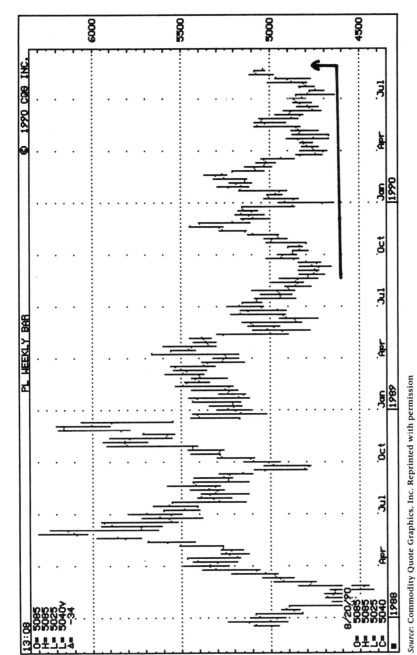

Source: Commodity Quote Graphics, Inc. Reprinted with permission

Figure 8-17 Typical chart patterns during the accumulation phase.

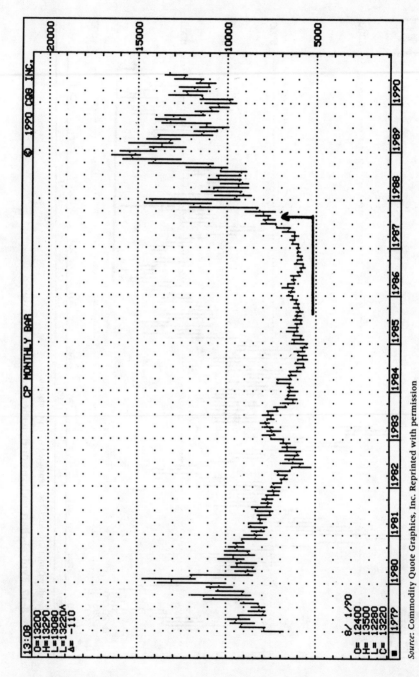

Source: Commodity Quote Graphics, Inc. Reprinted with permission

Figure 8-18 Typical chart patterns during the accumulation phase.

Within the framework of this relatively neutral to negative environment, insiders continue their accumulation activities. Informed investors take advantage of negative news, considering such news to be opportunities for additional accumulation of positions at relatively low prices. It is always easiest and most efficient to buy before an up move begins. Fundamentally there appears to be no apparent reason for buying and, in fact, reasonable economic explanations can be advanced to contradict bullish expectations.

Phase 3: Strong Growth The accumulation phase is usually followed by a phase of strong growth or price increases. During this phase, prices accelerate steadily at first and rapidly as they approach a peak. During this time, the average investor first demonstrates an awareness that metals prices are in a bullish trend. Those who buy early during this strong growth phase are likely to profit, provided they can exit the market at, or close to, the top. Professionals are relatively small buyers during this time other than for short-term in-and-out moves as they continue to hold their base position acquired during the previous two stages. Typically sophisticated investors are already thinking and planning ahead, looking for an opportunity to liquidate their positions to less experienced investors who are ready, willing, and able to buy.

Figures 8-19, 8-20, and 8-21 show metals markets in strong growth phases showing the upward acceleration of prices. Characteristically, the strong growth phase also contains specific elements that can help you identify it. Fundamentally, the news backdrop has turned bullish and, in fact, good case can be made for a sustained up movement in prices. The volume of trading and open interest in futures contracts increase dramatically, and public awareness of the bull market rises to high levels. This is reflected also in a growing public interest in metals stocks and metals-related investments.

Figure 8-22 shows various cyclic phases of the 1967–1968 bull market in silver.

Technical chart patterns attract a great deal of attention, and prices continue to gain upward momentum, reaching extremely high levels. The news backdrop is, as noted earlier, extremely

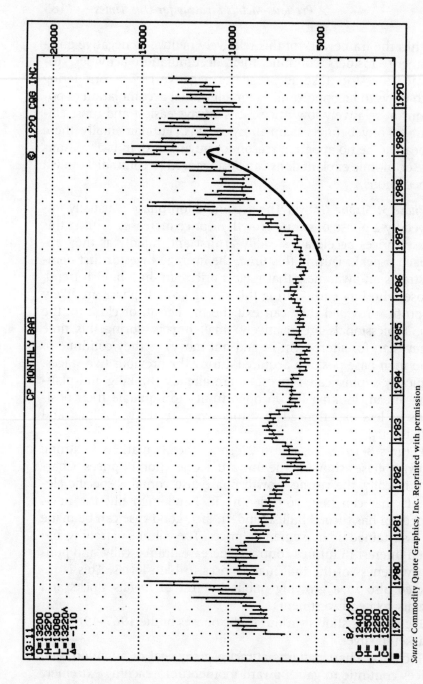

Source: Commodity Quote Graphics, Inc. Reprinted with permission

Figure 8-19 Metal market in strong growth phases, showing the upward acceleration in prices.

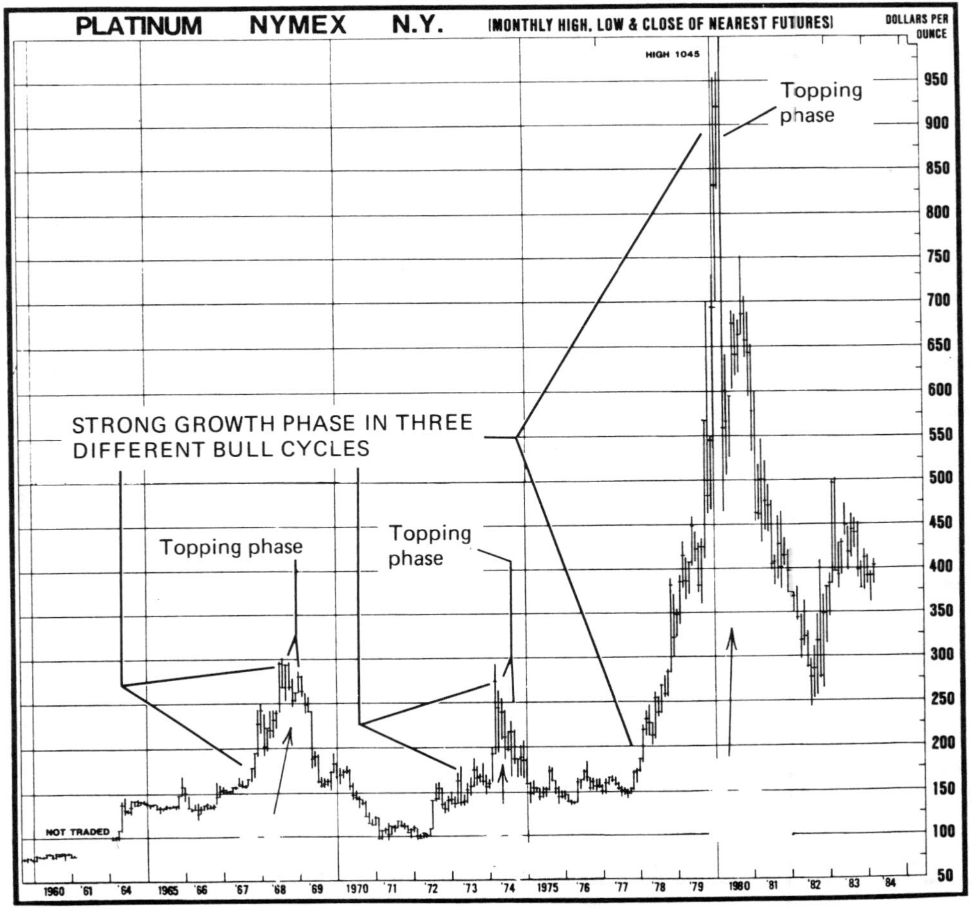

Figure 8-20 Metal markets in strong growth phases, showing the upward acceleration in prices.

Source: Commodity Research Bureau. Reprinted with permission

Figure 8-21 Metal market in strong growth phase, showing the upward acceleration in prices.

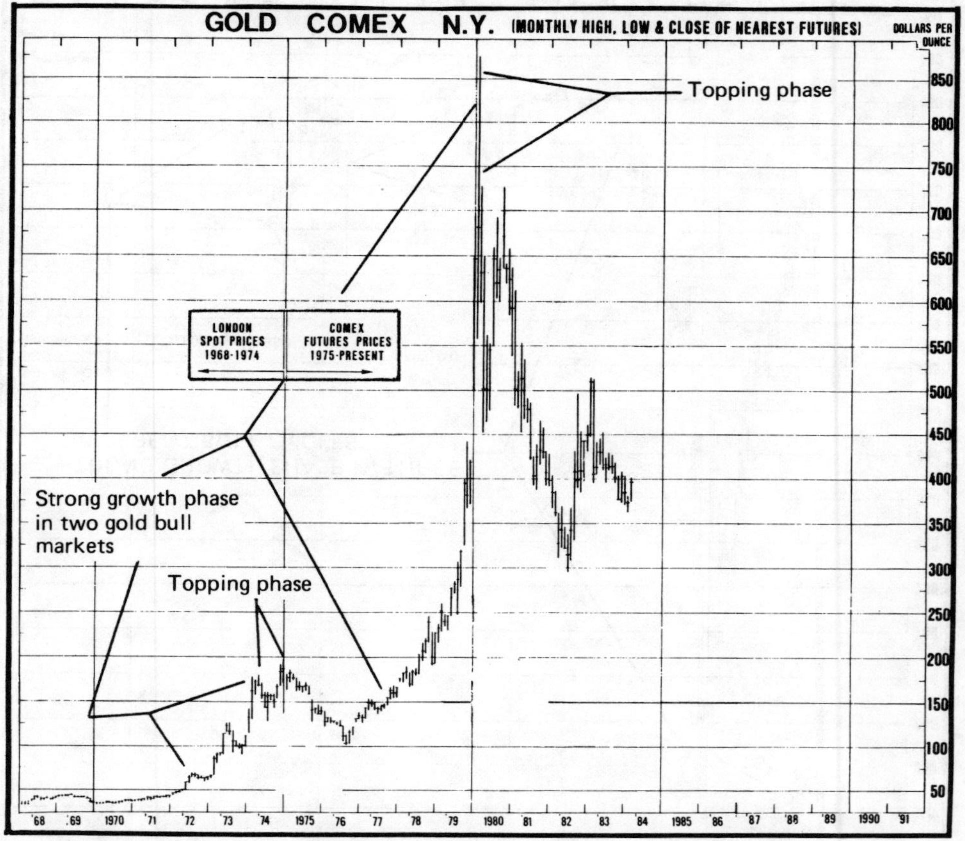
GOLD COMEX N.Y. (MONTHLY HIGH, LOW & CLOSE OF NEAREST FUTURES)
DOLLARS PER OUNCE
Topping phase
LONDON SPOT PRICES 1968-1974
COMEX FUTURES PRICES 1975-PRESENT
Strong growth phase in two gold bull markets
Topping phase
850
800
750
700
650
600
550
500
450
400
350
300
250
200
150
100
50
'68
'69
1970
'71
'72
'73
'74
1975
'76
'77
'78
'79
1980
'81
'82
'83
'84
1985
'86
'87
'88
'89
1990
'91

Source: Commodity Research Bureau. Reprinted with permission

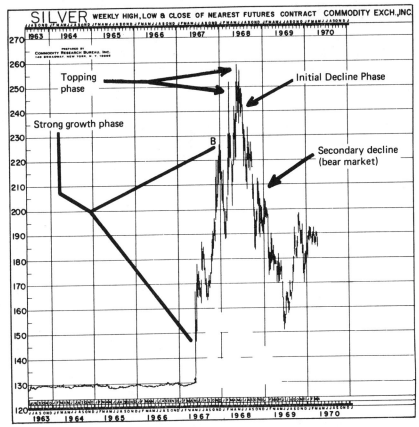

Source: Commodity Research Bureau. Reprinted with permission

Figure 8-22 Various cyclic phases of the 1967–1968 bull market in silver.

positive, and firms specializing in all types of precious-metal investments abound. There are heavy advertising campaigns, and positive commentary about metals investments in the financial press.

Another correlate of the strong growth phase is the daily price range in the futures and cash markets. In most bull markets, price range increases, along with margin requirements imposed by brokerage firms and futures exchanges. An examination of Figure 8-23 clearly shows price range prior to a gold bull market and price range during the strong growth phase. As you can see, there is a substantial increase in price range.

YEAR	MONTH	DAY	OPEN	HIGH	LOW	CLOSE
80	1	14	653.0	653.0	653.0	653.0
80	1	15	690.5	690.5	680.0	690.5
80	1	16	740.5	740.5	740.5	740.5
80	1	17	722.0	790.5	720.0	790.5
80	1	18	815.0	840.5	815.0	823.0
80	1	21	873.0	873.0	815.0	834.0
80	1	22	784.0	784.0	784.0	784.0
80	1	23	734.0	740.0	734.0	734.0
80	1	24	710.0	723.0	684.0	684.0
80	1	25	688.0	697.0	634.0	635.0
80	1	28	635.0	645.0	607.0	639.0
80	1	29	674.0	704.0	664.0	702.0
80	1	30	690.0	705.0	654.0	658.0
80	1	31	660.0	687.0	638.0	681.5
80	2	1	677.0	693.0	666.0	683.3
80	2	4	670.0	677.7	659.0	660.0
80	2	5	670.0	698.0	667.0	687.0
80	2	6	705.0	721.0	705.0	713.0
80	2	7	705.0	708.0	685.0	689.5
80	2	8	691.0	700.0	688.5	694.5
80	2	11	720.0	729.0	702.0	702.0
80	2	12	700.0	704.5	693.0	697.5
80	2	13	697.0	700.0	681.0	688.0
80	2	14	688.0	689.0	663.0	670.5
80	2	15	670.0	671.0	656.0	663.0
80	2	19	660.0	660.0	625.0	632.0
80	2	20	603.0	664.0	599.0	661.5
80	2	21	662.0	670.0	646.0	656.5
80	2	22	650.0	652.0	612.0	615.0
80	2	25	621.0	655.5	607.5	648.9
80	2	26	645.0	646.0	625.0	625.5
80	2	26	645.0	646.0	625.0	625.5

YEAR	MONTH	DAY	OPEN	HIGH	LOW	CLOSE
80	10	16	157.9	158.5	157.4	157.4
80	10	17	159.5	160.0	159.4	159.4
80	10	20	159.4	160.2	159.1	160.2
80	10	21	161.3	161.3	158.3	158.3
80	10	22	158.1	159.4	158.1	159.4
80	10	23	157.8	157.8	157.8	157.8
80	10	24	156.6	156.4	156.4	156.6
80	10	27	155.3	155.5	154.6	154.6
80	10	28	154.2	154.2	153.6	153.6
80	10	29	154.5	155.2	154.5	155.2
80	10	30	155.2	155.2	154.5	154.5
80	10	31	153.7	153.7	153.3	153.3
80	11	3	154.3	154.4	153.9	153.9
80	11	5	157.5	160.0	157.5	159.7
80	11	6	158.9	158.9	157.2	157.2
80	11	7	156.0	157.4	156.0	157.4
80	11	10	156.0	156.3	156.0	156.0
80	11	12	155.1	155.3	154.9	155.2
80	11	13	155.8	155.8	154.0	154.0
80	11	14	154.2	154.2	152.7	152.7
80	11	17	153.3	153.4	150.0	150.1
80	11	18	150.7	151.1	150.0	151.1
80	11	19	153.0	153.8	152.5	153.8
80	11	20	153.7	153.7	152.8	152.8
80	11	21	152.4	152.4	152.2	152.3
80	11	24	151.6	152.8	151.6	152.6
80	11	25	152.7	152.7	151.5	151.5
80	11	26	151.0	151.0	150.4	150.7
80	11	28	147.5	149.1	147.5	147.8

Figure 8-23 Price range prior to a gold bull market and price range during the strong growth phase.

Phase 4: Topping A great deal has been written about the history of markets and the manner in which prices may be predicted. Little, however, has been written about the manner in which markets top. Major tops in the metal markets are characterized by massive buying hysteria, large increases in trading volume both in stocks and futures, significant up movement in prices, and extreme public and professional bullishness. Tops are ordinarily characterized by large upward movement of prices.

Figure 8-24 shows the strong growth phase of three different metals bull markets.

There are many things that the long-term investor must do as prices enter their cyclical peak. Markets do not linger at the top and there is, therefore, limited time during which to act in liquidating a long-range position. Timing is crucial, and specific techniques must be employed in taking profits on positions previously established during the accumulation and bottoming phases. Market tops emotional; purchases are justified on fundamentals, and the consensus of experts, as well as the public, is unfailingly bullish. There are few obvious signs of a top. However, a top is surely developing and often arrives much more quickly than expected.

Phase 5: Decline The first indication that a bull market is ending is usually signaled by an initial sharp decline, usually from record high levels. The decline can be as much as 20 percent of price within a matter of days. Typically, such a reaction after an extremely bullish move is considered by the public and experts as a buying opportunity, and few believe that the initial decline phase marks a significant market top. The initial decline, however, is a warning sign that the bull market is not healthy and that a protracted decline is likely to follow. The long-term investor following the metals strategy proposed in this book must be alerted to the development of this technical development and should take appropriate action.

Be aware of the fact that the initial decline phase can be particularly brief and, in some cases, totally absent. Few bull markets, however, peak without an initial decline phase preceding a secondary test of the top. Figures 8-25, 8-26, and 8-27 show how the initial decline phase appears in a number of markets and what ordinarily transpires subsequent to the initial decline.

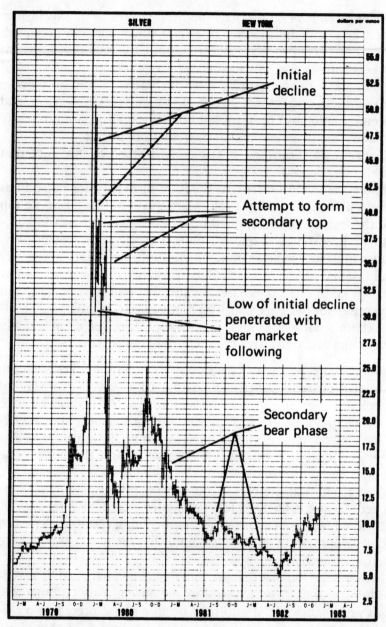

Source: Commodity Research Bureau. Reprinted with permission

Figure 8-24 Strong growth phase of three different metals in bull markets.

Source: Commodity Research Bureau. Reprinted with permission

Figure 8-25 Initial decline phase before a secondary test of the top.

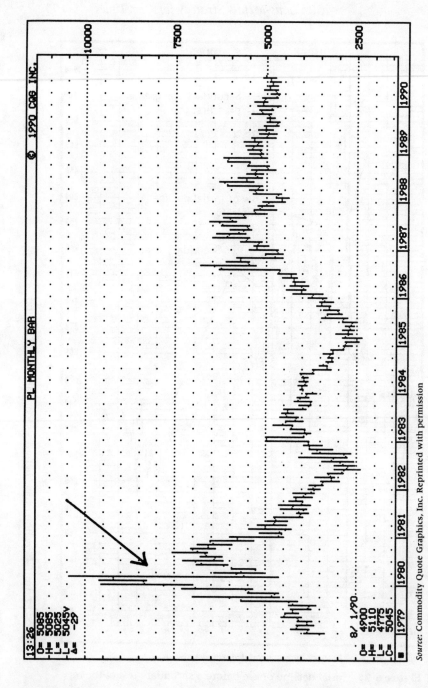

Source: Commodity Quote Graphics, Inc. Reprinted with permission

Figure 8-26 Initial decline phase before a secondary test of the top.

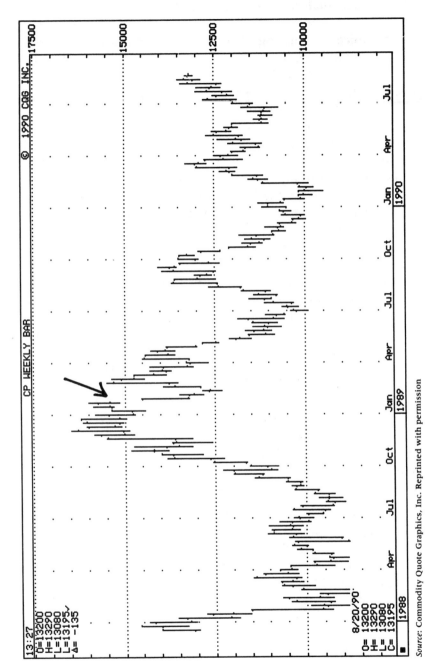

Source: Commodity Quote Graphics, Inc. Reprinted with permission

Figure 8-27 Initial decline phase before a secondary test of the top.

In technical terminology, the initial decline is usually followed by a secondary top, and when the low of the initial decline has been penetrated, a double top is said to have been confirmed. In practice, few secondary tops penetrate their previous peak, or do so only briefly. Since the initial decline phase and its subsequent test of the top is a highly emotional period for investors, it is always best for long-term traders to be entirely out of their metals investments at this time in order to minimize the likelihood of being caught with large positions. It has been said that "market tops and bottoms are made by wise men and fools"; this saying is particularly relevant in discussing the secondary peak and initial decline in the metals markets. We can assume, therefore, that to participate in the market during the formation of major tops and bottoms is a foolish undertaking.

Remember that the best action to take during this phase is action contrary to popular thinking. As you know, of course, I favor contrary thought and behavior at most turning points in the markets, since contrary action is frequently the correct action at major market turns. Investors who are persistently successful are those are not interested in holding out for the last dollar or in buying at the exact low.

The initial decline phase and its secondary or subsequent recovery and tests of highs characterize not only precious-metals markets, copper, and strategic metals, but virtually every market known to investors, whether stocks, bonds, futures, or options. Figures 8-28, 8-29, and 8-30 show several markets in their initial decline phase.

Phases 6 & 7: Recovery and Final Decline Following what is usually an unsuccessful attempt to penetrate the existing top, prices often begin an extended period of deterioration, during which they decline more quickly than they had gained during the growth phase. Characteristically, declining markets drop much faster than bull markets rise. It is, therefore, possible for a bear market to erase, in several months or less, most, if not all, that it has taken several years to gain. It is perhaps the force of gravity at work, but more likely the persistent liquidation that causes bear markets to continue with such force. Figures 8-31 and 8-32

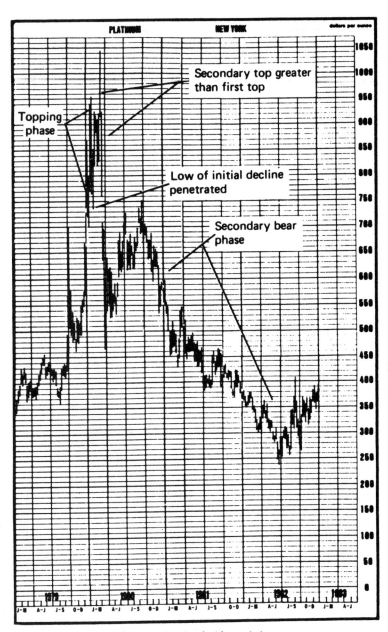

Figure 8-28 Several markets in their initial decline phase.

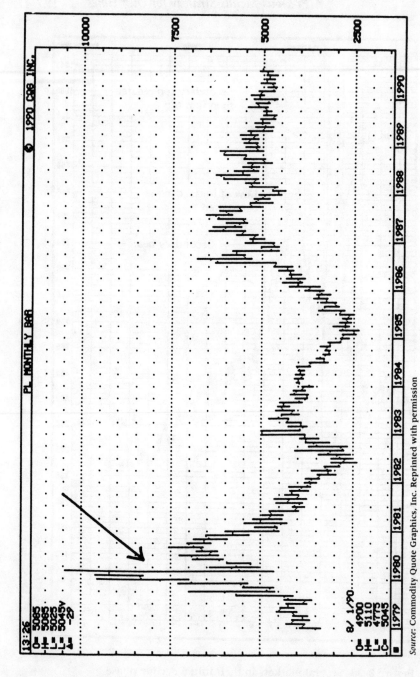

Source: Commodity Quote Graphics, Inc. Reprinted with permission

Figure 8-29 Several markets in their initial decline phase.

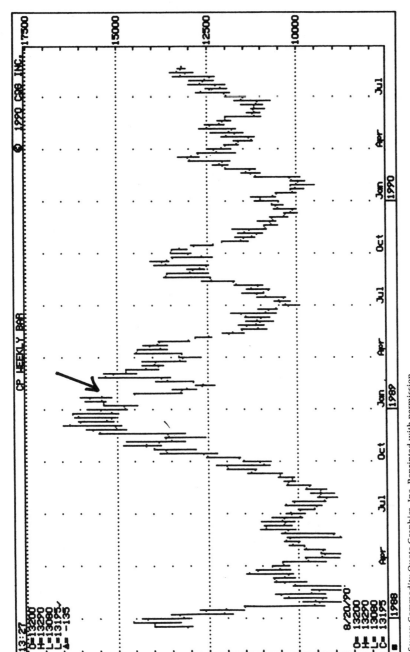

Source: Commodity Quote Graphics, Inc. Reprinted with permission

Figure 8-30 The initial decline phase and its various aspects.

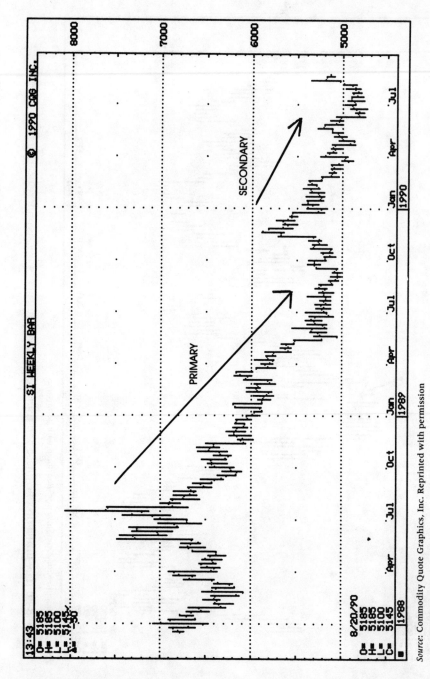

Source: Commodity Quote Graphics, Inc. Reprinted with permission

Figure 8-31 Recent bear market phases in silver and general tendency of the secondary bearish phase.

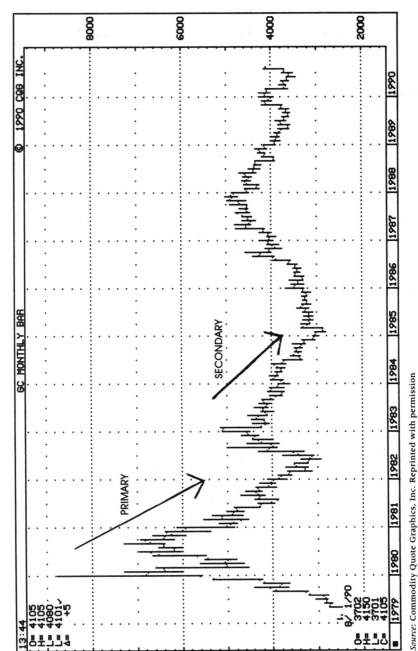

Source: Commodity Quote Graphics, Inc. Reprinted with permission

Figure 8-32 Recent bear market phases in gold and general tendency of the secondary bearish phase.

show recent bear-market phases in the metals and the general tendency of the secondary bearish phase.

Investors who have not liquidated their positions in advance of a decline are in a particularly bad situation. One of the most dangerous things to do if you are holding a long position in a bear market is to "wait for a rally." Bear-market rallies will rarely be long enough or large enough for you to take appropriate action, and you may still find yourself holding the position when the market finally bottoms. The tendency at the bottom, of course, will be to liquidate your position because the pain has reached an intolerable level.

The long-term investor who is not inclined to sell short is usually not trading at this time. His or her position should have been closed out well in advance of the secondary decline phase, and a wait-and-see stance should be maintained during the drop. Technically and behaviorally, there are many aspects which characterize the decline phase. In addition, specific actions may be taken by the more aggressive speculator. The secondary decline phase, of course, has its attendant rallies, but these usually last for only brief periods of time and constitute nothing more than mere selling opportunities. In retrospect, objectivity is easy to achieve; however, in the heat of battle, most investors lose sight of the fact that markets do indeed move in waves and they do indeed have specific personality traits in addition to their specific cyclical phases.

The information and general explanations provided in this section should help alert you to what can occur during cyclical phases in the metals markets. Remember that they pertain primarily to active markets. In other words, inactive or "thin" markets such as the strategic metals may not exhibit the wave characteristics.

The purpose of this section has been primarily to acquaint you with the cyclical stages and to provide a general orientation within which prices can be seen, so that you may determine how and when to allocate your funds. Here are some steps you may wish to incorporate into your evaluation of the markets and your decision-making process:

1. Study market prices and trends regularly by keeping your own price charts or by subscribing to any of the various services.
2. Determine the probable stage of each market.
3. Allocate your funds on a dollar-cost-average basis, once prices enter the bottoming phase or when they begin their initial rally.
4. Exit all metal investments when the final rally stage is in process
5. You may want to consider the fundamentals; however, be careful about the fundamentals, since they will usually appear to be the most bullish at the top.

Risk and Reward in Metals Investing

Losses and risk are primary considerations in every investment program. No one can give you the perfect investment program or vehicle. And no one can guarantee you no risk, particularly in the metals markets. There are times when things do not go well. In such cases it becomes necessary to take one's losses; however, the probability of ending up with a loss, if you have done your homework, is not as significant as it is if you make investment decisions on whims, tips, or rumors.

In addition to having a consistent program of selecting and timing your metals investments, the key to effective money management is based on three basic principles:

1. Your metals investment portfolio should be diversified, and you must avoid the "all eggs in one basket" syndrome. Try to use the guidelines I have provided, remembering, of course, that they are not rigid.

2. Purchases should be made on a scale-in or dollar-cost-average basis as previously described.

3. Margin allotted to each position must be more than the amount required by the exchange and/or brokerage house. Regarding this last point, I advise you to be particularly careful

when trading futures, because of the very high leverage. Leverage and low margins can work for you; however, all too often they will work against you.

There are, in addition to the points discussed above, particular and unique aspects of both reward and risk for each area of metals investing. While these may change as the markets change, I'd like to give you an overview of the risk and reward potential of each particular area. Remember that even in cases of relatively low risk, an overly aggressive or unsound investment strategy can be destructive.

Bullion and Cash Metals

While the thought of owning bars of silver or gold is a romantic one indeed, I urge you not to do so. There are a number of problems with this type of investment in precious metals, and foremost among them are storage and certification of authenticity. The storage of metals is a costly proposition. Not only does it cost money to store metals, but they must also be insured against theft, loss, or damage. And when it comes time to sell your metal bullion, it will need to be assayed once more to verify its authenticity. This is a costly procedure, and it may also be time consuming. If you want to sell quickly, you may not be able to do so.

The potential rewards of owning bullion are no greater than the potential rewards of owning bullion coins. In terms of the metal, they are one and the same thing. These comments, of course, apply only to precious metals. The risks and rewards of investing in copper and the strategic metals will be discussed later on. Regarding the precious metals, however, there is no reason to venture into bullion. While the risks may be considerably greater than those of owning bullion coins, the potential rewards are the same.

Bullion Coins

For most investors one of the ideal ways in which to participate in the precious metals markets is through bullion coins. As with all investments there are risks as well as rewards, however, there are some risks unique to bullion coins. Here is a synopsis of the risk factors:

1. No immediate return on investment. When you buy bullion coins, you must remember that there will be no return on your investment other than the potential increase in bullion value. In other words, there is no numismatic value, no dividend, and no yield. In fact, once you buy the bullion coin and pay the broker's commission, you are actually behind the game. The only way you will profit is if the bullion value of the coins increases.

2. No leverage. Since bullion coins are bought for 100 percent of their value, there is no possible leverage as one would have with stocks and futures. This means that you will not be able to maximize your dollar return.

3. Liquidity may be limited depending upon the types of bullion coins you have selected. If you buy coins that are not so well known, then their liquidity will be poor. It will be difficult for you to sell them unless the market changes and becomes very active.

4. Counterfeit coins are always a danger; however, doing business with a reputable dealer who will certify the authenticity of the coins you buy will go a long way toward reducing the likelihood of this problem.

The potential rewards are, of course that prices will move in your favor. This is the whole point of your investment.

Metals Shares

As in the case of bullion coins, the risk of loss is always a consideration, particularly in cases where margin is used. When investing in metals stocks, however, there are some unique considerations. Some of the potential risks are as follows:

1. Selectivity. While you may have correctly identified the start of a new bull or bear market in metals, you may have not picked the stock or stocks that will best participate in the trend. If you have limited capital, you are even more likely to select a stock that will move more slowly than the underlying cash markets or other stocks. The best way to avoid this problem is to invest in a mutual fund.

2. Margin. This can be an asset or a liability. The use of margin must be carefully considered. It can work for you or against you. Many investors can use margin effectively, thereby maximizing their return on investment dollars; however, there are still many investors who ride their losses too long, and margin purchases work against them, encouraging them to hold their losing positions too long.

3. Bankruptcy. This is a potential problem that must always be considered when buying mining shares, particularly those of smaller producers. When trading in the so-called penny-mining share market, this is a particularly important risk. If you owned bullion or bullion coins, then you have a tangible asset that cannot disappear. Shares in a corporation, however, are only pieces of paper that can be rendered worthless in a matter of days.

4. Liquidity can also be a problem, especially if you are dealing in shares for which there is a limited or inactive market. The best way to avoid this problem is to deal only in better-known shares.

   The potential rewards of investing in mining shares are similar to those of any investment in metals; however, there are more stocks to choose from, and you can also diversify by buying shares of producers that have interests in many different metals, as opposed to just one of the metals.

Strategic Metals

With the possible exception of futures and futures-options trading, this is the single most risky area of metals investing. The potential for returns in the thousands of percents is certainly a real and attractive one, but the risks are immense. While there is always the risk of loss, there are also several other risks of which you should be aware:

1. Liquidity is a major risk. There are not many firms or investors who deal in strategic metals with the public. Typically these firms deal in larger quantities of product with end users. When you buy, you'll pay a high premium, and likewise when you sell.

2. The area of strategic metals is highly specialized. There are few bona fide experts and even fewer knowledgeable advisors. Consider this carefully before putting money into this market.

3. The possibility of fraud is a real and ever-present danger. Since not much is known about the strategic metals and since there are few dealers or experts, it is possible that you will be cheated. I urge you to be particularly careful about any program. Do your homework and carefully check the details of any such program you are considering, and make certain that you also are familiar with the expertise and background of the program or fund managers.

4. Volatility can be immense in these markets. Prices can fluctuate wildly not only within one market, but within one day as well. The price you are quoted is not always the price you can get.

5. Limited availability of information is another problem. Price information is often hard to come buy, and even when you are quoted a price it is not necessarily a price that is real in terms of what can be obtained.

In all, while the potential for profit in strategic-metals investing is immense, the risks far outweigh the rewards. Until and unless this market becomes more active, I recommend extreme caution for all but the most intrepid and well-capitalized investors.

9 SEASONAL PRICE TENDENCIES IN METALS

BECAUSE OF ITS highly repetitive seasonal and cyclical tendencies, copper is an excellent vehicle for both the long-term investor and the short-term speculator. Copper is a particularly good investment alternative for those who shy away from the precious metals because of their risk and volatility. In this chapter, we will examine the price trends and tendencies affecting several of the most important metals, starting with copper.

Copper

Copper prices have had a long and volatile history. During periods of war, copper prices have fluctuated dramatically. Strikes, political instability, and wide swings in supply and demand have contributed to the long, and at times erratic, history of copper prices. Figure 9-1 shows the monthly history of cash-average scrap copper prices from 1820 through 1990. While the price chart itself fails to reveal any clearly repetitive or predictable price pattern, copper has for many years exhibited some of the most reliable cyclical patterns in any of the commodity markets, and in particular, in the metals markets. The foundation for the Study of Cycles has documents at least 8 reliable cyclical patterns among which are included the 54 year, 11–12 year, and 5.7 year cycles.

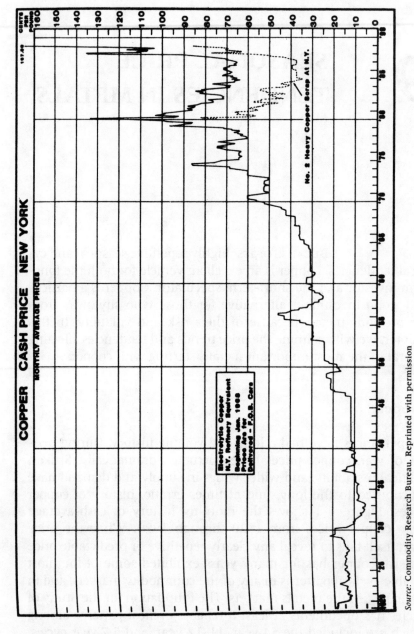

Source: Commodity Research Bureau. Reprinted with permission

Figure 9-1 Monthly history of cash average scrap copper prices, 1920–1990.

My analysis of the cyclical patterns in copper appears in the previous chapter.

In addition to the cyclical patterns in copper prices, the market has also had a lengthy history of fairly predictable seasonal fluctuation. Typically, copper-futures prices tend to make their lows in mid to late summer, as shown in Figure 9-2, the weekly composite December seasonal futures chart. The cash market has shown a slightly different seasonal tendency, however, as you can see from an examination of Figures 9-3 and 9-4. These figures show cash copper seasonals for different time spans. Industrialization and increased consumption of copper due to a sharp increase in residential and commercial building has altered the seasonal tendencies in copper prices since the late 1940s.

In addition to studying the general seasonal tendencies for copper prices, I've also conducted more concise seasonal research in the form of what I call "key date" seasonal analysis. This analysis employed a computerized search of daily copper prices from the mid-1960s through 1989. The analytical technique involved searching every possible combination of buy-and-sell dates for copper futures, as well as over 10 different stop-losses. The number of possible combinations was immense; however, this is the kind of work for which a computers is ideal. This analysis yielded numerous ideal buy-and-sell dates for copper futures using combinations that have shown a high probability of repetition since the 1960s. Given the relatively limited number of years used in my analysis, the pure statistician could question the results, and the doubts would be reasonable. If, however, the cash market is used to verify the results, then we find that they are more likely to be true seasonal tendencies as opposed to random events.

The "key date" seasonals in Table 9–1 appear to have been most reliable since the 1960s. Each listing shows the key-date rule, the synopsis of results, and the yearly profit/loss, entry-and-exit analysis, and cumulative performance. You will note that there are both long-side and short-side trades. While I've isolated these tendencies as among the most reliable during the given span of years, there is no guarantee that these seasonal tendencies will continue to perform as well in the future as they have in the past. Given, however, my study of copper prices and my experi-

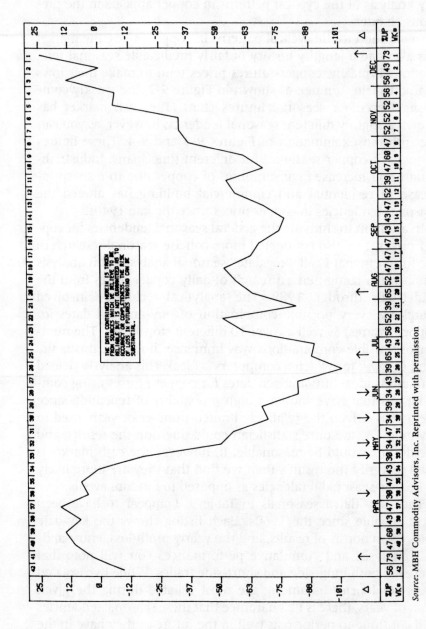

The data contained herein is from file sources which we believe to be reliable but is not guaranteed as to accuracy or completeness. The risk of loss in futures trading can be substantial.

Source: MBH Commodity Advisors, Inc. Reprinted with permission

Figure 9-2 Weekly seasonal composite futures chart for copper, 1967–1990.

JAN	FEB	MAR	APR	MAY	JUN	JUL	AUG	SEP	OCT	NOV	DEC
JAN	-50.5	53.0	-51.8	50.0	-53.6	-55.9	-54.3	-54.0	50.9	52.6	52.4
	FEB	-50.5	51.1	50.3	-55.0	-56.2	-51.6	-52.1	-51.2	50.3	52.1
		MAR	51.8	-55.2	-60.3	-58.5	-56.5	-51.9	-51.5	-51.2	-50.3
			APR	-56.4	-61.5	-60.8	-56.1	-53.7	-53.4	-53.6	-50.6
				MAY	-59.6	-58.2	-57.1	-52.8	-51.9	-51.8	51.2
					JUN	-53.4	51.6	54.8	53.0	52.2	53.5
						JUL	57.5	59.7	51.5	52.7	54.1
							AUG	56.8	51.2	50.4	53.9
								SEP	-54.3	-50.8	53.7
									OCT	54.0	60.5
										NOV	60.8

MONTHLY SEASONAL CASH TENDENCY: COPPER   Years 1796–1990

High % Seasonal Up Months: None   Ideal Seasonal High: Dec
High % Seasonal Down Months: None   Ideal Seasonal Low: Jun

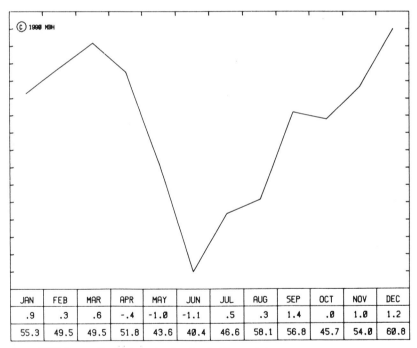

© 1990 MBH

JAN	FEB	MAR	APR	MAY	JUN	JUL	AUG	SEP	OCT	NOV	DEC
.9	.3	.6	-.4	-1.0	-1.1	.5	.3	1.4	.0	1.0	1.2
55.3	49.5	49.5	51.8	43.6	40.4	46.6	58.1	56.8	45.7	54.0	60.8

Source: MBH Commodity Advisors, Inc. Reprinted with permission

Figure 9-3 Monthly seasonal chart for copper, 1796–1990.

JAN	FEB	MAR	APR	MAY	JUN	JUL	AUG	SEP	OCT	NOV	DEC
JAN	60.0	66.7	70.8	76.0	70.4	70.4	61.5	59.3	60.7	60.7	53.6
	FEB	78.9	76.2	83.3	69.2	61.5	64.0	57.7	55.6	57.7	50.0
		MAR	80.0	69.6	56.0	65.4	50.0	56.0	55.6	50.0	-51.9
			APR	60.0	-54.5	52.2	-52.2	50.0	-52.0	-57.7	-55.6
				MAY	-60.0	50.0	-52.4	56.5	-52.0	-60.0	-63.0
					JUN	52.6	55.6	50.0	50.0	-56.5	-58.3
						JUL	-55.6	52.6	-54.5	-54.2	-54.2
							AUG	52.9	52.6	50.0	-52.4
								SEP	-52.9	-52.6	55.0
									OCT	-55.6	52.6
										NOV	52.6

MONTHLY SEASONAL CASH TENDENCY: COPPER   Years 1796–1990

High % Seasonal Up Months: Mar Apr   Ideal Seasonal High: Oct
High % Seasonal Down Months: None   Ideal Seasonal Low: Jan

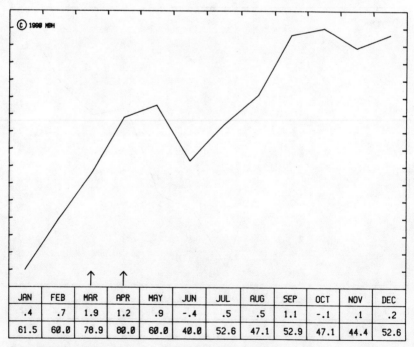

JAN	FEB	MAR	APR	MAY	JUN	JUL	AUG	SEP	OCT	NOV	DEC
.4	.7	1.9	1.2	.9	-.4	.5	.5	1.1	-.1	.1	.2
61.5	60.0	78.9	80.0	60.0	40.0	52.6	47.1	52.9	47.1	44.4	52.6

Source: MBH Commodity Advisors, Inc. Reprinted with permission

Figure 9-4 Monthly seasonal chart for copper, 1960–1990.

Table 9-1. Summaries of Six Key-Date Seasonals for Copper

1.

LONG Mar Copper ON THE CLOSE 02/07 WITH A 6% STOP-LOSS CLOSE ONLY, OR EXIT ON CLOSE 02/18

Entry Date:	02/07	Exit Date:	02/18
Positive Trades:	19	Negative Trades:	6
Starting Year:	1966	Ending Year:	1990
% Positive Trades:	76.00	% Negative Trades:	24.00
Average Gain:	3.48	Average Loss:	−1.49
Average Trade:	2.28	Profit/Loss Ratio:	7.38
Years Analyzed:	25	Cumulative Gain*:	$14,275.00
Maximum		Calculated Stop:	0.00
Drawdown:	−$812.50		

2.

LONG Jly Copper ON THE CLOSE 01/10 WITH A 6% STOP-LOSS CLOSE ONLY, OR EXIT ON CLOSE 03/29

Entry Date:	01/10	Exit Date:	03/29
Positive Trades:	17	Negative Trades:	7
Starting Year:	1966	Ending Year:	1989
% Positive Trades:	70.83	% Negative Trades:	29.17
Average Gain:	8.58	Average Loss:	−6.06
Average Trade:	4.31	Profit/Loss Ratio:	3.43
Years Analyzed:	24	Cumulative Gain*:	$25,837.50
Maximum		Calculated Stop:	0.00
Drawdown:	−$4,687.50		

3.

LONG Jly Copper ON THE CLOSE 02/26 WITH A 6% STOP-LOSS CLOSE ONLY, OR EXIT ON CLOSE 03/30

Entry Date:	02/26	Exit Date:	03/30
Positive Trades:	18	Negative Trades:	5
Starting Year:	1967	Ending Year:	1989
% Positive Trades:	78.26	% Negative Trades:	21.74
Average Gain:	4.21	Average Loss:	−6.03
Average Trade:	1.99	Profit/Loss Ratio:	2.52
Years Analyzed:	23	Cumulative Gain*:	$11,425.00
Maximum		Calculated Stop:	0.00
Drawdown:	−$2,750.00		

(continued)

Table 9.1 (*continued*)

4.

SHORT Jly Copper ON THE CLOSE 05/24 WITH A 6% STOP-LOSS CLOSE ONLY, OR EXIT ON CLOSE 06/27

Entry Date:	05/24	Exit Date:	06/27
Positive Trades:	17	Negative Trades:	7
Starting Year:	1966	Ending Year:	1989
% Positive Trades:	70.83	% Negative Trades:	29.17
Average Gain:	4.23	Average Loss:	−5.25
Average Trade:	1.47	Profit/Loss Ratio:	1.96
Years Analyzed:	24	Cumulative Gain*:	$8,800.00
Maximum		Calculated Stop:	0.00
Drawdown:	−$5,900.00		

5.

SHORT Jly Copper ON THE CLOSE 04/05 WITH A 4% STOP-LOSS CLOSE ONLY, OR EXIT ON CLOSE 04/28

Entry Date:	04/05	Exit Date:	04/28
Positive Trades:	18	Negative Trades:	6
Starting Year:	1966	Ending Year:	1989
% Positive Trades:	75.00	% Negative Trades:	25.00
Average Gain:	4.07	Average Loss:	−4.63
Average Trade:	1.89	Profit/Loss Ratio:	2.63
Years Analyzed:	24	Cumulative Gain*:	$11,362.51
Maximum		Calculated Stop:	0.00
Drawdown:	−$2,800.00		

6.

SHORT Dec Copper ON THE CLOSE 10/15 WITH A 4% STOP-LOSS CLOSE ONLY, OR EXIT ON CLOSE 10/27

Entry Date:	10/15	Exit Date:	10/27
Positive Trades:	18	Negative Trades:	6
Starting Year:	1966	Ending Year:	1989
% Positive Trades:	75.00	% Negative Trades:	25.00
Average Gain:	2.41	Average Loss:	−3.22
Average Trade:	1.00	Profit/Loss Ratio:	2.24
Years Analyzed:	24	Cumulative Gain*:	$6,012.50
Maximum		Calculated Stop:	0.00
Drawdown:	−$2,187.50		

---

ence with the market, I would expect these seasonal tendencies to continue in the future, and I would not be surprised if they became more pronounced and reliable.

Silver

Figure 9-5 shows the monthly cash average price of silver from 1882 through 1990. As you can see, silver prices moved in a relatively narrow price band until the 1950s. The last 40 years have witnessed a dramatic increase in silver prices, as well as several highly volatile periods of price fluctuation. The 1980s in particular were marked by a substantial rise and fall in prices as speculation increased considerably and as the Hunt brothers' silver-manipulation scheme raised prices to historically high levels.

Many investors consider the mid to high $4-per-ounce range to be an important fundamental support zone for silver prices, since as this is the approximate cost of production. Typically when prices fall below the $5 level, U.S. and Canadian mines begin to scale down production and, in fact, entirely stop production in some cases. This, of course, eventually reduces supplies and gives rise to a new bull market.

Through the years there has been much discussion and analysis of the silver-versus-gold price ratio. The feeling among speculators is that when the ratio becomes too high (i.e., gold too high in relation to silver), then it is probably wise to buy silver as opposed to gold, and vice versa when the ratio is too low. While there are some market analysts and investors who feel that the ratio is important, I maintain that there is insufficient historical data to arrive at a firm conclusion. Given the fact that U.S. gold prices were fixed for many years, it is difficult to compute a valid ratio. Although there are numerous sources for additional information on the gold/silver ratio, one which you may wish to investigate further is Roy Jastram's *Silver: The Restless Metal.*

Silver prices have exhibited several cyclical tendencies since the 1800s. Among the most prevalent are the approximate 5- and 10-year patterns. In addition to the above, the Foundation for the Study of Cycles and other researchers have proposed the exis-

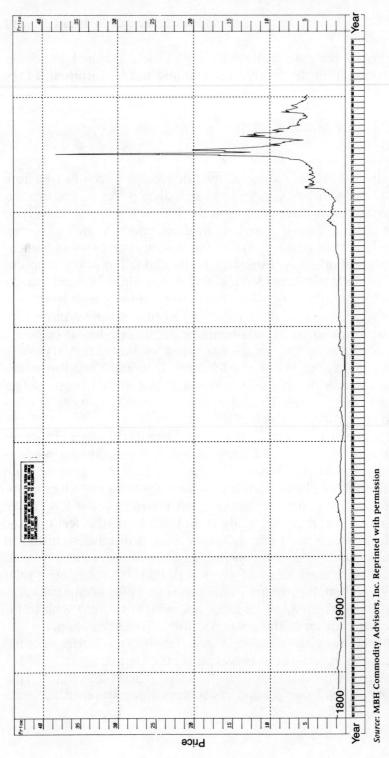

Source: MBH Commodity Advisors, Inc. Reprinted with permission

Figure 9-5 Monthly cash average price for silver, 1882–1990.

tence of other long term cycles. Here is a synopsis of the most reliable silver cycles as analyzed by Lieutenant Commander David Williams.

It will also be noted . . . that all four cycles, i.e., 31, 15.36, 9.26 and 5.58 years, peaked in 1919. In addition, the 31- and 15.36- year cycles peaked in 1859, 1890 and 1951, while the 9.26- and 5.58- year cycles peaked together in 1912, 1935, 1946 and 1974. The 1951 peak of the 5.58-year cycle also coincided with the peaks of the 31- and 15.36-year cycles in that year. These cycles are believed to be real because: (a) There have been 3 repetitions of the 31-year cycle and 7 repetitions of the 15.36-year cycle since 1850; (b) there have been 8 repetitions of the 9.26-year cycle and 12 repetitions of the 5.58-year cycle since 1900. Shirk estimates the next ideal peaks to occur: 31-year cycle in 1980.5, 15.36-year cycle in 1981.58, 9.26-year cycle in 1983.5, and 5.58-year cycle in 1985.62. By a slightly different method, the author's forecast is: 1981.7, 1983.7, 1983.09 and 1985.66 for the respective cycles. The ideal low of the 5.88-year cycle is due at 1982.8 according to Shirk.*

The previous chapter includes my analysis of the silver cycles. While the cycles have been fairly predictable in the past, there is no guarantee that they'll be as reliable in the years to come. I suggest, therefore, that if you plan to make investment decisions based on these cyclical patterns, you update them and investigate them further. As a point of information, I'd suggest joining the Foundation for the Study of Cycles, 3333 Michelson Drive, #210, Irvine, California 92715. The low cost of an annual membership is one of the best bargains available, considering the wealth of research which comes with your membership.

Silver prices have also exhibited a distinct *seasonal* tendency since the 1800s. The monthly cash seasonal price chart (Figure 9-6) shows that lows tend to come during the summer months, most often in August. This has been a prevalent pattern since the 1800s and, as you can see from the 35-year seasonal cash price chart in Figure 9-7, the pattern has not changed appreciably in recent years. Additional validation of the seasonal tendency is obtained from an examination of the weekly composite seasonal futures chart in Figure 9-8.

* See *References,* Williams, p. 8.

	JAN	FEB	MAR	APR	MAY	JUN	JUL	AUG	SEP	OCT	NOV	DEC
JAN		52.7	51.9	-51.2	54.0	50.0	-52.2	-51.1	-51.1	51.6	52.0	-50.5
FEB			-51.9	-56.4	50.6	-57.1	-52.3	-54.8	50.0	54.9	51.6	-51.1
MAR				-56.3	-50.6	-50.6	50.6	51.1	50.6	50.0	50.0	-54.7
APR					59.4	50.6	-50.6	-52.4	54.8	53.9	52.7	-52.7
MAY						-61.0	-60.2	-59.3	-54.9	50.0	52.1	51.1
JUN							-52.1	54.4	61.6	56.8	58.0	52.8
JUL								61.8	60.8	64.0	58.1	-50.6
AUG									63.9	61.4	54.1	-51.1
SEP										50.7	-53.2	-57.0
OCT											-62.7	-63.0
NOV												-60.5

MONTHLY SEASONAL CASH TENDENCY: SILVER   Years 1882–1990

High % Seasonal Up Months: None	Ideal Seasonal High: Jan
High % Seasonal Down Months: None	Ideal Seasonal Low: Jul

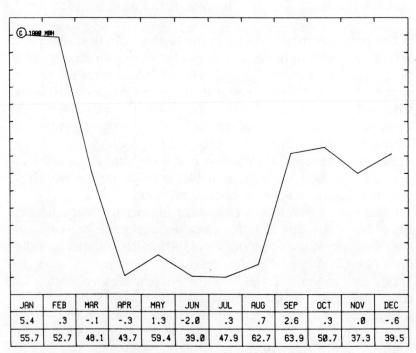

JAN	FEB	MAR	APR	MAY	JUN	JUL	AUG	SEP	OCT	NOV	DEC
5.4	.3	-.1	-.3	1.3	-2.0	.3	.7	2.6	.3	.0	-.6
55.7	52.7	48.1	43.7	59.4	39.0	47.9	62.7	63.9	50.7	37.3	39.5

Source: MBH Commodity Advisors, Inc. Reprinted with permission

Figure 9-6 Monthly seasonal chart for silver, 1882–1990.

MONTHLY CASH ARRAY ANALYSIS: SILVER   Years 1960–1990

JAN	FEB	MAR	APR	MAY	JUN	JUL	AUG	SEP	OCT	NOV	DEC
JAN	56.0	60.0	56.0	64.0	56.0	50.0	53.8	53.8	50.0	55.6	-51.9
	FEB	52.0	-52.0	56.0	52.0	50.0	50.0	57.7	57.7	55.6	-51.9
		MAR	-52.2	-52.2	50.0	50.0	50.0	57.7	-57.7	-55.6	-59.3
			APR	52.2	52.0	53.8	-53.8	57.7	53.8	55.6	-53.8
				MAY	-62.5	-53.8	-57.7	-53.8	50.0	55.6	51.9
					JUN	57.7	58.3	65.4	50.0	55.6	51.9
						JUL	68.0	56.0	60.0	57.7	50.0
							AUG	52.2	54.2	56.0	56.0
								SEP	50.0	54.2	52.0
								•	OCT	50.0	-60.0
										NOV	-52.0

MONTHLY SEASONAL CASH TENDENCY: SILVER   Years 1960–1990

High % Seasonal Up Months: Aug   Ideal Seasonal High: Feb
High % Seasonal Down Months: None   Ideal Seasonal Low: Apr

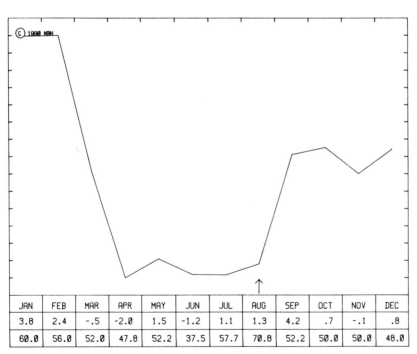

JAN	FEB	MAR	APR	MAY	JUN	JUL	AUG	SEP	OCT	NOV	DEC
3.8	2.4	-.5	-2.0	1.5	-1.2	1.1	1.3	4.2	.7	-.1	.8
60.0	56.0	52.0	47.8	52.2	37.5	57.7	70.8	52.2	50.0	50.0	48.0

Source: MBH Commodity Advisors, Inc. Reprinted with permission

Figure 9-7 Monthly seasonal chart for silver, 1960–1990.

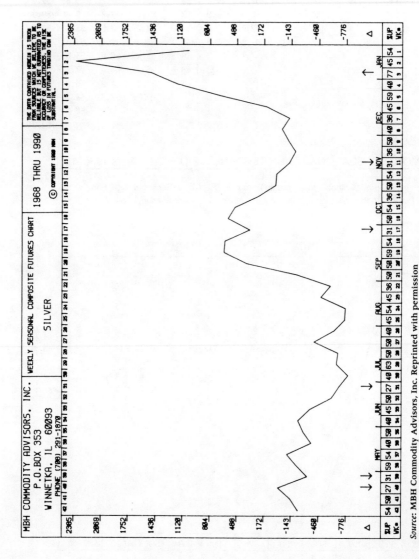

Source: MBH Commodity Advisors, Inc. Reprinted with permission

Figure 9-8 Weekly seasonal composite futures chart for silver, 1967–1990.

Gold

Since gold prices were fixed for many years, it is difficult to analyze the gold cycles with complete confidence. An extensive analysis of gold cycles has been provided by Lieutenant Commander David Williams through this work in *Cycles*. Figure 9-9 provides a synopsis of his work with the various long-term gold cycles. As you can see, there are many cycles, but I must remind you to be particularly cautious if and when you use these cycles for the purpose of investing or speculating since their length can vary considerably. It is always best to consult a current source for the most up-to-date cyclical analyses and projections.

The previous chapter includes my analysis of gold prices and cycles. As you can see, the history is not entirely that of cash gold prices. It is a combined historical record of a gold stock price index through 1972 when gold ownership was again legalized in the United States, after which the chart shows monthly cash-average gold prices. As I've stated before, cycles are not perfect. They vary in length and reliability, and it is always best to consider additional factors in conjunction with cyclical patterns.

Figure 9-10 shows the seasonal tendency of gold prices since the 1940s, and Figure 9-11 shows the seasonal pattern for futures prices on a weekly basis. As you can see, there are some distinct patterns that can be used to the advantage of speculators and investors. In addition to the above general seasonal patterns, I've conducted more in-depth research into gold seasonal tendencies in the form of key-date seasonal analysis as discussed earlier. The list of gold key-date seasonals in Table 9-2 may serve as a guide for your investing and/or speculation. Please remember, however, that the gold analyses are based on considerably less data than those for silver or copper, since the price history is more limited.

Platinum

Figure 9-12 shows the history of platinum prices from 1920 through 1990. You can see that platinum prices have had a more volatile history than have gold prices. Given the higher price of

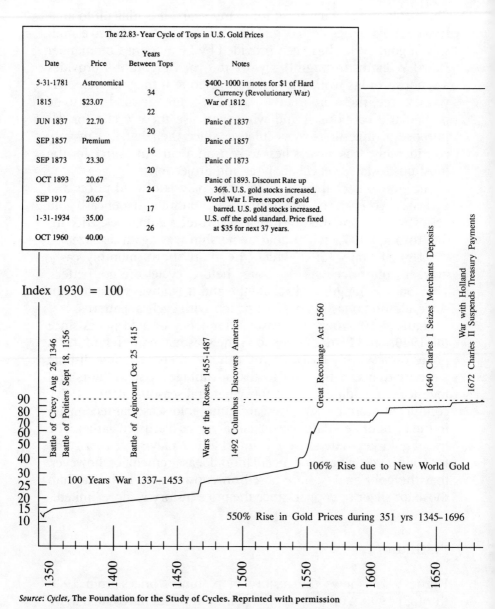

Date	Price	Years Between Tops	Notes
		The 22.83-Year Cycle of Tops in U.S. Gold Prices	
5-31-1781	Astronomical		$400-1000 in notes for $1 of Hard Currency (Revolutionary War)
		34	
1815	$23.07		War of 1812
		22	
JUN 1837	22.70		Panic of 1837
		20	
SEP 1857	Premium		Panic of 1857
		16	
SEP 1873	23.30		Panic of 1873
		20	
OCT 1893	20.67		Panic of 1893. Discount Rate up 36%. U.S. gold stocks increased.
		24	
SEP 1917	20.67		World War I. Free export of gold barred. U.S. gold stocks increased.
		17	
1-31-1934	35.00		U.S. off the gold standard. Price fixed at $35 for next 37 years.
		26	
OCT 1960	40.00		

Index 1930 = 100

Battle of Crecy Aug 26 1346
Battle of Poitiers Sept 18, 1356
Battle of Agincourt Oct 25 1415
Wars of the Roses, 1455-1487
1492 Columbus Discovers America
Great Recoinage Act 1560
1640 Charles I Seizes Merchants Deposits
War with Holland
1672 Charles II Suspends Treasury Payments

100 Years War 1337–1453

106% Rise due to New World Gold

550% Rise in Gold Prices during 351 yrs 1345–1696

90 80 70 60 50 40 30 25 20 15 10

1350 1400 1450 1500 1550 1600 1650

Source: *Cycles*, The Foundation for the Study of Cycles. Reprinted with permission

Figure 9-9 Gold prices in England, 1343–1980, as compiled by Lt. Comdr. David Williams.

Chart 1: Gold Prices in England, 1343–1980

Index: 1930 = 100 = £3.17s.10.5d.
Ratio Scale
Statutory Price: £3.17s.10.5d.
Acts of 1717, 1819, 1925
Source: R.W. Jastram *The Golden Constant*
Drawn by: LCdr. David Williams

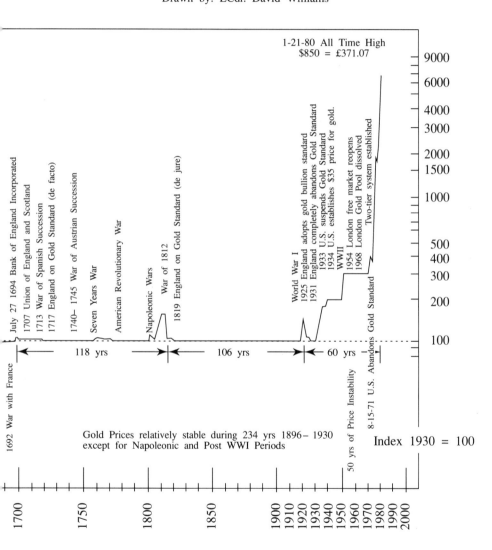

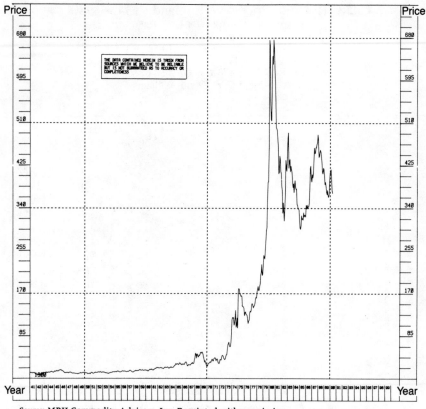

Price

THE DATA CONTAINED HEREIN IS TAKEN FROM SOURCES WHICH WE BELIEVE TO BE RELIABLE BUT IS NOT GUARANTEED AS TO ACCURACY OR COMPLETENESS

Year

Source: MBH Commodity Advisors, Inc. Reprinted with permission

Figure 9-10 Monthly cash average price for gold, 1941–1990.

platinum, as well as its exotic uses and increasing popularity both in coinage and jewelry, the demand for platinum has increased more steadily than demand for gold or silver. In recent years Japanese investors have taken a particular liking to platinum in bullion, coin, and retail applications. Such growing interest has, I feel contributed to the higher price volatility.

Another important consideration in platinum prices (as well as in gold prices) has been the ratio or spread between gold and platinum. Figure 9-13 shows the monthly spread between platinum and gold from 1980 through 1990. As you can see, this spread has varied considerably, yet there are several noteworthy aspects of the spread chart. First and foremost, when platinum

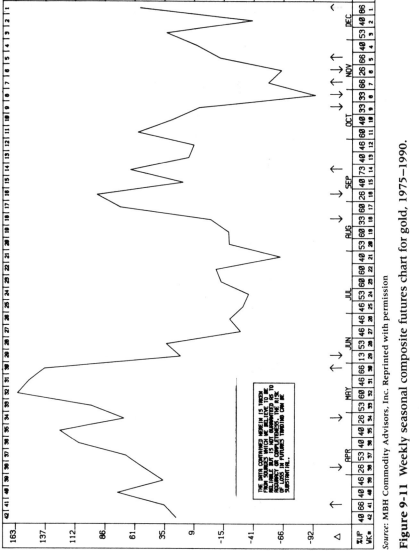

Source: MBH Commodity Advisors, Inc. Reprinted with permission

Figure 9-11 Weekly seasonal composite futures chart for gold, 1975–1990.

Table 9-2 Summaries of Two Key-Date Seasonals for Gold

1.

LONG Dec Gold ON THE CLOSE 09/01 WITH A 3% STOP-LOSS CLOSE ONLY, OR EXIT ON CLOSE 09/21

Entry Date:	09/01	Exit Date:	09/21
Positive Trades:	11	Negative Trades:	4
Starting Year:	1975	Ending Year:	1989
% Positive Trades:	73.33	% Negative Trades:	26.67
Average Gain:	24.62	Average Loss:	−9.17
Average Trade:	15.61	Profit/Loss Ratio:	7.38
Years Analyzed:	15	Cumulative Gain*:	$23,409.99
Maximum		Calculated Stop:	0.00
Drawdown:	−$1,370.00		

2.

SHORT Jun Gold ON THE CLOSE 04/17 WITH A 5% STOP-LOSS CLOSE ONLY, OR EXIT ON CLOSE 05/09

Entry Date:	04/17	Exit Date:	05/09
Positive Trades:	12	Negative Trades:	3
Starting Year:	1975	Ending Year:	1989
% Positive Trades:	80.00	% Negative Trades:	20.00
Average Gain:	7.58	Average Loss:	−5.93
Average Trade:	4.87	Profit/Loss Ratio:	5.11
Years Analyzed:	15	Cumulative Gain*:	$7,310.01
Maximum		Calculated Stop:	0.00
Drawdown:	−$1,290.00		

prices and gold prices are at a par (i.e., no price difference) and in particular when platinum prices have been lower than gold prices, it has been reasonable to buy platinum, since the price is relatively low. It has been a most reasonable and profitable strategy to buy platinum when it is at a discount to gold and to buy liquidate both metals when the premium of platinum over gold has been considerable. While this strategy may not always be effective for the futures trader, it may be effective for those who invest in mining stocks, coins, mutual funds, or bullion, since

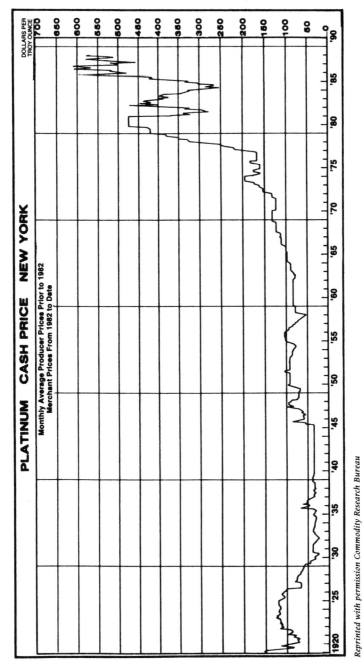

Reprinted with permission Commodity Research Bureau

Figure 9-12 Monthly average prices for platinum, 1920–1990.

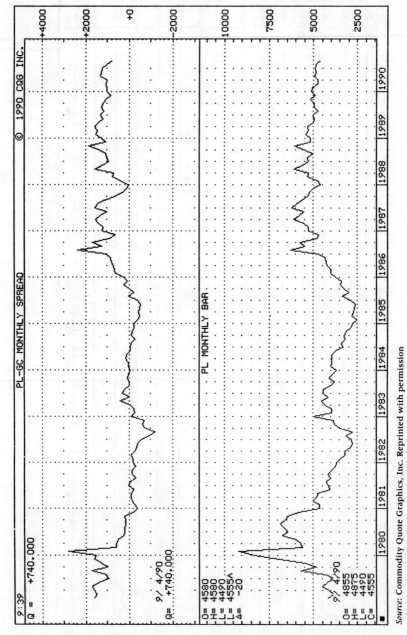

Source: Commodity Quote Graphics, Inc. Reprinted with permission

Figure 9-13 Platinum/gold spread, 1980–1990.

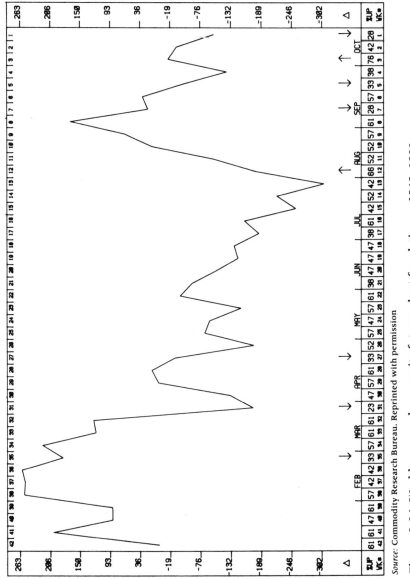

Source: Commodity Research Bureau. Reprinted with permission

Figure 9-14 Weekly seasonal composite futures chart for platinum, 1968–1990.

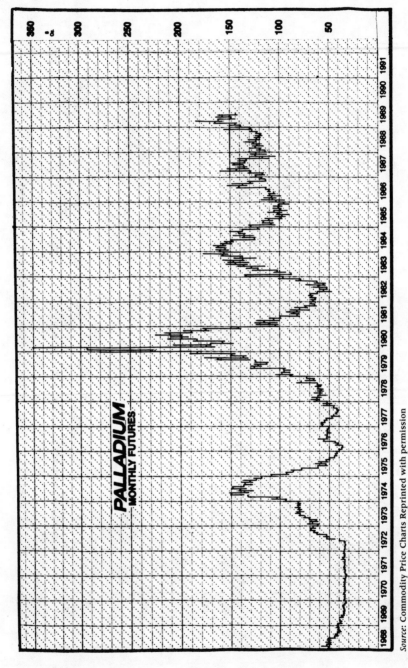

Source: Commodity Price Charts Reprinted with permission

Figure 9-15 Monthly futures prices for palladium, 1968–1990.

Table 9-3. Summaries of Two Key-Date Seasonals for Platinum

1.

SHORT Jly Platinum ON THE CLOSE 04/16 WITH A 6% STOP-LOSS CLOSE ONLY, OR EXIT ON CLOSE 05/01

Entry Date:	04/16	Exit Date:	05/01
Positive Trades:	17	Negative Trades:	5
Starting Year:	1968	Ending Year:	1989
% Positive Trades:	77.27	% Negative Trades:	22.73
Average Gain:	13.22	Average Loss:	−13.58
Average Trade:	7.13	Profit/Loss Ratio:	3.31
Years Analyzed:	22	Cumulative Gain*:	$7,839.98
Maximum		Calculated Stop:	0.00
Drawdown:	−$1,345.01		

2.

LONG Oct Platinum ON THE CLOSE 08/10 WITH A 3% STOP-LOSS CLOSE ONLY, OR EXIT ON CLOSE 08/20

Entry Date:	08/10	Exit Date:	08/20
Positive Trades:	18	Negative Trades:	4
Starting Year:	1968	Ending Year:	1989
% Positive Trades:	81.82	% Negative Trades:	18.18
Average Gain:	16.36	Average Loss:	−11.43
Average Trade:	11.30	Profit/Loss Ratio:	6.44
Years Analyzed:	22	Cumulative Gain*:	$12,435.00
Maximum		Calculated Stop:	0.00
Drawdown:	−$1,670.00		

timing is not nearly as critical a factor as it is with futures-related activities.

Platinum prices have also exhibited some distinct seasonal tendencies. Figure 9-14 shows the seasonal tendency in weekly platinum futures. Note also the key-date seasonal tendencies in Table 9-3 based on my concise seasonal research as described previously.

Palladium

We have less history for palladium prices than we do for any of the other precious metals. Although there is considerably less history for palladium, its recent growing popularity has stimulated some large price movements, particularly since 1988 when the use of palladium as a substitute for platinum in catalytic converters began to increase. Given the virtual stranglehold of the Soviet Union on palladium production, it is likely that volatility will continue to increase and, in fact, it is very possible that palladium prices could increase considerably in the years ahead. Figure 9-15 shows the recent futures-price history for palladium.

10 THE FUTURE OF METALS PRICES

As YOU CAN SEE from the chapters you have just read, the metals markets have had a long and volatile price history. It is likely that the behavior of precious metals will continue to be affected in dramatic ways and that there will be significant opportunities to profit. But you must remember, above all, that the opportunity for profit is not a one-way street. Where there is the probability for profit, there is also the risk of loss. As you know, investments in precious metals are generally considered non-income-producing investments. They carry considerable risk and, as a result, most analysts and financial planners agree that perhaps no more than 5 to 10 percent of your investment portfolio should be placed in metals-related investments. While I agree with these conclusions, I must emphasize that this holds true for the uninformed public. If you have taken the time to study the metals, and if you are aware of the fundamental, technical, and timing considerations, then you are in a significantly better position than is the average investor. You may decide to place a greater percentage of your risk capital and/or of your investment capital into metals-related investments. The results can be significant not only in capital appreciation, but also in dividend income as well, provided you buy at the right time.

I would be misleading you if I told you that I could predict the future of metals prices; however, I feel that I am in a position to acquaint you with the various forces and factors that may affect metals prices in the months and years ahead. I suggest you consider the following items in your study and analysis of future metal price trends.

International Conflict

In the past, international conflict has been one of the major stimuli of bullish moves in prices. While many investors feel that international unrest affects only precious metals, such events have, in fact, also affected copper prices as well as strategic-metals prices. Copper has had a long history of upward price movements in response to military actions, whether localized or global. In such situations the investor should also consider the fact that governments may act to freeze certain metal prices in the event of a declared war. This would effectively limit profit potential in bullion or physical holdings, but it will probably not have the same effect on such things as bullion coins or mining shares. I've indicated previously that bullion or physical holdings in any of the metals is not a good idea in most cases, and this may be particularly true in the event of international conflict.

If you feel that the world is destined for times of peace, then you must also conclude that international conflict will not be a significant factor in future metals price movements. With the many changes in Eastern Europe and the U.S.S.R. (which is slowly but surely disintegrating), many investors may feel that international conflict will diminish, and with it, one of the primary stimuli for higher metals prices. Yet this may be precisely what causes the metals to explode. Historically, the element of surprise has always been an important factor in pushing metals higher. The world has been slowly lulled into a sense of security by the events of 1980 and early 1990. A sudden and "unexpected" conflict such as the 1990 Iraq invasion of Kuwait, could easily send metals prices soaring. Consider this as a real possiblity in evaluating the potential price movement of all metals, particularly the precious metals, copper, and the strategic metals.

Inflation

Perhaps the single most important upward stimulus for higher metals prices has been inflation. During times of inflation, currency tends to lose its buying power, and investors tend to flock to precious metals as a safe haven for their funds. Given the state of world economies in 1990, and in particular the huge U.S. budget deficits, inflation will continue to be a problem in the years ahead. Long-wave cyclical analysis suggests that the mid-1990s are likely to bring with them a bottoming of the recessionary economic trend in the United States which has been in effect since the early 1980s. And with inflation will come a general increase in all commodity prices, but in particular in the precious metals. It should be remembered that the most substantial portion of price increases in precious metals is during the latter half of an inflationary economic trend.

Bear in mind an additional point of information regarding which precious metals might fare best during an inflationary period. Historically, platinum has experienced the largest dollar-price moves, while gold has come in second. Along with platinum, palladium may very well make large dollar moves as well during the next bull cycle, particularly if the Soviet Union, which now controls a considerable majority of the world's production, holds back supplies. In the latter stages of a bull market, silver prices have been inclined to move sharply higher, often showing the largest percentage gains.

The most sensible way to participate in an inflation-inspired metals bull market is to accumulate a portfolio of metals preferably as shares, mutual funds, coins, futures, and options. This would hold true for the precious metals; however, it would only be possible to hold bullion or mining stocks in the base and strategic metals, unless the availability of new investment vehicles in these metals expands in the future.

Another consideration during inflationary times is the platinum versus gold spread. I've indicated previously that platinum tends to gain on gold during bullish moves. Futures traders should consider buying platinum futures and selling gold futures in bull markets, expecting platinum to gain a healthy premium on gold. Should the popularity and consumption of palladium increase in the coming years, the possibility of using a palladium-versus-gold spread might also be considered for those futures traders who are more speculatively inclined.

Inflation has also proven an ideal stimulus for sharply higher bullion coins and bullion numismatic coins. Traditional bullion coins such as the Krugerrand, Maple Leaf, or Panda will increase in value commensurate with increases in bullion. There are, however, numerous numismatic issues such as the U.S. St. Gaudens which have both bullion value as well as value acquired by their scarcity and quality. In addition to the well-known U.S. numismatic bullion coins, there are literally hundreds of foreign numismatics that tend to appreciate sharply during inflationary periods. Should you venture into this area, however, I recommend you consult a qualified and reputable coin dealer.

An ideal inflation-era portfolio in metals might be as follows:

20 percent platinum coins and mining stocks
20 percent gold coins and mining stocks
10 percent strategic metals
10 percent other metal mining stocks
15 percent silver coins and mining stocks
20 percent bullion and numismatic coins
5 percent futures and futures options

As the inflationary market progresses, you might consider changing the mix somewhat in order to capitalize upon the unique aspects of each metal during different phases of the bull market. You might, for example, increase the silver percentage once the bull move has been in effect for some time. You can study the previously discussed cyclical lengths to help you make this decision.

Industrial Usage

The base of scientific and technological progress is expanding substantially every day, and with these increases, applications for metals will also increase. Recently, for example, platinum has been used in a new and promising cancer medication. Pollution control, electronic components, and a variety of chemical processes continue to provide a steady demand for metals. Strategic metals will continue to grow in importance as new discoveries are made and as new applications are found.

As humankind begins to realize that it is polluting the world with plastics and other nonbiodegradable products, we may find that metal containerization will regain its prominent role. We may even find that the current use of lumber will diminish markedly in construction because of concerns about destruction of the world's forests. Metals may eventually take the place of lumber in many construction projects.

Stock Market Trends

There has been a distinct tendency for stock-market prices to move contrary to precious metals prices. Figure 10-1 shows the Dow Jones Industrial stock average plotted against gold prices on a monthly basis, and Figure 10-2 shows the Dow Jones Industrial stock average plotted against silver bullion prices. As you can see, there has been a generally inverse correlation between the precious metals and stock prices. Hence, we might reasonably conclude that when stocks are in a generally rising trend, precious metals would not be favored investments, but that when stocks are in a generally falling trend, precious metals would be good investments. I suggest, therefore, that you also consider the direction of stock prices in making your decisions about precious metals.

Some market watchers, on the other hand, have claimed that copper price trends tend to correlate highly with stock price trends. Figure 10-3 shows monthly copper prices plotted against the Dow Jones Industrial stock average. As you can see, there has been a reasonably positive correlation, which suggests that copper stocks as well as copper futures might be good from the long side during periods of rising stock market, and good short sales during falling stock markets.

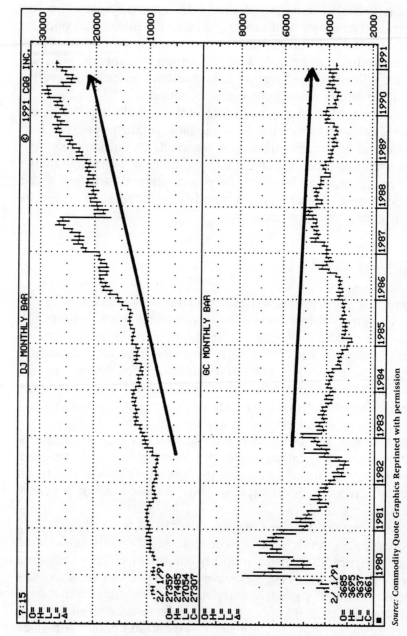

Source: Commodity Quote Graphics Reprinted with permission

Figure 10-1 Inverse trend correlation between stocks (top) and gold prices (bottom).

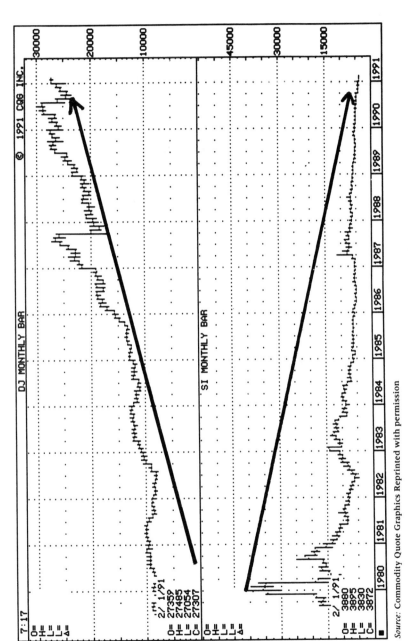

Source: Commodity Quote Graphics Reprinted with permission

Figure 10-2 Inverse trend correlation between stocks (top) and silver (bottom) prices.

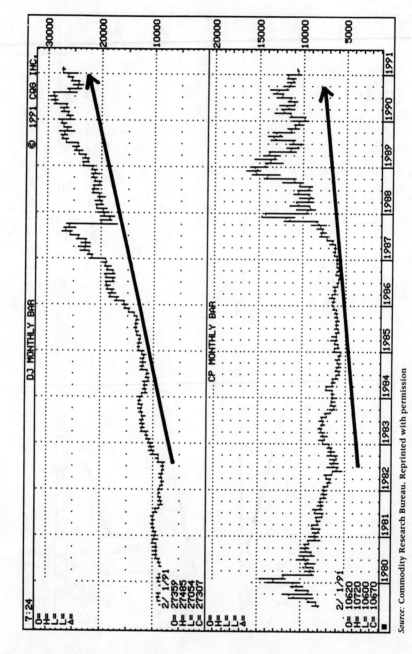

Source: Commodity Research Bureau. Reprinted with permission

Figure 10-3 Positive trend correlation between stocks (top) and copper prices (bottom).

Currency Instability

Since the 1970s international currency fluctuations have markedly affected precious-metals prices trends, particularly those in the gold market. Concerns about currency stability have prompted banks as well as speculators to buy or sell gold depending upon the exact nature of the currency situation. Swiss banks in particular have been very active in the gold market through the years. Should situations arise that threaten the strength of world currencies, investors will probably move heavily into precious metals, the most likely one of which would be gold. While moving funds into gold as a response to instability of any kind is not necessarily valid from a strictly economic point of view, the fact remains that as long as an overwhelming majority of large investors, bankers, and governments consider gold to be a safe haven, then it will serve its purposes.

Japanese Economic Trends

During the period from 1970 through 1989, the Japanese economy has grown almost exponentially. A majority of international trade is now dominated by Japanese firms who are among the largest, the most successful, and the most profitable in the world. Japanese banks are among the most highly capitalized banks in the world, and they have provided considerable funds for leveraged buyouts and other acquisitions of foreign firms. The massive influx of wealth into Japan has given the Japanese consumer sufficient funds for investing in many different areas, the most favored of which have been precious metals, particularly platinum and gold. In addition, Japanese consumers are perhaps the most avid jewelry buyers in the world. If the Japanese economy begins to turn negative, or if it begins a severe crash, the long-run effect on precious metals could be negative as investors begin to sell their metals holdings and as consumers decrease their demand for gold and platinum jewelry. In the event of a severe crash in the Japanese stock market, precious metals could actually decline unless international buying is enough to offset the Japanese selling that may result as an effect of a sharply declining stock market.

11 SUGGESTIONS FOR THE METALS INVESTOR

NOW THAT YOU'VE HAD an opportunity to learn most of the important facts about metals, from both fundamental and investment perspectives, you may decide to venture into the markets. Here are some guidelines to consider before putting any money into metals:

1. Determine how much you want to invest. Keep in mind that a majority of metals-related investments will not return any income. While some stocks do pay dividends, dividends should not be your primary consideration. You must remember that your goal is capital appreciation and not income. A well-planned investment portfolio will take many factors into consideration, among them, the amount of capital you have available for higher-risk ventures and/or speculations. This is the portion of your portfolio that should be considered for metals investing and speculation.

2. Futures and options trading are the most speculative areas of investing. In fact, they should not even be considered as investments, but rather as speculations. While they can return large percentage gains, in most cases they will turn out to be losing propositions for a variety of reasons, most commonly a lack of trader discipline and lack of a thorough plan or program.

3. Know your plans and objectives before you invest. This means that you must know the potential of your investments. If you have not determined ahead of time which vehicles you will buy or sell, then you will be prone to act on impulse; and acting on impulse is not a wise strategy.

4. Diversification is important. I recommend, therefore, that you spread your investment dollars into a number of different metals-related investments. A suggested portfolio mix has been discussed previously.

5. Be patient and await ideal opportunities. You may find yourself very impatient, but don't give in to the feeling! The successful metals investor is patient, methodical, and persistent. Positions are accumulated slowly, most often when the consensus of opinion is negative on metals, and they are liquidated gradually, although more quickly than they were acquired, and most successfully when the consensus of opinion is very bullish.

6. Don't consider the opinions of others unless they are professional, well-established advisers with proven performance records in the metals. What you hear from your broker, brother-in-law, boss, newspaper, attorney, or taxi driver is usually wrong. You must do your own research, you must believe in it, and you must act accordingly. But bear in mind that this will be difficult to do since you will likely be going against the consensus.

7. Be careful of futures options, penny mining stocks, and other metals-related programs that you don't understand. The more promising the return, the higher the risk of loss. Remember this motto and you will not fall victim to the many scams, high-risk investments, and low-probability investments. While many programs have profit potential, you are always better off if you investigate the programs, understand them thoroughly, and attempt to determine the probability of success.

8. Ask for references and check credentials before you do business with anyone you don't know. If you are solicited by tele-

phone, and if the claims sound too good to be true, then they probably are too good to be true. Never send money to anyone unless you have checked them out thoroughly. Don't be afraid to ask for references and/or credentials, and don't hesitate to check with government and regulatory agencies.

9. Be especially carefully of high-commission programs that promise incredible returns with limited loss. Futures-options programs, in particular, are notorious for high commissions.

10. Strategic-metals investment programs tend to become popular when metals are in bull markets. There are numerous problems unique to investing in strategic metals. You must carefully consider these limitations. While it is easy to buy into these programs, it is frequently difficult to get out unless the markets are moving higher, and even then you may not be able to exit at a good price, and you may have to pay large commissions will eat into your profits.

11. If buying bullion or numismatic coins, remember to deal with ethical brokers who come highly recommended. In bull markets, forgeries flourish, and the cost of buying and selling can vary considerably from one dealer to another; so shop around before you make any transactions.

12. Take advantage of the news. Make the news work for you. When the news is unusually bullish or positive, take the opportunity to sell some of your holdings if your technical work suggests that a top is likely. When the news is most negative and prices are falling sharply, take the opportunity to add to your long-term position.

13. Do your homework. If you fail to do your homework regularly, you will one day awake to find that the move you expected has started and that you have missed your opportunity to get on board. If you plan to be in on a major move in the metals, then you must study the market regularly.

14. Think ahead. Try to understand what will make metals move in the direction you have anticipated. While you can't imagine every possible outcome or scenario, you can be prepared for many possible outcomes if you think ahead.

The successful metals investor often has to rely on instincts and intuition developed through long and hard experience. By following some of the guidelines in this book, you will be more prepared to profit from investing in metals. But remember, above all, that there is no substitute for direct experience, consistency, persistence, and caution.

Major Metals Producers in the United States and Canada

United States

ASARCO Incorporated, New York, New York
Battle Mountain Gold Company, Houston, Texas
Callahan Mining Corporation, Phoenix, Arizona
Coeur d'Alene Mines Corporation, Coeur d'Alene, Idaho
Freeport-McMoRan Gold Company, Elko, Nevada
Gold Fields Mining Corporation, New York, New York
Hecla Mining Company, Coeur d'Alene, Idaho
Homestake Mining Company, San Francisco, California
Inspiration Consolidated Copper Company, Scottsdale, Arizona
Kennecott Corporation, Salt Lake City, Utah
Newmont Mining Corporation, New York, New York
Pegasus Gold Incorporated, Spokane, Washington
Phelps Dodge Corporation, New York, New York
St. Joe Minerals Corporation, St. Louis, Missouri
Sunshine Mining Company, Voise, Idaho
Tenneco Minerals Company, Lakewood, Colorado
Vanderbilt Gold Corporation, San Mateo, California

Canada

Agnico-Eagle Mines Limited, Toronto, Ontario
American Barrick Resources Corporation, Toronto, Ontario

ASAMERA Minerals (U.S.), Inc., Calgary, Alberta
BP Canada Incorporated, Selco Division, Toronto, Ontario
COMINCO Limited, Vancouver, British Columbia
Consolidated CSA Minerals Ltd., Timmons, Ontario
Dickenson Mines Limited, Toronto, Ontario
Dome Mines Limited, Toronto, Ontario
D'Or Val Mines Limited, Val d'Or, Quebec
Echo Bay Mines Limited, Edmonton, Alberta
Giant Yellowknife Mines Ltd., Yellowknife, Northwest Territories
Hudson Bay Mining & Smelting Co., Ltd., Toronto, Ontario
INCO Limited, Toronto, Ontario
Kerr Addison Mines Limited, Toronto, Ontario
Noranda Sales Corporation Ltd., Toronto, Ontario
Northgane Minerals Limited, Calgary, Alberta
Northgate Exploration Limited, Toronto, Ontario
Pamour Incorporated, Timmins, Ontario
Placer Development Limited, Vancouver, British Columbia

Reference and Reading List

Bernstein, Jacob. *The New Prosperity.* New York: New York Institute of Finance, 1989.

Bernstein, Jacob. *How to Profit in Precious Metals.* New York: John Wiley and Sons, 1985.

Blake, William P. *The Production of the Precious Metals: or Statistical Notices of the Principal Gold and Silver Producing Regions of the World; with a chapter upon the Unification of Gold and Silver Coinage.* New York: G.P. Putnam and Son, 1869.

Browne, Harry. *The Economic Time Bomb: How You Can Profit from the Emerging Crises.* New York: St. Martin's Press, 1987.

Busschau, W. J. *The Measure of Gold.* South Africa: Central News Agency, Ltd. 1949.

Butterman, W. C., and J. M. Lucas. "Gold" in *On Golds.* Ed. H. Alan Lipscomb and Donald R. Libey. DeKalb, Ill.: The Waterleaf Press, 1982.

Fagan, Brian. *New Treasures of the Past.* New York: Barron's Educational Series, Inc. 1987.

Gent, Ernest V. *The Zinc Industry: A Mine to Market Outline.* New York: The American Zinc Institute, Inc., 1949.

Get Rich Investment Guide. Vol 6, No. 2. Chicago: Consumer's Digest, Inc. January, 1985.

Green, Timothy. *The New World of Gold,* rev. ed. New York: Walker and Company, 1984.

Groseclose, Elgin, Ph.D. *The Silken Metal. Silver: Past, Present, Prospective.* Washington, D.C.: Institute for Monetary Research, Inc., 1975.

Jackson, Robert S. *North American Gold Stocks: New Investment Opportunities and Strategies in U.S. and Canadian Gold Mining Stocks.* Chicago: Probus Publishing, 1988.

Jastram, Roy W. *Silver: The Restless Metal.* New York: John Wiley and Sons, 1981.

Kehrer, Daniel M. *The Cautious Investor's Guide to Profits in Precious Metals.* New York: Times Books, 1985.

Lasser, J. K. *Personal Investment Annual—1989–1990.* New York: J. K. Lasser Institute, 1989.

Leontif, Wassily, et al. *The Future of Nonfuel Minerals in the U.S. and World Economy: Input-Output Projections, 1980–2030.* Lexington, Mass.: D.C. Heath and Co, 1983.

Lipscomb, H. Alan, and Donald R. Libey, Eds. *On Gold.* DeKalb, Ill: The Waterleaf Press, 1982.

McDivitt, James F., and Gerald Manners. *Minerals and Men.* Baltimore: Johns Hopkins University Press, 1974.

Metal Statistics 1988, The Purchasing Guide of the Metal Industries. New York: Fairchild Publications, 1988.

Mikesell, Raymond F. *The World Copper Industry: Structure and Economic Analysis.* Baltimore: Johns Hopkins University Press, 1984.

Money Maker: Complete Guide to Successful Investing. Chicago: Money Maker, 1988.

Money Maker: Get Rich Investment Guide. Chicago: Money Maker, 1985

Prain, Sir Ronald. *Copper: The Anatomy of an Industry.* London: Mining Journal Books Limited, 1975.

Sarnoff, Paul. *Trading in Silver: How to Make High Profits in the World Silver Market.* Chicago: Probus Publishing Co., 1988.

Wagenhals, Gerhard. *The World Copper Market* in *Lecture Notes in Economics and Mathematical Systems.* Ed. M. Beckmann and W. Krelle. New York: Springer-Verklag, 1984.

Williams, Trevor I. *The History of Invention*. New York: Facts on File, Inc., 1987.

Zimmerman, Erich W. *World Resources and Industries*. rev. ed. New York: Harper and Row, 1951.

INDEX

A

Accumulation Phase 175
Aluminum 20
Antimony 84–86

B

Bankruptcy 206
Base Metals 11–35
  As Investments 31
Beryllium 86–88
Bottoming Phase 175
Bronze Age 12, 23
Bullion Coins 143, 144, 205–205

C

Cadmium 88–90
Capital Gains 127
Chromium 90–92
Coins 143–151
Cobalt 92–94
Columbium 95–96
Commissions 3
Copper 11, 18, 21, 32–22, 34, 154,
    160–163, 168, 209
  Mining 23

Counterfeit Coins 205
  Uses of 15
Cycles 157, 172–173

D

Declining Phase 191
Dewey, E. R.
Dines, Jim 5
Dividends 127
Dollar—Cost Av   ᴐing 125
Dow Jones Aᵛ   `9
Drawdown

E

Edwards, Robert D 133
Emotions, 1, 4

F

Final Decline Phase 196–198
Financial Condition 155–156
Foundation for the Study of Cycles
    7
Fraud, 207
Futures Magazine 135
Futures Options 241

Futures Trading 127–130
    in Metals 131–132

G

Gallium
Germanium 97
Gold 37
    marketing 53–55
    mining 50–52
    sources 38–49
Growth Phase 185–186

H

Hafnium 99
High Pressure Sales 3
Hunt Brothers 6

I

Indium 100
International Conflict 236
Instability 240
Investing in coins 149
Iridium 109–110

J

Jackling, Daniel C 13
Japanese Economic Trends 176

K

Key Date Seasonals 215–216, 228,
    233

L

Leverage 205
Liquidity 205
Lithium 101

M

Magee, John 133
Magnesium 103–104

Manganese 104–106
Managed Account Reports 135
Margin 206
Mercury 106–108
Metals Shares 124, 205
Molybdenum 108–109
Money Manager 134–135
Myers, Verne 5

N

Numismatics 143, 148

P

Palladium 76–79, 232
Panic Liquidation 180–182
Partnerships 144
Platinum 9, 76
Portfolio, 238
Psychology 8

R

Recovery Phase 196–198
Reward 203
Regulatory Agencies 4
Rhodium 110
Risk 2, 3, 203

S

Schultz, Harry 5
Seasonals 209–234
Selenium 111–112
Slicion 112
Silver 63–68, 157
    scrap 69
Strategic Metals 4, 83
    Investing in 121
Strategy 153
Success, odds of 3
Storage 146
Supply and Demand 17, 28, 55, 69,
    79, 85, 80, 95, 99, 100, 102,
    105, 111

T

Tatalum 113–114
Technical Factors 163–164
Tellurium 114
Timing 172
Tin 22, 24, 25
  Role of 29
  Uses of 26–27
Titanium 115–116
Topping Phase 191
Tungsten 117–118

V

Vanadium 118–119

W

Williams, David 223–225

Y

Yttrium 120

Z

Zirconium 120